A WORD IN YOUR EAR

and

JUST ANOTHER WORD

A WORD IN YOUR EAR

AND

JUST ANOTHER WORD

by

IVOR BROWN

With a Foreword to the American Edition by
J. DONALD ADAMS

IN TWO PARTS

E. P. DUTTON & COMPANY, INC.
New York, 1945

First Printing . . . . September, 1945
Second Printing . . . . October, 1945

FOREWORD
TO THE AMERICAN EDITION

THIS is a good time to think about words. During wars, and immediately after them, words, and particularly those that stand for big and ideal concepts, are likely to have a hollow sound and to have grown fuzzy and frayed at the edges, if not a little rotten at the heart. Words, except the simplest and most direct, are not much good in time of war, and yet we are pelted with them to an even greater degree than in the intervals of peace. However much we may talk about them as weapons, when armies are on the march and the earth shakes, words assume a triviality which belies their true nature. They have a lot to do with making wars, but not much, I fear, with winning them. The best kind of words in war are like these of Field Marshal Montgomery: "I am never anxious when I fight my battles. If I am anxious, I don't fight them. I wait until I am ready." Or words like those of Marshal Foch — "They shall not pass," or of the American submarine commander who quietly ordered, "Take her down," before the seas washed over him.

But if it is better to be sparing in their use when there is grim work to be done, it is well to be thinking about them and the power which they have when the guns are silent. And not alone the power which they hold, but the delight which they can give. I can think of no other medium of communication or, indeed, any other expression of man's creative spirit, in which delicacy and strength, explosive force and soothing assurance are as remarkably combined as they are in words.

Nothing, surely, is more alive than a word. They are man's purest creations, of a visible or audible kind. They depend not at all upon material aids for their effectiveness, as do all other fruits of the human mind. Architecture, painting, sculpture, music, science — all demand a material intermediary of some sort; words alone are as disembodied as when man first plucked them from the air. Nothing in man's progress from his bestial beginnings seems to me as fascinating, as teasing to the mind, as the process by which he developed these counters for his thought. All of us who use them as tools in our work must sometimes pause to ponder over their beginnings and to wonder over the frequently brilliant suggestiveness of the symbols chosen by those remote ancestors of ours who looked with fresh eyes upon the phenomena of nature and sought to find in speech sounds that would convey appropriately what they saw. How admirably and how often they succeeded! And I think the coiners of Anglo-Saxon speech were uncommonly gifted in that respect, though it is enormously difficult to compare the quality of a word in one's own tongue with that of another, because of the long and intimate, deeply imbedded associations of the native word.

Yet, think of words like "dawn" and "dusk." They are beautiful in themselves, and still, after long centuries of wide and continual use, untouched by time, fresh as the day when they were minted. There is slowly spreading light in the word "dawn," both in the sound and the look of it. And the soft and stealthy darkening that is conveyed by "dusk" is not merely the mental reflex occasioned by the sight or sound of the accustomed symbol. As you look at it, as you hear it, you are aware of the perfect appropriateness of the word. So too, is "thunder" one of the most evocative words in the language. And though *Donner* in German, *grom* in Russian, and *tonnerre* in French are good too, is not "thunder" the best of the four? It seems to me to have more reverberation in its sound than the others. Another excellent word of this kind is the Russian *prostor,* for which there is no real equivalent in English, French or German. It denotes a wide, far-horizoned prospect, such as that offered by the Russian steppes, or our own Great Plains. The absence of such a word in English, so responsive to natural phenomena, seems strange, for its early makers, though they did not know such great spaces inland, must already have looked on the sea when their language was taking form.

The Greeks, we say, "had a word for it." Indeed they did, as evidenced by such fine creations as *thalassa,* for the sea. Is it not reasonable to suppose that the word derived from the sound of water slapping against rocks, or the side of a boat? How dead beside it seems the Latin *mare,* coined by a people of far less imagination, much less originality. How few indeed — though here, no doubt, I may encounter indignant protests — are the Latin words woven into the texture of English which have fibre and life! They seem to have about them a synthetic, laboriously created quality which is absent from the words of Anglo-Saxon or of Greek origin.

We never tire of the words which man in his folly and stupidity cannot smirch and debase. Words like those I have mentioned and many others like them never grow drab or stale. It is, for the most part, the words which express mental concepts that we tire of, that we come to use with misgiving or distaste — the words that we have sullied and betrayed, words like "liberty" and "honor," "freedom" and "democracy," "faith" and "glory." These are the words that need renewal and repair from time to time, that need to be thought about as we use them.

Words are such sensitive things that even the way in which we spell them matters. I have always, for example, had a bitter prejudice against the spelling "gray." To my eyes, and I think to many others, the word "grey" is mistreated and misrepresented by the "a" spelling. "Gray" is not grey. Somehow, the letter "a" lets in light, so that a "gray" wall is definitely lighter in tone than a grey one. Why this should be so is impossible, for me at least, to determine, but however intangible the reason, the effect is clear.

I think it was listening to the lectures of George Santayana at Harvard, many years ago, that first made me keenly aware of the magic there is in words. More vividly than I recall the substance of the lectures, I remember the charm and skill of their delivery. It was fascinating to watch the grace and precision with which he expressed his thoughts; the slight but never awkward pause while he reached for and inevitably found the word or the phrase perfectly suited to his meaning. Santayana made visible for you that feeling for words which is one of the greatest gifts a speaker or a writer can possess. For that feeling *is* a gift; it is something that no amount of training and hard work can supply if the potential capacity is lacking. The majority of writers use words as they would lay bricks; they are at best competent craftsmen familiar with their tools and skilled in their use, but they employ them unimaginatively. Their words are never winged; they never ignite.

Ivor Brown, who in his capacity as editor of the *London Observer,* is a highly skilled manipulator of words, is a lover of them as well. He is also, as he puts it, a "collector" of them, and these two little books, here offered as one to American readers, are the fruit of his war-time collecting. With that admirable sanity with which the British have behaved through the terrific stresses they have endured for the past four years, Mr. Brown has culled from his war-time reading several hundred words which, for one reason or another, have particularly interested him because of the sea-changes through which they have passed since they first became a part of English speech. He has written about them with so much sympathy and understanding, with so much imaginative appreciation of the life that is in them, with so wide-ranging an acquaintance of the best uses to which they have been put, that I have found *A Word in Your Ear* and *Just Another Word* two of the most delightful volumes to appear in a time when the world was never more emptied of delight.

The quality of words, the company they keep, their strange and sometimes unaccountable fortunes as they journey down through the centuries, are rewarding fields of exploration, and too little has been written about them that has the juice of life in it. Most of the literature of etymology wears a forbidding aspect, and that's a pity, for the material with which it deals is the living tissue of communication. By right of its intrinsic interest it should stir the imagination no less than the mysteries of radio and television. This, I think, Mr. Brown has beautifully accomplished in his two "anthologies" of words. He is not one of your inflexible purists and stubborn conservators who turn their backs upon any innovations in language. His approach to words is warm, receptive, and unpedantic. But wide though his sympathy and appreciation is, it is not wide enough, praise be, to harbor the circumlocutions and heavy Latinities of the bureaucrats and social scientists whose dreadful inroads upon the English tongue rouse him to such unbridled wrath. We have their counterparts here, and I think none of Mr. Brown's heavy artillery will be wasted upon American readers, any more than the graceful charm of his more light-hearted moments. I have trespassed on his province long enough, and I leave you with the hope that you may find as much pleasure and stimulation in his pages as have I.

J. DONALD ADAMS

New York City

ix

Contents

PART ONE

A WORD IN YOUR EAR

THE book which follows is an anthology of words. Anthologies of prose and verse abound: but there is, I think, no such volume of their raw material, which is words. If it be deemed pleasant to gather bouquets of the former, why should the latter be left only in the cold storage of the lexicon? The phrase 'flowers of speech' has been unhappily applied with jocosity and even contempt to what Mr. Wells's Mr. Polly so nicely entitled 'verboojuice'. But 'flowers of speech' is an exact description of an anthology of words. Words, like flowers, have colour and bloom and aroma. They are to the writer as paint to the artist and, while they have been scientifically examined and listed and defined without cease by learned men and lexicographers, they merit also the purely affectionate approach of the collector who assembles his favourites in order to gratify both his sense of meaning and his sense of beauty in verbal shape and sound.

My method has been simple, personal, and vagrant. I have noted and collected the words which caught my fancy during my casual war-time reading, much of it re-reading of half-forgotten acquaintances and of abiding friends. I have not gone exploring for strange and striking terms. Had I chosen to do so, I could have made a whole anthology of rareties merely by raking the surface of Urquhart, Burton, and Ben Jonson. Once attracted by a word and looking into antecedents and parentage, I have grubbed in the Dictionary. But is grub a fair description? Scarcely. One is dealing with the flowers as well as with their native earth. Dictionaries are green and blossoming pastures, wherein any fancier of curious and delightful things can meander contentedly for days.

In my selection I have made no rules. What pleased, was noted: what noted, sifted: what survived the sieve, is here. I have in most cases quoted one passage or more in which the word appeared and gave pleasure. I have quoted freely because words, like precious stones and cut flowers, depend upon their grouping and the choice of neighbours. They may be strange or beautiful or amusing in isolation, but they will be doubly so when an author of judgment has put them in the right company.

Strange, beautiful, amusing — I have made my pick for all sorts of reasons. I have not barred American or Scottish or dialect words: I have included archaisms and obsolete terms as well as modern slang. No rule but personal relish has guided me. In general, I have chosen words which I would like to see employed more often or more accurately, rescued from neglect and restored to their appropriate power.

My taste, it will at once be seen, is catholic. I like the short and Saxon: I like the long and Latin. Domestic or alien, farmyard or courtly, all that has distinctive quality goes into the bowl. So long as a writer knows what he means and can express it, he can delight me as a Puritan stylist, with his English as close-cropt as his hair, or he can affect the laces and the ribbons of language and display all the panache of a Cavalier: he can be classical or romantic, urbane as Pope or rustic as John Clare. The abomination in the use of words is obscurity. This tiresome quality may be caused by a pose, as in the earlier work of sprouting genius, or by a brain that works too fast and cascades its clauses and images in a torrent, as in some later work of Shakespeare, or it may be the result of muddled thinking. Be it affectation or incompetence, it is a more common and more afflicting nuisance than is pomposity, which suits its own epochs and has its own enjoyable grandeur, as shows upon a stage may be portentous, even vulgarly massive, and yet somehow likeable. I have read that Mr. Winston Churchill, who can be florid as well as tremendous with his pen, based his style on a young addiction to Gibbon and Macaulay. There is a case for the sounding period to suit the high, substantial theme.

In a Country Churchyard

An easy way to study the ups-and-downs of language and the different tastes of different generations in the use of words is

6

to take one's gentler exercise in churches and churchyards, which are indeed the marble-index of a nation's mind voyaging in strange seas of valedictory emotion. This is a pastime open to all and one leading to serene and not altogether melancholy places.

The church and its tombs are a chronicle of style and state of mind. As such they may be depressing because they reveal, at least during the last hundred years, a steady decline of taste in material, in sentiment, in diction, and in lettering. The oldest stones have a native modesty: their grey simplicity emerges without fuss: they seem to grow as naturally as the daisies in the grass beside them. Even when fresh-cut they cannot have been out of place or flashily demonstrative, as are the sepulchres of alien marble which came into a later vogue. The words which they carry have a quiet dignity, and so has the lettering of these sincere and tranquil tributes. Men in those days were allowed to die: death need not be disguised with larger words.

True, the eighteenth century had its pomps; it would put into an English village the amplitude of a Roman gesture and bid farewell to a Georgian Squire with an Augustan flourish. But there was style in the gesture, and, after all, our culture came very largely by way of Rome. The lover of words will forgive the pleasing classical rotundity and even delight in the fine formality of a dismissive phrase. Recently in a church of the Shakespeare country, to which I was the more attracted because so many of its dead were called by the name of Lively, I found a tablet upon the wall in honour of a young Georgian doctor's skill. By his art and science, it said, 'He prolonged the lives of others to lament his own dissolution'. The compliment may or may not be just; the phrasing is certainly perfect.

A touch of eighteenth-century scepticism crept in later when the memorial tablet added, 'He was removed, we trust, to immortality'. The potentially sardonic 'we trust' would not have been admitted in an age of real faith. The inscription concluded with conventional lines in heroic couplets.

7

> For thus Religion softly murmurs peace
> And bids the sorrows of the mourners cease.

Any quick schoolboy could churn this out by the page. But it has an atmosphere: it marches with the phrasing of the prose and the graving of the sentiments.

During the eighteenth century, according to my churchyard observations, people were allowed, quite simply, to die. Towards the end of that period they begin to 'depart this life'. That is a fuller term, but there is no evasion about it. All this time the valedictory compliments paid to these departed have a classical dignity on the more august sepulchres and a native good sense on the humbler stones. But about the year 1830 everything goes. It has often astonished me how sudden and all-inclusive was the collapse of taste. In a churchyard you notice no gradual decay, but a complete break.

The craft of Journalism, like that of epitaphy, employed at that period a sounding vocabulary and a great sense of cadence. There were space and leisure for the ample phrase and this magniloquence was to be discovered as much in a local sheet as in one of the more august London journals. In a bar-parlour in a remote Derbyshire dale I once noticed on the wall a cutting from a local paper. It was an obituary notice, written in the early nineteenth century about a gamekeeper who had become a centenarian and had executed some high feats of agility and endurance even when he was reaching three figures. It was written of his habits — I must quote from memory —

> Until the age of sixty he consumed but one gallon of malt liquor a day: but later he began to drink plentiful, which he found both agreeable to his constitution and an abiding comfort to himself.

Such prose employs no rare words, but it patterns the familiar terms to a noble surge of sound. The modern form of farewell to such a veteran of the chase and tankard would probably be some mean string of clichés, far less candid and without the sap of feeling or the dignity of phrase.

8

The historian of word-usage notes that in a year or two everything is spoiled. The classical grandeur is softened and turned sentimental. The calamity happened round about 1830. Simplicity vanishes, as well as the stately and sonorous rhythm. People no longer die, like Adam: they pass over, they go home, they are carried to rest, they fall asleep, they are removed to the divine bosom, or whisked to other celestial and possibly embarrassing niches. Anything but the plain fact of death. Their virtues are no longer stated with any regard for truth: the dead are all possessed of moral excellence beyond belief and their village must have been a communion of very tiresome saints. The epitaphic English becomes affected, ornate, and odious. Humbug, no doubt, was always with us. But now a particularly florid humbug has arrived. One wanders from sepulchre to sepulchre whose inscriptions suggest that Chadband has been burying a Tite Barnacle or that Podsnap has said 'Vale' to Veneering. The vulgarity is general and affects the quantity and quality of commemorative stone as well as the lettering and the language upon it. The churchyard, which used to be a piece of English country, grey and green, now glitters hideously with Italian marble.

Verboojuice

There is no reason why the long and weighty word should be a bad one. The craving for such mental implements is natural. The lad who wants the biggest missile in the biggest catapult is like a writer in the flush of youth. Marlowe's 'mighty line' was just such a weapon. To make a thundering noise, to use pen and lungs to the full, is an irresistible temptation to young nations as to young people. There seems to be no slow evolution of artistic skill. The cave-men painters emerged supreme at the start. Their animal murals are immediate masterpieces. So with language and poetry. The Greek epic arises, like Aphrodite from the wine-dark sea, complete in beauty and elaborate in eloquence. But not eloquent only in the simple style of mariners' song or peasant fable. It is rhetorical, verbose, many-syllabled song. The earliest Greek poetry has a treasury of long, large, musical phrases. The insurgent genius of the race reveals the young and lusty appetite for glorious and gigantic words. 'Poluphlois-boisterous Homer of old!'

It continually happens. Boyhood loves to use its lung-power. Mr. Wells's Mr. Polly, that Boy Eternal of English democracy, revelled, as I said, in 'sesquipeddle verboojuice'. He was behaving like William Shakespeare before him. Shakespeare began with the 'taffeta phrases, silken terms precise' of the modish Euphuism and proceeded to the terrific verbal detonations of his battle-pieces in the Histories, in which his munitions were an unquenchable gift of metaphor and a colossal vocabulary. In his major tragedies he still splashed freely in the 'verboojuice', while discovering the full powers of simplicity. *King Lear* contains magic of both kinds, spilling cataracts and hurricanoes, sulphurous fires and oak-cleaving thunderbolts as fitly on the horrid heath as it sheds the simplest tears over the corpses on the soil of Kent. Lear fooled away his kingdom with as much waste of noble words as of ignoble temper: then died to the sad, slow music of humanity, which was as native to his withering as to Wordsworth's thoughts at Tintern Abbey.

Long words only become offensive when they are also tired and dull. Who would have the dialogue between Hamlet and his father's Ghost written out in words of one syllable? Who would confine Othello to a lackey's lingo or have Hotspur speak only for the ears of modern Tottenham? But enjoyment of 'verboojuice', the grand 'sesquipeddle' stuff, does not excuse the dreary prolixity of our own time, as it is splashed across the pages of official forms, reports, propaganda, and Governmental scripts of all kinds. In loathing this I am a good constituent of Mr. A. P. Herbert, whose fight for decent English has properly befitted the Parliamentary representative of Oxford University. But it was not a total victory and much remains for tears.

A Journey in Jargantua

In our time the official has created a language, a fearsome and ponderous dialect which I once christened the Barnacular in memory of the Circumlocution Office and its Tite Barnacle Controllers. But let us be fair to the Civil Servant: the official is not the only dealer in officialese. There is in this country an enormous and semi-official bureaucracy which deals in social welfare and all manner of educational and uplifting matters. It is rapidly developing a jargon of its own, a semi-officialese which is even worse than anything to be discovered within the envelopes marked O.H.M.S. It has the pomposity of style favoured by the self-important Business Man mixed up with the pretentiousness of those who dabble vaguely in Social Sciences. While the Government afflicts us with the Barnacular, the Uplifters and Welfarists are assaulting us with the similar horrors of their Jargantuan.

Let me quote a sentence from a document of this type. It was not composed by any member of the much-abused Civil Service. It is sad to think that it was concerned with a form of education, and, since it was composed by one of our would-be educators, we may well shudder at the notions of English speech that are now to be instilled. When the author of this piece of prose wished to say 'How the young now live' he put it thus: 'Material descriptive of conditions at present governing the lives of under-twenties (cross-sectional).' He thus used twenty-eight syllables instead of five and two or three lines instead of half a line at a time when saving of print and paper was said to be most necessary. Whenever he intended to talk of 'sundry people' he had to write 'a cross-section of the community'. Indeed, this word 'cross-section' so much went to his head (because of its length and Latinity) that he even talked of a family as a 'cross-section of the community', although that is exactly what the family is not, if the word has any point whatever.

So it ran on. The cumbrous phrase was invariably preferred to the simple. Are we to sympathize with the young? Certainly, if we are good citizens. But need this be called 'Self-identification with the experience, interests and problems of other young people (over a wide range) and also with their points of view and emotional attitudes'? One begins to believe that a man who can write this stuff would rather eat his own typewriter than call a feeling a feeling. It must be an 'emotional attitude'. Another tiresome habit in which such folk revel is the use of an adjective as a noun, presumably because it sounds unusual and therefore imposing. They have to lengthen everything, but you would think it enough to call an order a direction. No, they have to make it 'a directive', just as reforms have to be 'correctives'.

Needless to say, the word 'reaction' occurred constantly. 'Bringing correctives to bear upon reactions to war-time experience' probably means something. But, being an innocent abroad in this land of Jargantua, I would not care to say what. However, I am a poor hand at this whole business of spinning syllables. I have always preferred 'naughty children' to 'juvenile delinquents' and 'mend' to the now universal 'recondition'. What parent ever asked his boy not to be 'delinquent', or told him to 'recondition' his manners? I would rather 'start a talk and sum up' than 'promote discussion and synthesize the various categories of reaction'. But I am beginning in sorrow to believe that there are few on my side. Certainly the War Office is in the opposite camp and strongly entrenched in Jargantua. Why do its 'spokesmen' never call a ridge a ridge but always an 'escarpment'? Would these same fellows, if proposing a peace-time picnic, suggest some neighbouring 'escarpment' as a scene for lunch? Old-fashioned regiments and companies now seem to be always 'operational units'. 'Operational' has become a very operative word.

How does this Jargantuan stuff come to get written? The composers of it have, as a rule, had university educations. Were they permitted (or even encouraged) by their tutors to employ this mess of pointless and polysyllabic classicism instead of plain, brief English? It certainly is the case that, once you intimate to a student that the proper study of mankind is man, he immediately concludes that the proper English for setting down his views about the lives of his fellows is that which no normal Englishman ever did speak in actual life and, let us hope, never will.

Not long ago there was a broadcast about war-time on the farm which was delivered by Wiltshire cowmen, shepherds, and labourers in a natural way with an agreeable burr to their speech and a sensible reliance upon the vocabulary of the village. But suddenly, in the midst of it, one cowman said, 'We, with our depleted staff . . .' instead of 'We, with many away'.

Depleted staff! It is the very hall-mark of officialese, with its Latinity and its use of a formal and imposing word, staff, instead of the simpler 'hands' or 'men'. We need not suppose that the cowman wished to be imposing and to seem a fine, book-learned speaker at the 'mike'. He might have used the phrase any day at his own fireside, because words of this kind come pouring over the air and are inserting themselves into the common talk 'unbeknownst', as they used to say. The Ancient Greeks had a nice phrase about the man who 'escaped his own notice becoming drunk'. So nowadays we escape our own notice becoming verbose. All the Ministries encourage this vice. Why, for example, say of a certain food that it is 'in short supply' when all you mean is that it is scarce? I have not yet heard a housewife tell her husband that eggs are 'in short supply' this week, but that, like 'depleted staff' upon the farmer's lips, may come.

Some of Our Conquerors

The war, through the power it gives to bureaucracy and to the industrialists turned public administrators, will certainly add to our language — or rather inflate it. The tendency of such people is always to prefer a new and heavy word to an old and short one. In doing that they are following a habit particularly dear to our time, that is, to take the noun belonging to a verb and then to turn that noun into another and a longer verb. The most absurd and offensive example of this is the use of the word 'to decision'. 'Decide' is not nearly swollen enough for the swollen-headed Napoleon of a Film Corporation. 'Have you decisioned this?' he inquires, with a happy illusion of appearing the Educated Man. The American up-lifters have turned 'inspiring' into the ghastly 'inspirational', and their opposites, the American gangsters, who are supposed to talk quick,

13

'peppy' language, are often as long-winded and Latin-loving as any. They use 'to suspicion' instead of 'to suspect' (see James Cain's brilliantly horrible story *The Postman Always Rings Twice*). Nowadays the motor-trade has made a silly verb on similar lines, 'to service'.

There is, of course, a good case for keeping the language fluid and receptive. Mr. H. L. Mencken justly points out that Shakespeare and Ben Jonson enriched English frequently by their use of nouns as verbs. What an excellent word, for example, is the Shakespearean 'to spaniel' — that is, to follow in a flattering, fawning way, as the officers under Antony 'spaniel'd him at heels'! But such a trick is quite different from the abominable malpractice of taking the abstract noun made from a verb and then using that as a verb — e.g., 'to decision'. Mr. Mencken does indeed dismiss as silly such a usage as that, but he notes with satisfaction the official usage of 'to contact' in his country and the American Navy's acceptance of the verb 'to message'. Perhaps these are justified. There is no word which covers approach by telephone, letter, and speech, and 'contact' and 'message', used as verbs, are self-explanatory and concise.

He gently dismisses 'to signature' as 'redundant'. It is, in fact, as odious a waster of breath and space as 'to decision', since it adds two more syllables to a perfectly good word of one. That ridiculous habit of making additions, in order to seem important, is to be seen again in the film trade's use of the word 'to author' instead of 'to write'. 'Finalize' for 'end' is a new horror of this kind. The object here is to have a Latin word of two or three syllables instead of a Saxon word of one, the notion being that the simpletons to whom the films appeal will be vastly impressed by polysyllabic 'blurbs'.

Many words which were scolded on their first appearance have since lived on to acquire a good character as well as to perform a good function. Mr. Mencken quotes 'belittle', first used by Thomas Jefferson in 1787 and violently derided in London, and mentions as others once tabu in orthodox quarters but now accepted, freely employed, and allotted dictionary status, 'influential, handy, mileage, dutiable, lengthy, to advocate, to legislate, to progress,

14

and to locate'. 'To progress' is, perhaps, the most interesting of this list. It is a verb formed from a noun, but it is not long or clumsy. But in a short time an eminent Film 'Executive' will dismiss it as paltry and insufficient for the trumpeting of his forward-looking purposes and proceed to regard 'progression' as a more imposing verb. 'The fact that we have finalized a Six Months All-America Conference on Consumer Reaction to Art Pictures and have decisioned to create an All-Star Motion-Picture in Glorious, Glamorous Stereoscopic Technicolour, authored and signatured by Nelson Schmalzheimer and planned to run for eight hours with only two intermissions, indicates the rate of progressioned exhibitioning envisaged by Super-Superlative Pictures.' Such writing is increasingly with us.

Britain seems now to have swallowed and digested the American use of 'executive' as a noun. Being long and Latin, it is a natural favourite with those who so learnedly call a lift an 'elevator' and bid you 'operate' instead of work it. There was a time when American could fairly claim to be a 'snappy' language. But now it prefers prolixity to 'pep'. Have not its 'bosses' all become 'Executives'? Incidentally, 'an Executive' for a man who decides, a boss, is not only pompous but incorrect. Executive action is that which carries out somebody else's orders, a humble matter of following out, which is what the word originally meant. Our own Civil Service rightly grades its Administrative Class above its Executive Class.

How far American has been overwhelmed by this passion for classicism is revealed by the holy man of Harlem, who has called himself in turn The Messenger, Major J. Devine, Father Divine, and finally, and simply, God. This celestial coon, who has an immense following, bids the flock 'contact me harmoniously' and assures them that he is 'visibilating and tangibilating' their fondest imaginations. The gentleman may act as a very fine influence on the ethics and happiness of Harlem, but he is plainly doing the American language no good at all. The Negroes who once made their spirituals out of Bible English were fortunate to avoid this gas-bag stuff of the new evangelism at large in Jargantua.

The itch for length in diction becomes continually more powerful. Take the case of the final, the usually unnecessary, preposition. When I was a boy we checked figures: next we checked them up: now we 'check up on' them. Test and try once sufficed. Now everybody 'tries out' or 'tests out' this or that. Shall our cricketers have 'Test-Out' Matches? People no longer win. They 'win through' or even 'win out'. Vilest of all, perhaps, are 'face up to' for 'face' and 'meet up with', which says nothing more than 'meet.'

The Quick and the Dead

Words, like all other creatures, can be worked to death. The more we write and print — talking is hardly so lethal — the more words do we reduce to weaklings and even to corpses. What happens is that the words which are supposed to be specially picturesque or exciting appear so often that they are taken for granted. The image behind them ceases to be effective: they dwindle, despite their once great vigour and value, into the cliché class.

The first man, for example, to talk of a 'sickening thud', employed a vivid metaphor for acutely physical terror. But its success was its ruin. Every thud is now sickening and the idea of a fright producing actual nausea has quite gone. So with 'stony silence'. There are people who cannot use the word 'silence' without automatically prefixing 'stony'. What they mean by it they could not say. For stones are not notably silent. If struck, they clang. If trodden on, they make more noise than grass. If thrown, they produce 'sickening thuds'. Vegetable matter or cloth is much more quiet stuff than any mineral. Why not say 'a grassy' or 'a velvet' silence? It would be more accurate and more effective. Stony silence is really as dead as a neolithic flint.

I do not propose to wander further into the gigantic forest of Cliché. It has been carefully explored and charted by that active lexicographer, Mr. Eric Partridge, whose *Dictionary of Clichés* is a wonderful graveyard of the good phrase killed by kindness. For most clichés are tremendously vivid when they are born. Consider such a phrase as 'beggaring description'. It was a tremendous metaphor when first used by Shakespeare. Now it is valueless.

We should, however, observe one particular form of word-slaughter in the hope that we may occasionally rescue a nice term from this butchery. Journalism, pouring out its millions of words daily, is inevitably a murderer. In the game of word-making and word-taking it takes (and destroys) far more than it makes. What it takes nowadays is usually the short word, for the obvious reason that the formidable 'verboojuice' is of no use to those making up headlines for columns and captions for posters. Their business is to say as much as possible in the least possible space. Hence they seize on brevities, even if they happen to be antiques, such as 'slay' for murder or assassinate, 'parley' for conference or discussion, and 'key' for important. (In war-time everybody seems to be a key man, doing a key job, in a key town.) This cult of brevity may result in choices strangely unsuitable, such as lively for exciting when the subject is death. Thus a Trade Union Conference becomes on bills and headlines 'T.U. Parley' — well might a foreigner wonder who the fellow is — and a class-war riot is reported under 'Reds Slay Whites. Thousands Dead in Key Town. Lively Scenes'.

One of the words recently flattened out by the excessive attentions of journalism has been thrill, which is so much shorter than excitement or suspense. Thrill has had a specially hard time because it is the business of newspapers, especially in peace-time when things are dull, to discover excitements. If there is no news, news must be whipped up. Breakfast and supper without a ration of sensation are unthinkable. Therefore excitements are duly provided and, for sake of brevity, thrill is the chosen word. Pity the poor cricket-reporter sent to watch a dull game. Nothing whatever happens all day, but it is his job to record high lights and great deeds. At last, after hours of tedium, somebody misses a catch or is run out. Despairingly, he makes a feature of it. Next morning he sees that the sub-editor has headed his tale 'Thrills at Lord's'. Does this annoy spectators who had sat there all day swooning with boredom? Apparently not, but it infuriates me.

The unhappy history of 'thrill' is noted later in this book. So is that of glamour, a lovely victim of shocking misuse and constant over-work. Epic is another unfortunate. In the most humdrum times newspapers abound in 'Epic Struggles'. Do we not read 'Police Trail Bandit. Epic Chase', or 'Girl-Wife in Court. Epic Scenes'? We do, but the adjective, being dead, does not set us thinking of the major poets or of warriors spearing and spouting on the windy plains of Troy. Alas, poor Homer! He is not only caused to nod; he is totally floored. Any bit of nonsense can be 'epic' now, while some hiker's holiday outing may be absurdly dignified with the truly epic and honourable title of an 'Odyssey'.

That sort of thing is inevitable. When tools are blunted the best policy is to give them a rest. So, no doubt, with our words. If we could lay aside the thrills and glamours and the like for a very long period of repose, they might be able to return revived. But the life of words cannot be organized. The difficulty is to create suitable new words in societies which have been subjected to a formal education. For this education usually limits the creative capacity. Peasants make words easily — good, vigorous, picturesque words. But our urban and mechanical life is rarely inventive in this way: all its wits are going into its machines and so, apart from occasional bursts of slang-creation, it works with featureless abbreviations of long classical terms, like 'mike' for microphone, or else it does not even shorten at all but is loyal to the ponderous. It is queer that people so much concerned with speed as are motorists should be content with long and lumbering terms, such as limousine, accelerator, and carburettor, none of which is commonly shortened. Motors, as Mr. Osbert Sitwell has pointed out, entered this country as very odd, foreign contraptions which only some very odd creature like a foreigner could be supposed to understand. Hence the use of 'chauffeur', which has lingered on in our language, like hotel, chef, and valet. Perhaps some snobbery was at the back of this. The fact remains that the mechanization of our lives has weighted our English down far more than it has speeded it up. Compared with our ancestors we are a tongue-tied generation.

It is unfortunately true that people interested in words, which, as the vehicles of thought and feeling, are as vital to our lives as food and drink and fire and shelter, become unconsciously conservative. Many people instinctively resent new words and usages. That may be the product of an education which is so largely an immersion in traditional things. When any novelty of speech arrives, even a lively and serviceable novelty, there is certain to be strong protest. It is dismissed as a vulgar modernism, without much consideration as to the proper meaning of vulgar and the necessity of modern words for modern things. I hope that I shall never be caught condemning a good new word simply because it is new, but the virus of conservatism is powerful and one frequently finds oneself opposing what may turn out to be a valuable piece of creation.

In what follows far more will appear about old words than about new. My anthology has been made rather as a record of personal pleasures than as a weapon for linguistic reformers. I have amused myself with word-collection. But that does not indicate any lack of appetite for word-creation. Let us have new words in abundance, but not the kind of word which is merely an old and short and stout one made long and flabby. Why, for example, call a job an assignment?

Until our tongue has become fecund again we may profit by some revivals of the just word unjustly neglected. This anthology suggests a few which seem to merit a glorious resurrection. One profitable line of procedure would be to recover from America some of the good, simple words which the Pilgrim Fathers took in their cabin-trunks. American is either the best of English or the worst, the best when it preserves the vigour of the seventeenth century, the worst when it is mixing Social Science with 'inspirational' sentiments. The dabblers in matters of the Psyche have created a truly abominable 'psychologese', in which responses are always reactions, every sort of desire is a complex, and to be fond of mamma is inevitably called possession by a mother-fixation.

(So far has this nasty lingo permeated from the lecturer's dais to the common convention that nobody now asks me my opinion of this or that. It is always 'What is your reaction?') I have at hand a work composed by one of this School on *The Nature of the Soul* in which thought is always called opinionation, while the word integration appears in almost every paragraph, though I doubt whether the author knows what it means. Here is a powerful specimen of that gentleman's curious vocabulary and creed:

> And as for the fertilization of one soul-integration by another — look how *that* process is collectivized by the Article of Covenant governing External Synthesis. There we see provision for The Society of Life (the world's first seeding group) to enter into serious fertilizing relations with the appropriate external group. This is not a mere metaphor. The spirit of the seed is in it. It *is* fertilization. It *is* the road to unfoldment, in place of the stony integrations which lead to opposition of a hatefilled kind.

That is one sort of American English. But the English need not vaunt themselves. They have their own masters in this kind. The other sort is the sensible, concise Tudor English which uses 'beat it' for go. Ben Jonson's characters are to be discovered 'beating it' down the cobbled street. Sidewalk, again, which is seventeenth-century English, is a much better term than our pavement since it describes what it is meant to be, whereas pavement might mean any paved surface. It is astonishing how the modern American, not the modern English, usage turns up when one is reading the Elizabethans. When I play cards, my English friends talk of a pack. When I go to the pictures, the American gangsters ask for 'a deck of cards'. So, when he wanted a game, did Shakespeare — or who ever it was that wrote 3 *Henry VI*, v, 1.

> But, when he thought to steal the single ten,
> The king was slily fingered from the deck.

am not suggesting that deck is a better word than pack, but merely citing a striking case of the emigrants' verbal luggage.

In addition to hinting at the need for revivals and reimportations, I may, I hope, persuade a few more people to be interested in words, whose oddity and beauty, whose strange parentage and exquisite aspects and rhythms make them excellent material for collectors. Man is an acquisitive animal and nearly everybody amasses and dotes upon something in addition to his grievances. The collecting tribe has applied itself to an extraordinary range of articles, ranging from eggs and orchids and butterflies to stamps and coins and walking-sticks. If the locks of hair and shoe-buckles of the great are meet for hoarding, what of their words, often the prime instruments of their power? If it is good to collect first editions, why not the stuff of which that precious print is made?

To be a collector of language is an innocent occupation. The snatchers and hoarders of birds' eggs and of flowers first create a scarcity, then hunt down the rareties (or, even worse, hire others to go marauding for them) and finally exterminate the beauty which they crave. To go a-fowling on the slopes of Helicon with those flashing, sounding beauties, the words, as coveted prize invades no rights and does no violence to life. To hunt words is to do no trespass. Rather does it keep or elicit good things for the common use and public pleasure instead of destroying them or making them scanty for a privy satisfaction. Words can be as rich to the senses as a Painted Lady, Purple Emperor, Bird of Paradise, and the most orchidaceous blooms of domestic marsh or alien jungle. Like coins in the purse and stamps on letters, which also men covet and collect, they serve a simple need. They throw colour on to paper and make music in the air. Words are wind and fire: but those are difficult articles to collect. They are also the seed of action and the blossom of thought, which are easier for the anthologist. I have found some words which are withering and deserve to recover their old strength and liveliness, others, more scarce, which are rising to power and merit that emergence. I have found, and hope to go on finding, the droll specimen and the thing of beauty. Readers of Shakespeare know to their great comfort that they are never finished with him. They turn to a passage which they had heard or read a thousand times; every syllable is stale: yet suddenly a new beauty leaps out from the famous and familiar lines. The English vocabulary, like Shakespeare its matchless employer and its giver of increase, has always some untapped or neglected mines of precious metal. It is the El Dorado of collectors.

ACKNOWLEDGEMENT

THE right to quote from copyright work is a matter teeming with legal complexity. Authors to whom I have appealed because I was quoting more than a phrase or a few lines have shown me the greatest kindness, and I would like to express my gratitude to Miss Bambridge, Mr. A. P. Watt, and Messrs. Methuen (in the matter of quoting from Rudyard Kipling), to Mr. Hilaire Belloc, to Mr. John Betjeman, to Mr. Edmund Blunden, to Messrs. Laurence Housman, Jonathan Cape, and the Society of Authors (in the matter of quoting from A. E. Housman), to Messrs. Macmillan (in the matter of quoting from Kipling and Ralph Hodgson), and to Mr. Siegfried Sassoon; also to Mr. Arthur Ransome for helpful suggestions.

ALLAY

ALLAY is a verb of richest variety. In its time it has signified a fine assortment and even confusion of meanings, to overthrow or to appease, to dilute wine or to lay on hounds. I have also found it as one of a covey of Elizabethan verbs proper to the serving and carving of meats. These verbs run like the famous nouns of assembly, a pride of lions, skulk of foxes, gaggle of geese, and so on. Robert May, author of *The Accomplisht Cook*, thus parades them:

> Lift that Swan; Rear that Goose; Dismember that Hern; Unbrace that Mallard; Unlace that Coney; Allay that Pheasant; Wing that Partridge; Display that Quail; Unjoynt that Bittern; Unlatch that Curlew; Break that Egript; Thigh that Woodcock.

One can imagine them rolled with a sonorous rapture on a Malvolio's tongue as he overlooked the ordering of his lady's table for a day of high entertainment. Sir Toby, too, would have gladly and imposingly commanded the allaying of a young roast pheasant.

ALOOF

ALOOF, to me a vividly expressive word, is a gift from the sea: it is derived from the nautical 'luffing', one of whose meanings is to get the windward side of your opponent in a race or battle. So aloof meant 'away to the windward', and then apart from or away in any sphere. Milton used it almost as a preposition, calling the sun 'alooff the vulgar constellations thick', and that implies the sense of pride and superiority which the word now so nicely carries. I owe to Mr. James Agate an admirable quotation from a wine-merchant's list, 'This claret is so distinguished as to be almost aloof'. There are always authors and artists to whom aloofness is a natural or a desirable and cultivated pose. They take to themselves the exquisite refinement of the vintage aforesaid. Milton's 'vulgar constellations thick' suggests the kind of stage-party which is called a galaxy. To be aloof at such a gathering admirably describes the faint participation of a literary gentleman who believes himself to be above such matters, say a Henry James bidden to a feast of that starry, but breezily benignant Music-hall companionage, The Water Rats.

ANIMATION

ANIMATE, for quicken, was known to Marlowe and Milton, but, rather strangely, unused by Shakespeare. In the eighteenth century it acquired a technical sense which has charm as well as pertinence. The various recognized antics and capers of a Harlequin in the pantomimes of the period were known as his several 'animations'. Great actors, like all great artists, have their various tricks, nowadays called technique, for obtaining their effects. In the case of so vivid an art as acting, it would be appropriate to preserve the word once so picturesquely bestowed on Harlequin. What playgoer does not know and relish the 'animations' of Sir Seymour Hicks?

ANNOY

COMMON enough surely, but weakened now by its restriction to personal vexation. Once it meant to harm or corrupt and was applied to all nuisances.

> As one who long in populous City pent
> Where Houses thick and Sewers annoy the Aire

is Milton's usage of annoy. There was wont to be a Jury of Annoyances to decide about such public pests as 'Houses thick and Sewers'. Nowadays the would-be solitary, who seeks to be lonely in the hills, finds the air 'annoyed' with aeroplanes, and we have all seen golfers, annoyed in our sense, who appeared to be most obviously annoying the turf.

ARRANT

ARRANT comes very trippingly off the tongue as an adjunct and aggravation of abuse. There is some real satisfaction in adding 'arrant' to one's description of a knave or rogue. The word has a curious history. It was a form of errant, which means vagrant or wandering, and it was thus especially applied to strolling thieves. Then, by a mistake as to the origin, an arrant thief was taken to mean a particularly guilty or shameless specimen, a very thievish thief. So arrant began to be put in front of any adjective, even a friendly one, to add to its weight. First we have arrant thief, i.e. wandering pilferer, then arrant scoundrel, i.e. a very wicked wretch with no suggestion of movement, and lastly, an arrant good fellow, stressing simply his genuine excellence. But arrant was best and most commonly used with opprobrious intention. Shakespeare's texts abound in arrant knaves, thieves, and whores. Was it arrant folly on our part to let it slip?

AWFUL

IN *Some Miseries of Human Life*, an admirable compilation of social calamities made by 'Samuel Sensitive and Timothy Testy', there is set down as one of the main horrors of a rural ride,

> Visiting an Awful Ruin, in the company of a Romp of one sex or a Hun of the other.

It is curious to discover this use of Hun, presumably as a boorish, uncultivated fellow, with the old and good use of Awful as awe-inspiring. No word has been more foully mishandled than the latter. Romp, for a chattering, facetious adult, instead of a turbulent child, seems to be another good thing lost.

BABBLE

BABBLE is descriptive of childish or senile babble. Dying Falstaff babbled of green fields as any babe of his food and trinkets. But babble is not a mean or ugly word and it is justly applied to the songs of birds, not merely to the cuckoo's prattle, as Wordsworth applied it, but to the master-singers themselves. Mr. Ralph Hodgson has invented the babble-wren; at least orthodox ornithology is ignorant of this voluble mite.

> There, sharp and sudden, there I heard —
> Ah! some wild, lovesick, singing bird
> Woke singing in the trees!
> The nightingale and babble-wren
> Were in the English greenwood then,
> And you heard one of these?

For Gerard Manley Hopkins the lark is a babbler,

> Not that the sweet-fowl, song-fowl needs no rest,
> Why hear him, hear him babble and drop down to his nest.

Inanimate things can be likewise vocal.

> The stripling Thames at Bablock Hythe

What a name for what a place! The water-music of the Upper River babbles in the memory of all who have loved Oxford.

BARKABLE

THE use of adjectives ending in -able is peculiar. They are usually passive, as in lovable, eatable, drinkable, and so on. But knowledgeable, which used to mean knowable, has of late been commonly employed to mean 'knowing'. This I took to be an affectation or a faulty modernism, until coming across such a word as barkable for able to bark, which is as old as the thirteenth century. Eileen Power quotes this exquisite passage from a treatise of that period on Estate Management.

It profiteth the lord to have discreet shepherds, watchful and kindly, so that the sheep be not tormented by their wrath but crop their pasture in peace and joyfulness; for it is a token of the shepherd's kindness if the sheep be not scattered abroad but browse around him in company. Let him provide himself with a good barkable dog and lie nightly with his sheep.

Was John Davidson's 'runnable stag' fit to be hunted or actively fleet? In either case it might be a cause of barkability.

BARNACULAR

T H I S will not be found in the dictionary and its inclusion is a piece of vanity. While writing once of the Tite Barnacles, the great clan of office-holders satirized by Dickens in *Little Dorrit*, I had reason to mention that they are habitually cited by modern journalism to mock the Civil Service. As a matter of fact, the whole point of the Dickensian attack is that the Barnacle clan had its clutches on everything, ruled and exploited all the services and professions, and expected to have the fattest pickings of Church, Law, Medicine, etc. as well as of the Government Departments. However, one of its chief fortresses was the Circumlocution Office and so the Barnacles have become especially associated with bureaucratic dalliance and pedantry and the issue of complicated forms composed in an abominable jargon. I have the greatest respect for the British Civil Service, which recruits and retains many of the best brains in the country, but I must confess to sharing Mr. A. P. Herbert's abhorrence of their 'officialese' English. This lingo I ventured to call 'The Barnacular'.

BEREAVE

A C O M M O N word and beautiful, which you can. if you are a strict zealot of etymology, trace back to Com. Teut., O. Teut., and O. Eng. origins and link up with vocables like 'bereafian'. Being no such zealot, I merely observe that to bereave meant to pill and rob before it meant to make orphans or remove kindred. I include it because it touches no line of poetry which it does not decorate. A. E. Housman explained how certain sounds and phrases gave him such a shiver of ecstasy that he dare not mutter them while shaving. Not so physically susceptible, I find many lines of his to work less like earthquakes and more like anodynes. When afflicted with the ugliness of things it is a comfortable exercise to murmur almost anything of Housman's, not least

> With the great gale we journey
>   That breathes from gardens thinned,
> Borne in the drift of blossoms
>   Whose petals throng the wind;
>
> Buoyed on the heaven-heard whisper
>   Of dancing leaflets whirled
> From all the woods that autumn
>   Bereaves in all the world.

I cannot, and would not, take a walk in October without at least the final couplet of this lovely noise some time upon my lips.

BLAZON

THE whole peacock world of tabards and trumpets is blazoned in a single word. Blazon begins as a shield or banner, heraldically marked, and then comes to mean a description of such things: at last, a description or report of anything. As a term for tidings it has the full sonority of powerful brass. The Ghost of Hamlet's father, having threatened to 'harrow up the soul' with his news of life beyond the grave, remembers that such hair-raising information is not for the living.

> But this eternal blazon must not be
> To ears of flesh and blood.

This is, as I interpret it, a magnificently condensed phrase to signify report of the long hereafter. George Russell used blazoned in the commoner sense in a quatrain of uncommon quality in his lines 'On behalf of Some Irishmen not Followers of Tradition'.

> No blazoned banner we unfold —
> One charge alone we give to youth,
> Against the sceptred myth to hold
> The golden heresy of truth.

Shakespeare was fond of blazon. Cassio calls Desdemona 'One that excels the quirks of blazoning pens'. Words dear to the richest wordman of them all must surely command the general affection.

BLIMPISH

WILL blimp and blimpish survive? (I prefer the adjective to the noun.) The great cartoonist, Low, drew on the military balloon for his Colonel and we may draw on that notable walrus for our symbol of rubicund pomp and large, preposterous folly. Blimpish goes with a way of life, which has not been lacking in good looks. The Spa, the promenade, the croquet-lawns, the Club with its bald domes of Anglo-Indian silence sunk sleepily in leather arm-chairs — for these blimpish is no mere word of contempt. I recommend it to Mr. John Betjeman, whose lighter muse is so happy among the palings and balconies of the Victorian Colonel's paradise, where my own boyhood was spent.

> Shall I forget the warm marquee
> And the general's wife so soon,
> When my son's colleger[1] acted as tray
> For an ice and a macaroon,
> And distant carriages jingled through
> The stuccoed afternoon?

He wrote of Cheltenham. To call its region of Pittville 'blimpish' would be to honour the adjective, for Pittville is a charming model of early nineteenth century town-planning, blimpish of old, and

[1] Mortar-board.

possibly still, in its personnel, but for a century benign to the eye and offering to the leisurely observer a gracious calendar of 'stuccoed afternoons'.

BLITZ

BLITZ-KRIEG, the lightning war, means something when war is suddenly declared or made. To talk of 'blitz-krieg' when a war has been going on for several years is mere nonsense. But the British seized the word 'blitz' because of its expressive likeness to blast and applied it to bombing. Bomb evidently struck the average mind as too weak a term except when a lonely missile fell. A large attack needed a larger word and 'blitz', most acceptable because of its brevity to composers of newspaper headlines, was welcomed. It is certainly more descriptive to the British mind than the 'strafe' of the last war. 'A blasted area' is equivocal to us. 'Blitzed' now is definite and painfully picturesque. The word may survive the dreadful occasion of its birth. Brevity, as I noted, is on its side, but that may result in its being over-worked before long (see the note on 'Thrill'). Meanwhile it goes with a bang.

BLOWEN

THIS, with its similar blowze, is one of the enormous list of English words for a coarse woman. But, according to Mr. W. L. Hanchant, editor of *The Newgate Garland*, it was first of all a blown-up type of person, 'any showy or flaunting woman, but finally a prostitute only, in contradistinction to joiner, a term of friendship applied to a fancy girl'. Joiner is a simply and sweetly descriptive term, which might be more widely remembered and employed. Blowze, which Herrick liked, also tells its story well. Blowen, in its original sense of a puffed-up, pretentious creature, with its inevitable suggestion of some physical grossness and wheezy flatulence as well, is the best of all. No steady supporter of the tavern can have passed his life without meeting many a blowze (in the public bar) and many a blowen (in the saloon).

30

BOOBY

BOOBY appears to be the fruit of a victory. It came in from Spain soon after the Armada and a fine, heavy dolt the booby is. Dryden, in one of his dramatic prologues, denounced 'the booby faces in the pit'. To us now the word savours of the nursery and belongs rather to the previous generation. But I can imagine it making an effective return into high politics. 'The petulant boobies of the Opposition'. Bunyan used it well of the tiresome, repetitive cuckoo.

> Thou booby, says't thou nothing but Cuckoo?

This is even better than A. E. Housman's

> The cuckoo shouts at nothing all day long.

The cuckoo may be sly enough in evading its parental cares, but proclaims itself, by lumbering flight and monotony of speech, true booby.

BOSKY

BOSKY naturally became an exile when the Tennysonian school of minstrelsy was broken up. True it is that bosky and boskage adorned many abominable verses in school-magazines, verses written in the odious lingo which proclaimed of sunrise that

> Phoebus hath clomb.

But bosky, a straight derivation from the Italian bosco, is a sensible word for wooded. England has abundant tangles of bracken and briar, bush and tree, which are most admirably described as bosky. In a handsome part of the Midlands, a westerly ridge of Staffordshire overlooking Shropshire, a region which has memories especially sacred for devotees of the House of Stuart, is Boscobel of the historic hiding-place and royal oak. Boscobel is simply a verbal importation from Italy, and means the lovely woodland. It is certainly a lovely word and should move us to grant to bosky the restitution of its ancient dignity and favour.

31

BRAG

ELSEWHERE Milton's nice use of brag, in relation to physical grace, 'Beauty is Nature's brag and must be shown', is quoted. Since brag became a game of cards in which bluff was the chief element, this might be deemed a prophetic reference to strip-poker. Brag means a challenge as well as a boast and, as an adjective, lively. Garrick, in one of his many and fearsome Odes to Shakespeare, called him a 'Wag ever brag' (See note on Wag.) Shakespeare used brag in our sense and called Caesar's Veni, vidi, vici, a 'thrasonical brag'.

Bragless occurs at the end of that mint of strange words, *Troilus and Cressida*. Here is the passage:

DIOMEDE   The bruit is Hector's slain by Achilles.
AJAX   If it be so, yet bragless let it be;
             Great Hector was a man as good as he.
AGAMEMNON   March patiently along. Let one be sent
             To pray Achilles see us at our tent.
             If in his death the gods have us befriended,
             Great Troy is ours and our sharp wars are ended.

A modern Dick Whittington could scarcely do worse on Boxing Night. That Shakespeare wrote most of *Troilus and Cressida* is powerfully stamped upon the play's sour heart. But some of this rhymed stuff must surely have been taken over from, or vamped up by, another. Whoever wrote it obviously was not feeling very brag.

BROWNED OFF

NOT much Service slang became general speech during the first two years of the Greater War. 'Browned off', meaning bored, was an exception. I would like to think that it referred to the hue of the tired autumnal foliage. In that case it is the modern equivalent of Macbeth's decline into the sere, the yellow leaf. More probably it is a kitchen metaphor. To 'do brown', i.e. cheat, apparently comes from the notion of an ample roasting, which raises an interesting point. Why should the kindly craft of cookery be so ill thought of and applied to the forging of accounts and robbery of men? I like to regard 'browned off' as a trope from the October garden: no doubt I sentimentally delude myself.

BUMBASTE

BOMBAST, which is now used exclusively in this form and for a swollen kind of speech, is much more persuasive in its old spelling and might have retained its old meaning. Bumbaste was cotton-stuff used for stuffing garments and the heavily-quilted Tudor folk were bombastic indeed: still more so, James I, who bumbasted himself all over and wore immensely padded clothes in order to defeat the dreaded assassin's dagger. The word was then common as a verb. Greene accused the 'prentice Shakespeare of 'bumbasting' blank verses and Heywood wrote of plays bumbasted out with all manner of noisy irrelevance and mummerish titivations. He boasted his own austerity.

> A Strange Play you are like to have, for know
> We use no Drum, nor Trumpet, nor Dumbe Show:
> No Combate, Marriage, not so much to-day
> As Song, Dance, Masque to bumbaste out a play.

In the same way Shakespeare spoke of certain kinds of wit as 'The bumbaste and the lining of the time.' Our bombasine, a magnificent word considering the type of lady once addicted to this fabric, comes from the same origin, and might often with point have kept the old spelling. This leads to the further and scholastic usage of bumbaste, 'to beat the posteriors'.

CANTLE

THIS, for segment or portion, a thing cut, seems to have pined away from usage since Charles Lamb employed it. Shakespeare

33

knew it and enjoyed its superior dignity and sonority. 'Part of the world' would not be much, but, when Antony's lieutenant says of his commander's dalliance,

> The greater cantle of the world is lost
> With very ignorance: we have kissed away
> Kingdoms and provinces,

the passionate squandering takes on imposing bulk. So there is a verb, to cantle, for cut; also a cantlet, for a tiny slice. Our restaurants would sound more richly did we but command 'a cantle of that pie'. Sliver is rare now for slice and rightly, for it is an ugly word. Let us keep cantle instead. Mention of slices reminds me of an old Scottish lady, described in a book of memories by J. J. Bell. When asked to take food at tea-time, she would at first decline and then accept what she called 'just a sensation of cake'.

CARAVEL

IT is odd that, while boating and sailing have so beautified the waters, they have so little adorned our language. Galleon was fine, but the smaller craft, gigs and brigs, sloops and schooners, cutters, frigates and pinnaces, yachts and yawls, are simply not good enough for the exquisite forms which they have represented. And as for our river-sports, canoe may pass, but skiff and punt and dinghy are deplorable. Why did we never promote coracle from the primitive tub that it was to serve our modern needs? Why, above all, did we let go the caravel, which sails with proper grace through the pages of Hakluyt and is occasionally remembered by our poets when dealing with the ancient mariner? Sir John Squire's sonnet 'There was an Indian' ends finely with the vision of the frightened aboriginal, who,

> His lips gone pale, knelt low behind a stone,
> And stared, and saw, and did not understand,
> Columbus's doom-burdened caravels
> Slant to the shore, and all their seamen land.

Caravel may be somewhat alien, but a wise Imperialism would have seized and kept it.

CHEVISANCE

MR. HAROLD NICOLSON has pointed out that most of the Elizabethan flowers, which wave and glisten in the lyrics of the time, are still with us. But what has become of Chevisance and likewise of Pawnce which Spenser sets dancing along with more familiar blooms in his 'Ditty in Praise of Eliza, Queen of Shepherds'?

> Bring hether the Pincke and purple Cullambine,
>> With Gelliflowres;
> Bring Coronations, and Sops-in-wine
>> Worne of Paramoures:
> Strowe me the ground with Daffadowndillies,
> And Cowslips, and Kingcups, and lovèd Lillies:
>> The pretie Pawnce,
>> And the Chevisaunce,
> Shall match with the fayre flowre Delice.

Flowre Delice', presumably pronounced dillice, is Shakespeare's flower-de-luce, better known to us as fleur-de-lis, the heraldic lily or iris. Pawnce seems, like chevisance, to have withered away. Chevisance originally meant achievement or provision of supply and then, most unromantically, the lending of money or goods for profit. Spenser seems to have confused chevisance with chivalry: it is certainly too gentle a word for the usurers' profession, and is happier in the flower-bed than the counting-house.

CIT

A LEARNED essay might be written on the Abbreviation Contemptuous. Who calls a Gentleman a Gent is sneering: who reduces citizen to cit is doing much the same. But, after all, sneering is a part of wit and to reduce the swollen is usually both medical and moral. Cit is an excellent dismissive term, suggesting something less than a man in stature and more in purse. The cit, as most eighteenth-century authors knew, was wont to grub money in a dark counting-house in his mean little way. Wrote Burns:

> A title, Dempster merits it;
> A garter gie to Willie Pitt;
> Gie wealth to some be-ledger'd cit,
>   In cent. per cent.,
> But gie me real, sterling wit,
>   And I'm content.

Moderns should return to Cit. It may also surprise some of them to learn from Ayrshire that real was, and should remain, a word of two syllables.

CLOUD

A COMMON climatic word, but no longer commonly employed, in its old and beautiful usage, to mean hill. At the southern base of the Pennines, in Cheshire and Derbyshire, it still is so applied and there you may climb a Cloud. That sounds magical and lyrical, but, as a matter of fact, cloud is, in origin, the same as clod. First a clod of rock, then a clod of air . . . but, with a stroke of genius or by accident, those designating clods of air started to use the far more gracious form cloud. And what an exquisite word it is, almost creating poetry with no more said!

> Like far-off mountains túrnéd into clouds

is not one of the best-known lines in a very well-known play of Shakespeare, but it is certainly one of the loveliest, being most simply descriptive as well as musically perfect. Demetrius, if you are curious, says it to Hermia. (*A Midsummer Night's Dream*, Act iv, sc. 1). It unites the two meanings of cloud and for me has an enduring suggestion of mist over Dovedale, where some of the fells are Clouds.

COG

A COGGING fellow is an excellent description of a cheating, cozening creature and pokes his nasty head up in the orations of the eighteenth century. To cog originally was to cheat at dice by manipulating the fall. Later it was simply to play the deceiver. Falstaff, courting Mistress Ford, puts cogging among the arts of the precious and the foppish.

> Come, I cannot cog, and say thou art this and that, like a many of these lisping hawthorn-buds, that come like women in men's apparel, and smell like Bucklersbury in simple-time;

It is queer that the word should have dropped out. The Victorians preferred pettifogging, which has not exactly the same sense since it implies smallness as well as duplicity. We should return to the attack on 'cogging politicians' and 'cogging, cozening, slaves'.

COMELY

To use Comely now would, perhaps, be slightly affected, at least in England. It springs more naturally and with less archaic suggestion on Scottish lips. In 'The Song of Solomon' the Biblical translators used it of rich physical beauty: later it acquired a flavour of sobriety and moral decorum, adding these to the implication of a sensuous beauty. Milton's 'civil-suited Morn' was not 'trick'd and frounced' but 'kerchieft in a comely cloud'. Shakespeare's

> He is a man, setting his fate aside,
> Of comely virtues

makes the word first cousin to the austere 'seemly'. But a love who is 'black but comely' need not be so strict and in Scotland the fair word appears often to have been more liberally used, even of pleasuring places. In Edinburgh in the eighteenth century there was a resort called Comely Gardens, full of raree-shows, the intended Vauxhall of its time and city. Meanwhile the four Carnegie Trusts in Dunfermline have one of the loveliest addresses that I know — Comely Park House — and there do they properly survey and assist the arts and learning as well as the moral and physical welfare of the nation.

COMFORT

THIS is one of the admirable words which have turned soft and it needs to be re-stiffened to its proper shape and value. It is, by origin, the giver of strength and valour. But the ubiquitous advertisement of 'All Modern Comforts' hints mainly at central heating and other niceties of plumbing. 'Comforts for the troops' would once have been allies and reserves: listen to Berners' Froissart, who wrote of companies, 'on a wyng in good order, ready to confort the prince's batayle'. Now such comforts are mainly chocolates, cigarettes, and woollies. One is not depreciating the pleasures and utility of these latter in wishing more substance and dignity for the grand old word. This has become so dwarfed and so insipid that the unlettered Christian of to-day may easily think of the Holy Ghost, the Comforter, as a rather sickly source of sentimental consolation, a celestial crooner almost, instead of as an ally in the good fight and bringer of mettle and resolve. Gerard, the herbalist, used comfortable to imply a tonic and strengthening power. 'If odours may work satisfaction, they are so soveraigne in plants and so comfortable that no confection of the apothecaries can equall their excellent vertue.' Our comfort, in short, needs conforting in the way of Tudor English.

COMPENDIUM

COMING across this word in some impolite contemporary observations on Oliver Cromwell ('That Landskip of Iniquity, that Sink of Sin, and that Compendium of Baseness'), I was reminded of a Christmas long ago when I received 'a Compendium of Games', i.e. a chest containing the material for every kind of table-sport.

What a majestically Roman phrase for a somewhat bizarre, but most serviceable article! Compendium usually means an abridgement or summary or short treatise (e.g. Compendium of Mathematics), but in the toy-market it is a collection, an Omnibus Volume, as the publishers would say with an equal devotion to Latin. It was an astonishingly august word to apply to a box of childish pleasures and properly belonged to a seigneurial world in which the channel of communication between drawing-room and nursery was the imported polyglot governess. 'With what, Fräulein, is Master Rupert engaged?' 'He is engaged, my lady, with his Compendium.'

CORDIAL

As a noun it is commonly used for any warming drink, but more rarely and effectively as any kind of life-sweetening and encouraging thing. So it comes to mean an inspiriting example, as one might describe a great comedian as 'the cordial of our stage'. Here it is in John Galt, used in his description of Nanse Banks, who did the village schooling for scholars' pence.

> She was a patient creature, well cut out for her calling, with blear een, a pale face, and a long neck, but meek and contented withal, tholing the dule of this word with a Christian submission to the spirit; and her garret-room was a cordial of cleanliness.

Dule is exclusively Scots, but thole is good Anglo-classical for endure. Cordial thus employed is 'a cordial of speech'.

COURTESY

I prefer courtesy to be pronounced not as the longer version of curtsey but in the Victorian manner, with the 'ou' somewhat Frenchified, as befits our cousin of the lovely 'courtoisie'. It means the habit of being gracefully considerate in personal relations. It is more than politeness; beauty breaks in. Chaucer set it beside truth, honour, and freedom. Belloc has an exquisite lyric on three pictures owned by the Storrington monks — 'and Courtesy was in them all'. He ends:

> Our Lady out of Nazareth rode —
> It was Her month of heavy load;
> Yet was Her face both great and kind,
> For Courtesy was in Her Mind.
>
> The Third it was our Little Lord,
> Whom all the Kings in arms adored;
> He was so small you could not see
> His large intent of Courtesy.

So fair a word deserves to be spoken finely and kept in honourable use.

CREATURE

CREATURES are of two kinds, those fashioned by Nature, which may be noble or base, well or ill-favoured, and those made by man, which are usually contemptible. This second use of creature may now savour of the antique, but it has sting in it. Looking recently at a programme of Shakespeare's *Richard II* I noticed Bushy, Bagot, and Green described as 'Creatures of King Richard', which is far better than the 'servants to King Richard' usually employed. Let us have our more servile Members of Parliament dismissed as Creatures, instead of Puppets, of the Party Whips. There is something, at least for me, luridly 'umble, creepy, and crawly about a creature of this kind. Shakespeare, by the way, deprives the king's creatures of their proper titles. Holinshed wrote:

> The common brute ran that the king had set to farme the realme of England unto Sir William Scroope, Earl of Wiltshire, and then treasurer of England, to Sir John Bushie, Sir William Bagot, and Sir Henry Greene, knights.

The common brute is good: it so bluntly forecasts for us one phase of the modern industry of information.

CRIMSON

WHEN I first read, in a fine Scots ballad,

> When we cam in by Glasgow toun,
>   We were a comely sicht to see:
> My love was clad in the black velvet
> And I myself in cramasie,

I would have answered any question about the nature of cramasie by saying that it was a species of gay cloth named after some foreign place, as cretonne is named after Creton in Normandy. But cramasie is the old Scots form of crimson, itself a comely word, but no aboriginal, however native it may sound. It is, in fact, a Middle-Eastern import and one of our many Arabians. It is also, like other arrivals from the gorgeous east, an insect. Cramasie and cremosin, later crimson, came from the Arabic Qerinasi, the cochineal insect which, on being crushed in quantity, yields a reddish-purple dye. Out of this sordid mush comes our rich and romantic name of crimson, a name which always reminds me of one of the most strangely beautiful Shakespearean passages. When Iachimo is standing over the sleeping Imogen he spies,

> On her left breast
> A mole cinque-spotted, like the crimson drops
> I' the bottom of a cowslip.

The next time you pick a cowslip, look within, not only to appreciate the imperial mixture of crimson and yellow, but the exquisite sharpness of Shakespeare's eye that went to the making of this simile.

CRINKUM-CRANKUM

HERE is a fine dismissive word for all the fussily over-decorated things. Lord Ogleby in Coleman's comedy, *The Clandestine Marriage*, thus dismissed the vogue of Gothic which, in the middle of the eighteenth century, was beginning to fill the grounds of an English Nobleman's Seat with sham ruins and twisty ponds. At that time canals, not yet industrialized, were still channels (the words are really the same) and the gardens of a great mansion had to be rich in such ornamental waters. Fashion continually made the canals more bizarre, equipped them with a false façade of bogus bridges, and even introduced the fantastic Italian style of grotto with curious fountains, vivarium, aquarium, and so forth. All, of course, to be designed 'with knobs on', as the modern slang so expressively describes a certain kind of architecture. In short, crinkum-crankum.

DAEDAL

DAEDAL is pure classicism, deriving from Daedalus, the inventive one, and used both of the contriving hand and of the multiplicity of things contrived, especially by Nature. *Natura naturans* is daedal in one sense, *Natura naturata* in the other. Evelyn, the Diarist, wrote of 'a Daedale' as a complicated device in the laying out of gardens. Landor liked the word with its suggestion of multitudinous and glittering growth or movement. To him a dance was daedal. Robert Louis Stevenson implied a gloriously daedal world in his famous

> God's bright and intricate device
> Of days and seasons.

To Lord de Tabley, that gifted as well as baronial bard, looking out over Tabley Mere in Cheshire, a county which long remained lordly in a quiet way, the month of May and the pinguid scene ('Earth's royal aspects of delight') suggested the classic epithet. He saw

The serene domes of mounting lime
The meadow's crest of daedal May
And deep-eyed morning ere the time,
Sleeking her curtain clouds away.

I am indebted to Sir William Beach Thomas and his rustic anthology
'The Squirrels' Granary' for being reminded of de Tabley's
excellence.

DAFF

THERE are two Daffs, apart from the abbreviation of Daffodil.
There is the Scottish Daff, which is to talk or behave sportively. In
Jane Elliot's *The Flowers of the Forest* when 'The English, for ance,
by guile won the day', the melancholy has reached the sheep-folds
and there is sad silence at the milking-pails.

Lasses are lonely and dowie and wae
Nae daffin', nae gabbin' . . .

A dowie, i.e. dismal, lass may be the opposite of a daffin' one in
meaning, but she is equal in felicity of phrase. The English Daff
is to put off, cast aside. Clothes are both daffed and doffed. Daffing
may be applied to far larger matters than a doublet. 'Canst thou so
daff me?' cries Leonato when Claudio is pushing him away.
Henry V was once the Mad-Cap Prince who 'daffed the world
aside'. Why did his posterity daff this trim, expressive term?

DAFFODIL

DAFF I have claimed to be twice virtuous, once on each side of
the Tweed. But it becomes abominable when used as an abbreviation of Daffodil, a word so fair that truncation is a vile malpractice.
Daffodil itself is a childish creation (daffadowndilly still more so)
and a nursery version, as it were, of Affodil, which, in turn, is our
conception of Asphodel. Poetry is forever candled with the light

43

of Asphodel, as Elysium was carpeted with its blooms. When I was introduced to Asphodel on the Greek mountains beside Mycenae, I was as much disappointed by the first as staggered by the majesty of the second. Presumably I was shown the wrong article, for it bore no resemblance to our 'lamp of beauty', Shakespeare's brave anticipator of the swallow. Asphodel shall remain for me a lyric love, a flower laid up in fancy, frequent in the grounds of Castle Bunthorne — as well as in the classic meadows. English lyric poetry sways and shines with the windswept gold of daffodils. They are summoned to a lamentation by Milton.

> Bid amaranthus all his beauty shed
> And daffadillies fill their cups with tears,
> To strew the laureate hearse where Lycid lies.

But for the most part they are vessels of rejoicing.

DAINTY

ANOTHER of the victims of softening. It comes from the old French version of dignity and means anything of merit, value, and esteem. It grew to include fastidiousness and then, for some reason, it was depressed to the signification of the softly pretty and quaint. 'Teas', for example, as served in Ye Olde Oake Tea Roomes or the God-Wottery Gardens of the Kozy Kafe, are inevitably 'dainty'. Dainty, indeed, in modern English, has become almost exclusively applied to this blend of 'arty' china and horrid little cakes, just as 'prime' has now become attached exclusively to the leading Minister of State and the better cuts of butcher's meat. An Elizabethan could have asked for a dainty steak and expected a fine, big one. Such an order to-day, if understood at all, would produce a mouthful, probably minced. 'Full many a deynte hors hadde he in stable' is the real Old English, and not 'Ye Olde' at all. John Fletcher linked dainty with the lusty spring, and he too wrote,

44

> Green woods are dumb,
> And will never tell to any
> Those dear kisses and those many
> Sweet embraces that are given:
> Dainty pleasures that would even
> Raise in coldest age a fire,
> And give virgin-blood desire.

The pleasures here are evidently vigorous.

When Prospero says 'That's my dainty Ariel' he is thanking the spirit for his aid, not commenting on ethereal fragility. The 'dainty dish' of old was a dish worth eating, not a pretty fragment.

DAMASK

THE Syrian city of Damascus has, through its crafts, added picturesquely to our lexicon. A sword, a silk, a linen, a rose, all these have at some time, and even at the same time, been damask. Because linen is bleached and blanched, damask suggests whiteness to some. It may have done so to Bacon when he wrote 'roses, damask and red are fast flowers of their smell, so that you may walk in a whole row of them and find nothing of their sweetness'. But the true damask rose, of which attar of roses was made, was a pink flower and so the lips and complexions of Tudor ladies were frequently damask to the poet. Who can forget Viola's,

> She never told her love
> But let concealment, like a worm i' the bud,
> Feed on her damask cheek?

The verb, to damascene, means to ornament with inlaid work or watered pattern. John Davidson, too little remembered, often combined the rich vocabulary of late nineteenth-century 'poetese' with his relentless reasonings. His

> arabesques of blue and emerald wave
> Begin to damascene the iron sea

dexterously links in its metaphors the Syrian city with the Arabian deserts adjoining. His was a period of damascened English, with Oscar Wilde, in his flowery phases, as first practitioner.

DANDER

DANDER has a strange assortment of meanings. It can be a cinder or a piece of scurf or a show of temper. But it is also, and far better, a wandering or stroll. The Scots have retained this usage, and wisely — for what more expressive of an easy walk at dusk than 'a wee bit dander in the gloaming'? The very slowness of the movement is in the word. The English have preferred saunter, which is also happily expressive. But I always have the sense of the right noise for a slow and pleasant vagabondage when I read in a Scots book of a dander in the glen. The Mearns on a summer night, the Mearns so richly and rhythmically described in Lewis Grassic Gibbon's tremendous novels of the eastern Scottish coast and its dwindling crofter life, *Sunset Song* and *Cloud Howe*, is rare dandering country, as it ripples between the Grampians and the sea. When you read of such crofts and villages as Kinraddie and Bla-waerie and Peesies' Knapp and of the peewits and curlews above them, it's a dander that any wise man would be having in 'the lithe' of the hills, as Gibbon would say, lithe here meaning cover or recess.

DAPPER

DAPPER nowadays suggests a gentleman with patent-leather hair, well-creased trousers, and spats (if it be a good spat year). But Milton was not thinking of the best-dressed fairy when he wrote,

> The Sounds and Seas with all their finny drove
> Now to the Moon in wavering Morrice move,
> And on the Tawny Sands and Shelves
> Trip the pert Fairies and the dapper Elves;

Dapper to him meant quick and alert. Johnson defined it 'Little and active, lively without bulk'. Elves could not have an apter epithet. It is a pity that so vital a word has been annexed by haberdashery.

DAZE

IT is right that the North should have the best terms for cold. The South has lost the use of daze for numb, narrowing its usage to strong effects on eye and brain, just as it has limited 'starve' to matters of appetite. The Yorkshire child who, when settled in an air-raid shelter of the dank and draughty kind, cried out to his mother, 'Ee Moom, ba goom, ma boom is noom' might have called his posterior dazed had he lived a little earlier. In Scotland the use of daze does, I believe, linger. How well it sits in Gavin Douglas's sharp, clear, and tingling description of a Scottish winter.

> In this congealit season sharp and chill,
> The caller air penetrative and pure,
> Dazing the blude in every creature,
> Made seek warm stovis and bene fyris hot.
> In double garment cled and wyliecoat,
> With michty drink, and meatis confortive . . .

The last robust and reassuring word surely amplifies and justifies my earlier note on the original implication of comfort.

DEBAUCHEE

WORDS ending in -ee frequently give pleasure. Debauch is both expressive in sound and curious in origin. It comes from an old French word meaning 'to turn away from the workshop' and thus lead into idleness. The familiar connotation of idleness with sin followed and debauchery meant indulgence in the sensual joys. (This must remind many an old Oxonian, who followed philosophy under Canon Rashdall, of that rubicund divine's nice division of happiness into (*a*) Religious Rapture and (*b*) Violent, Sensual Pleasure.) Debauchee was a term which I loved to use when young in translating the observations of Cicero and Demosthenes on their opponents. I met it with delight recently in a series of anonymous eighteenth century 'Letters from Edinburgh', in which an English visitor described Scottish habits. He very strangely regarded the reel as a dance 'trifling and insipid'. Yet this trifle could evoke a thirst in at least its masculine practitioners, which disgusted the English looker-on. The Scottish gentry, he said, after the ladies are withdrawn,

> retire into a private room, where each sacrifices his understanding and health to wining, in full bumpers, the health of his fair partner; who, if she has any understanding, must ridicule, condemn, and abhor the custom. But the Scotch Gentlemen are so resolute in their determination, that many of them, immediately after the departure of the Ladies, retire for a short time, in order to change their dancing apparel, and put on a dress more adapted to the occasion of riot and excess.

Strange goings-on! Small wonder that the horrified Englishman wrote of his hosts as 'debauchees'.

DESCANT

MOST of our musical terms begin with a strict technical reference and then are applied, with a sentimental enthusiasm, to melody in general. (See later note on Madrigal.) Descant stood for the earliest form of counterpoint, but the Elizabethan poets, all of them musicians and primed with the lore and language of the art, seized it for song and harmony in general, and also made a verb of it. So, too, diapason, the concord through all the notes of the scale, comes to be used for all far-ranging agreement. Neither is a particularly attractive word, but the Elizabethans had a cunning and delightful knack of working the vocabulary of the music _aster into the music of the heart and Drayton, proclaiming the sad sighs of passion, cunningly employed such terms as these:

> My hollow sighs the deepest base do beare
> True diapazon in distincted sound:
> My panting hart the treble makes the ayre,
> And descants finely on the musique's ground;
> Thus like a Lute or Viol did I lye,
> Whilst he, proud slave, daunced galliards in her eye.

Descant was also used as a verb to mean simply talk or comment. Shakespeare has it both ways. Julia in *Two Gentlemen of Verona* is said to 'mar the concord with too harsh a descant', while Richard Crookback would 'descant' on his own deformity.

DIM

SHORT, simple dim, source of emotion in many a moving line, has had radically different meanings. To Shakespeare it mainly conveyed the idea of darkness. Tombs are dim, cloudy skies are dim, and 'violets dim' (magical phrase, as only Shakespeare could make magic of the simplest words) must refer to darkness of hue. Yet the notion of faintness was also implicit in his use of the word at times. 'As dim and meagre as an ague's fit', he says of a dying child. Milton's 'dim, religious light' perhaps unites both conceptions. Later the idea of something vague, weak, and transient begins to supplant the concept of darkness. In my undergraduate days dim, in our cant, stood for anything grey or dull. A witless or uninteresting man was voted dim. Dim in the sense of evanescent or ghostly occurs with magnificence in Siegfried Sassoon's sonnet 'On Passing the New Menin Gate'.

> Crudely renewed the Salient holds its own,
> Paid are its dim defenders by that pomp:
> Paid, with a pile of peace-complacent stone,
> The armies who endured that sullen swamp.

Browning finely alliterated it in his famous

> Still one must lead some life beyond,
> Have a bliss to die with, dim-descried.

Dim is but a meek, mild, midget of a word, but it has contributed to gigantic utterance, of which I take these to be examples.

DISASTER

A COMMON word and one which has lost its heavenly significance. The 'aster' is the Greek and Latin word for 'star' and so disaster is the ill-starred thing. To the writers of the sixteenth and seventeenth centuries it still had that significance of destiny proclaimed by the motions of the heavenly bodies. Edmund in *King Lear* links it with the skies.

> when we are sick in fortune, — often the surfeit of our own behaviour, — we make guilty of our disasters the sun, the moon, and the stars: as if we were villains by necessity; fools by heavenly compulsion: knaves, thieves, and treachers by spherical predominance; drunkards, liars, and adulterers by an enforced obedience of planetary influence; and all that we are evil in, by a divine thrusting on:'

Horatio in *Hamlet* reminds us how,

> A little ere the mightiest Julius fell,
> The graves stood tenantless, and the sheeted dead
> Did squeak and gibber in the Roman streets:
> As, stars with trains of fire and dews of blood,
> Disasters in the sun; and the moist star,
> Upon whose influence Neptune's empire stands,
> Was sick almost to doomsday with eclipse:

'Disasters in the sun' is a most curious phrase. The sky still enfolds the word, but the exact and starry meaning has vanished. In our time disaster has been unskied and belittled altogether. It used to be seen in Italy over Goods for Sale. Where we write 'Bankrupt Stock, Forced Sale', the Italians were apt to announce simply 'Disastro'. It has the ring of doom.

DISTASTE

NOT an impressive verb, perhaps, but it must be the peg for a note on Shakespeare's delight in the prefix dis-, which he often used where un- would be normal (e.g. dispiteous for unpitiful and disnatured for unnatural). Distasted means spoilt or put out of flavour and occurs in one of the least known among the loveliest of passages in Shakespeare. When Troilus and Cressida must part, Troilus cries,

> We two, that with so many thousand sighs
> Did buy each other, must poorly sell ourselves
> With the rude brevity and discharge of one.
> Injurious time now, with a robber's haste,
> Crams his rich thievery up, he knows not how:
> As many farewells as be stars in heaven,
> With distinct breath and consign'd kisses to them,
> He fumbles up into a loose adieu;
> And scants us with a single famisht kiss,
> Distasted with the salt of broken tears.

There is the very agony of war-time parting forever pictured, with poignancy unmatchable, the short, snatched kiss of the railway-platform or the quay-side as the train goes out or the ship sails. If anybody is interested in Shakespeare's exquisite and no doubt unconscious use of alliteration, let him note the use of 's', letter of sighs, in the last five lines; the 's' is most delicately interlaced with the many 'l's, three initial 'f's, two 'd's, two 'k's, and the plentiful 't's of the last line. To me the last couplet is as moving as anything that Shakespeare ever wrote and very nearly brings that physical shiver down the spine which A. E. Housman took to be the circumstance and proof of mighty poetry.

DOWIE

DOES dowie linger anywhere in northern English dialect? It was good Scots (and should stay so) for all things dull and heavy. Wrote Skinner, the author of *Tullochgorum*, of what he deemed to be 'dull, Italian lays':

> They're dowf and dowie at the best
> Their allegros and a' the rest,
> They canna please a Scottish taste
> Compared wi' Tullochgorum.

(Dowf is a word of almost similar meaning.) Skinner's vigorous salutation to the reel and contempt of Italian modes may show a less than subtle ear for fine music, but he knew fine words. Dowie is excellently used in Robert Fergusson's picture of the kind of winter morn when it is better to be 'canty' in the city of Edinburgh than 'cauldrife' on the farm. He knows and echoes his Skinner and bids the musicians

> Roset well your fiddle-sticks
> But banish vile Italian tricks
> Frae out your quorum,
> Nor fortes with pianos mix;
> Gie's Tullochgorum.

That is conventional Scots revel. What is not so ordinary and is indeed sharply descriptive is the first verse of this piece, 'The Daft Days'.

> Now mirk December's dowie face
> Glow's owr're the rigs wi' sour grimace
> While, through his minimum of space,
> The bleer-ee'd sun
> Wi' blinkin' light and stealin' pace
> His race doth run.

The first line has all mid-winter in its dank, tenebrous chill. Burns learned much from Fergusson, whose death at twenty-four, when the Ayrshire lad was fifteen, robbed Edinburgh of a master-singer.

DRAFFISH

DRAFFISH sounds like a telescoped form of dregs and raffish and that, in fact, does give its meaning. Draff, suggesting the lees or worthless residue, was a favourite of John Milton's, whose Samson asks only to drudge

> Till vermin or the draff of servil food
> Consume me.

The brood of Belial is also referred to as human 'draff'. Draffish, as an antiquity restored, would serve very well to describe not only the patrons of certain night-clubs, but the kind of food and drink which they are so eager to consume at preposterous prices.

DUDGEON

DUDGEON to Shakespeare was the wooden handle of a knife — 'And on thy blade and dudgeon gouts of blood', said Macbeth of his visionary dagger. Why did it come to mean peevishness and why is it now always high, though, in the seventeenth century, it could also be deep? I find no answer. Dudgen (without the 'o') is a now obsolete word for trash or trashy. Is our slang word dud an abbreviation of this or did it come from the notion that duds are ragged clothes? I had always believed that duds were the flashing clothes and haberdashery connected with dudes. Dude is set down as a recent American importation, but I suspect it of being reimported and possibly very old English.

DULCIFY

POLONIUS deemed beautify a vile word. Would he have been so sharply dismissive of the similar dulcify?

If we are ever to prefer the Latin to the Saxon term, surely we may sweeten sweetness by admitting dulcitude and dulcify, which make such a comfortable noise. 'Can you sublime and dulcify?' asks Subtle in *The Alchemist* of the astonished Ananias. Here, of course, the reference is chemical, but the words are most suitable for application to any fragment of man's business upon earth. Art, morals, politics — may we not hope to see them all, in their various ways, sublimed and dulcified? They make a handsome couple.

DUMPISH

THOUGH dumps and dumpishness sometimes refer to stupidity, they originally meant, as they do most commonly now, a dull form of melancholy.

> When griping grief the heart doth wound
> And doleful dumps the mind oppress.

How many Shakespeareans will place that quotation at a glance? (The source is *Romeo and Juliet*, Act iv. sc. 5, if you confess to ignorance and want the information. It is, however, a quotation from a poem 'In Commendation of Musick' by Richard Edwards.) One of the most captivating uses of the word is in the negative and as a verb. Here is Fuller on the great clown Tarlton, the Grimaldi of Tudor England. 'Our Tarlton was master of his Faculty. When Queen Elizabeth was serious (I dare not say sullen) and out of good humour, he could undumpish her at his pleasure.' Fortunate Tarlton, whose targets for to-night did not have to include professional dramatic critics, who creep like snails unwillingly to stall. True, they in the end give the droll his immortality, but they can be a terrible affliction in the meantime to those who would live by undumpishing. A Dump was a technical Elizabethan term for a lament. John Davies of Hereford wrote 'A Dump upon the death of the most noble Henrie, late Earle of Pembrooke.'

ENERGUMEN

To my astonishment I came across energumen in my morning paper and, though its general meaning was apparent, I had to consult the dictionary for the history and precise implication of this ugly but energetic word. It is a direct transliteration from the Greek. An energumen is not somebody ferociously working, but a person ferociously worked upon, chiefly by a devil or a frenzy. So an energumen is a demoniac enthusiast and raving devotee. The word, which was first employed in the beginning of the eighteenth century, may be rare, but the odious creature whom it depicts has been appallingly common in twentieth century Europe.

ESSENTIAL

This is a word which has been twisted away from its proper meaning. It should imply an article with essence, that is with genuine quality in it, and so substantial, important, full, pregnant. Now, of course, it is merely a synonym for necessary. It would be nice to hear again of an essential picture or poem. Milton magnificently gives us the negative side of the word.

> The void profound
> Of unessential Night receives him next
> Wide gaping, and with utter loss of being
> Threatens him plunged in that abortive gulf.

These lines most powerfully suggest to me the spectacle of my colleague in dramatic criticism, Mr. James Agate, sitting, under compulsion, at a musical comedy.

FANCY

Few words have so sadly come down in the world as fancy. It began (in its full form of phantasy) as the supreme quality of imagination. It is now an epithet for sugared or bedizened things, fancy bread (Scottish for cakes and biscuits) or fancy work, which implies any kind of irrelevant and hideous decoration. Fancy cooking is the 'good, plain cook's' dismissal of anything ambitious on the menu. Members of the fancy, now abbreviated to 'fans', may once have been connoisseurs of a sport, even of an art. (De Quincey used it of the bookish.) Now they are gaping, doltish creatures who make divinities of film-stars and scramble for autographs. That is the final degradation of fancy, which to Shakespeare meant the flight of mind and surge of feeling, the source of passion and of poetry too. To his Cleopatra fancy is the highest form of imagination. When asked if there might be another such as Antony she replies that Nature, in making such a man, defied all fancy, 'condemning shadows quite'. To Orsino, most musical of lovers, fancy is an honoured name for love itself.

FANGLE

FANGLE for a fashion has almost disappeared, surviving only in the adjective new-fangled and, less commonly, in the opposite, old-fangled. Shakespeare has the adjective fangled, Porthumus talking of 'our fangled world' in which the epithet has passed on from the meaning of affectation to that of deceitfulness. The dwindling use of fangle, except in a compound, reminds one of other useful words which have vanished, except in some negative or comparative form. The Scots have held to couth or couthy for kind, gentle, or cosy. ('Couthy and bien' — to rhyme with green — sang Stevenson of the sheltered house 'atween the muckle Pentland's knees'.) The English have let it go (absurdly, for 'a couthy farm' is a beautiful description of a steading lying snug in rich land) and retained the negative form, uncouth, applying it specially to roughness of aspect and manners. But if the lads of the village are to be uncouth, may not the lasses of the town be couth or couthy?

FAREWELL

THE word has dropped out of popular speech. We say 'Good-bye', which is decent, or decline into the democratic 'ta-ta's' and 'cheerios' and 'so longs', which are miserable. (What exactly does 'So long' mean?) Farewell is now rather literary or slightly jocose. Perhaps this is due to a kind of reverence. Do we hesitate to make common a word which sounds so beautiful? You have only to put it in a line that scans and poetry emerges.

> Farewell the tranquil mind: farewell content!
> Farewell the plumed troop and the big wars
> That make ambition virtue! O farewell!
> Farewell the mighty steed and the shrill trump
> The spirit-stirring drum, the ear-piercing fife,
> The royal banner and all quality
> Pride, pomp, and circumstance of glorious war
> . . .
> Farewell, Othello's occupation's gone.

Substitute good-bye for farewell in these lines, and the magic entirely vanishes. The word has the rich melancholy of Rome's 'Ave atque Vale', which must be pronounced with the 'a' broad. One of the loneliest sheep-farms in the noble wilderness of the North Yorkshire moors is called 'Farewell'. The people who so named it had the unconscious genius of the ballad-maker.

FASCINATE

MOST words descend in value: fascinate has actually climbed in reputation. It now refers mainly to attractive and radiantly enchanting things. To call a woman fascinating would be wholly complimentary. But once it would have been an accusation of witchcraft and even a stake-and-faggot matter. Fascinate originally meant to submit to the evil eye and exact writers, like W. H. Hudson, would still so apply it. He used it, for example, of the uncanny spell exercised on other animals and on small birds by the stoat and weasel. Either of these can paralyse the former, denying them power of motion, and leaving them staggering and screaming in terror, the latter they allure to come ever lower down the twigs, twittering in morbid ecstasy, until they are within striking distance of the fierce, blood-lusty fangs. In Hudson's *Hampshire Days* there is a wonderful picture of this fascination in progress in a wood near Boldre, where he watched a weasel chattering and spinning madly round the base of a tree, while an audience of birds, 'chaffinches, wrens, robins, dunnocks, ox-eyes, willow-wrens, and chiff-chaffs', fluttered spell-bound ever closer to the crazy cunning of their foe. After such fascination (Hudson calls it 'the good, old word') one might be inclined to avoid it in social compliment, but the ancient connection with the evil eye has been entirely forgotten. So let the greenwood tree, as well as the lady fair, be our fascinator now.

FEAT and FEATEOUS

To Shakespeare feat was an adjective as well as a noun. We have lost the adjective both in its brief form of feat and its longer one of feateous. Imogen became 'a page so feat, so nurse-like' and Perdita danced so 'featly' as to win the perfect tribute

> When you dance, I wish you
> A wave o' the sea, that you might ever do
> Nothing but that.

Feat as an adjective means neat, trim, efficient, and feateous (sometimes featous) also means well-shaped and becoming. The water nymphs of Thames in Spenser's stately 'Prothalamion' were feateous in their plucking of the bridal bouquets.

> And each one had a little wicker basket
> Made of fine twigs, entrailéd curiously,
> In which they gathered flowers to fill their flasket,
> And with fine fingers cropt full feateously
> The tender stalks on high.

Feateous would be a happy term for all actions in which skill and beauty run in beauty together. Games should have their feateous players as well as their feats and records. Prince Obolensky, who was killed in an air-crash early in the war, was feateous indeed upon the Rugby Football field. He touched some games that he could not win, none that he did not decorate.

FLOOSIE

SUCH terms as 'blowen', already mentioned, and 'frisgig' and 'giglot', yet to have their note, may be thought to cover sufficiently the frailty of women. But the American 'floosie' is so picturesque as to deserve a recognition. It may be Old English. You never know with American slang. So let us accept it as a novelty. It has a blousy, flowery atmosphere and, to me, at least, immediately and richly suggests a substantial charmer with plenty of good spirits and bad scent.

FOISON

OUR words for abundance do not abound and it seems regrettable that foison should be only an antiquity. It comes from the Latin for pouring and signifies the effusion of the horn of plenty. Perhaps its decay is due to an unhappy similarity to poison. Whatever the reason, we could do with it to help the painting of our summer landscape. I am writing this looking out on to English fields upon a 'glorious first of June' and what words have we to suggest the astonishing tangle and strength, the jungle-richness of early summer's growth in a soft and fruitful shire? Six weeks ago there was scarcely a sign of all this (it was a very tardy spring) and now we have Lucio's 'teeming foison', Gonzalo's 'all foison, all abundance', and the 'Earth's increase and foison plenty' sung by Ceres. There is general foison of crop and weed, of serviceable copse and ruinous briar. Perhaps another and more closely Latin word will help one to describe the lushness of the meadows and hedges. That is 'pinguid', a vivid word for fat pastures, but another Elizabethan casualty. 'From death to life thou might'st him yet recover', as Drayton sang of another matter.

FOXED

I⊤ is strange that foxy should mean cunning while foxed means baffled and stupid. In the latter sense it now has a Victorian ring. Only gentlemen of the oldest school would talk about being 'properly foxed' by liquor or calamity. It was a favourite of Pepys. After the Coronation of Charles II Pepys sat late with the Yeoman of the Royal Wine-cellar.

> With his wife and two of his sisters, and some gallant sparks that were there, we drank the King's health, and nothing else, till one of the gentlemen fell down stark drunk, and there lay, and I went to my lord's pretty well. But no sooner abed with Mr. Shepley, but my head began to turn, and I to vomit, and if ever I was foxed, it was now.

Later on,

> Waked in the morning with my head in a sad taking through the last night's drink, which I am very sorry for: so rose, and went out with Mr. Creed to drink our morning draught, which he did give me in chocolate to settle my stomach.

Chocolate, as antidote to a hang-over, would leave some of us queasy moderns more 'foxed' than ever.

FRIBBLE

To fribble is to act feebly, to be frivolous in a petty, fiddling way. The verb is also used as a noun, a fribble being a trifler. Its close rhyme with dribble suggests to me a dotard far-gone in years and folly. Mr. Justice Shallow was the fribble at his most likeable. Captain Charles Morris, who wrote some genial, toss-pot rhymes in the eighteenth century, observes:

> I find too when I stint my glass
> And sit with sober air,
> I'm prosed by some dull, reasoning ass
> Who treads the path of care;

> Or, harder tax'd, I'm forced to bear
>> Some coxcomb's fribbling strain,
> And that I think's a reason fair
>> To fill my glass again.

To be prosed, as a passive verb, is good and should appeal to all who have been much pent in conventicles and lecture-rooms.

FRISGIG

THIS, for a silly young woman, is not an orthodox dictionary word, but well it might be, for it is an excellent example of the vividness of Lancashire dialect. It so nicely telescopes the friskiness and giggles of a lively, vapid miss that it really ought to be taken into common English usage. It reminds me of the Elizabethan giglot, which began by meaning a wanton and then, because of its closeness in sound to giggle, went on to suggest a party both more innocent and more infuriating, the tittering, romping wench. Giglot, as well as frisgig, merits renewal, especially in its later sense. For wantons we had, and have, so many words. Ben Jonson alone will yield a column or so, of which callet is the chilliest and fricatrice the most candid. There are fewer terms for the titterers. So what Lancashire thought on this subject yesterday, England might well think again to-morrow.

FROLIC

FROLIC is almost always a noun or a verb to us, as it was to Thomas Woodcock who wrote of academic life and its oddities in the later seventeenth century,

> Of Dr. Thomas Goodwin, when ffelow of Catharine Hall. —
> He was somewhat whimsycall, in a frolick pist once in old
> Mr. Lothian's pocket (this I suppose was before his trouble of
> conscience and conversion made him serious). . . . He prayed
> with his hatt on and sitting.

It is perhaps as well that the donnish sense of a frolic has since altered. But it is a pity that the same century's use of frolic as an adjective has virtually disappeared. Milton's 'frolic wind that breathes the spring' is, of course, familiar. Herrick found wine to be both 'frolick' and 'frantick'. 'Come shake the frolic cocktail on the ice' would ring well to-day. There are occasions, no doubt, when frantic would be more accurately applied to that form of refreshment.

FRUITION

FRUITION, rightly used, is a delightful word. But how often is it so employed? Even the most august authors may be daily discovered confusing it with fruit and maturity. Leader-writers continually hold forth about plans 'coming to fruition'. The word, in fact, has nothing to do with fruit, but is derived from the Latin 'fruor', I enjoy, and means enjoyment. The meaning of ripeness, says the O. E. D. firmly, 'is not countenanced by dictionaries in this country, nor by Webster'. Fruition was rightly and exquisitely used by Marlowe.

> That perfect bliss and sole felicity,
> The sweet fruition of an earthly crown.

Charles Lamb in his rhymed 'Farewell to Tobacco' moaned, correctly as well as pathetically, that he had lost his seat among the 'blest Tobacco Boys'.

> Where, though I, by sour physician,
> Am debarr'd the full fruition
> Of thy favours, I may catch
> Some collateral sweets, and snatch
> Sidelong odours, that give life
> Like glances from a neighbour's wife;

We owe it to Marlowe and to Lamb to save fruition from the hackneyed misuse to which modern ignorance and carelessness have brought it.

GALINGALE

GOING back to boyhood's favourites, some of the more golden reaches of Tennysonian iambic (Why not? I find them delightfully rich in lullaby quality and excellent for perusal during air-raids), I ran into galingale. For Tennyson it decorated the land of the Lotus-eaters.

> Border'd with palm and many a winding vale,
> And meadow, set with slender galingale.

The galingale, which to us may suggest some 'period' boskage among which a lady in a farthingale listened to a nightingale, is an Eastern aromatic root. The Elizabethan men, so avid of all spices, used it carnally for cooking, but Tennyson, more loftily, for atmosphere. Remaking its acquaintance led to some dictionary-loitering in which I was reminded of the jovial and fine-sounding mixture of words beginning with 'gal'. Here is a question for a General Knowledge Paper. Distinguish between, Galingale, Gali-pot, Galligaskin, Gallimaufry, and Gallowglass. Also between Galliard and Galliass.

GALLIMAUFRY

ONE answer, at least, shall be given to the previous queries.

A good-sounding medley or hodge-podge is gallimaufry and one that came easily to the roaring play-boys and pamphleteers of Tudor London. Nashe, commenting on the stage of his time ('Our players are not as the players beyond sea, a sort of squirting bawdy comedians') goes on to complain that the ancient Romans always over-praised and over-wrote their native talent, 'thinking scorn to any but domestic examples of their own home-bred actors, scholars, and champions: and them they would extol to the third and fourth generation: cobblers, tinkers, fencers, none escaped them, but they mingled their all in one gallimaufry of glory'.

This last attractively alliterative phrase itself sums up the temper and achievements of Nashe's aspiring, brilliant, and cantankerous world, a gallimaufry of fiery particles. Incidentally, was ever a tedious stream of third-rate smut so brilliantly punished in a phrase as by 'a sort of squirting, bawdy comedians'?

GENIAL

WHAT an odd multiplicity of meanings has genial! 'Of or pertaining to the chin', for example. So a man may talk of 'a genial shave' or, with double truth, of Mr. Jack Hulbert as a most 'genial comedian'. But that is a different genial altogether from the commoner word, which, in its turn, has abundant variety of usage. 'Of or pertaining to marriage, nuptial.' 'Of or pertaining to a feast, festive.' So to our sympathetic, encouraging, jovial forms of geniality. Milton, loyal as ever to the original implication, spoke of the spirit presiding over marriage and fertility as 'The Genial Angel' and Spenser's description of matrimony as genial refers to the function as well as to the fun. Now good spirits have entirely usurped the term. There is a most solemn use of it in Collins's *Ode to Evening*, where he curiously links it with 'The pensive pleasures' brought by evening's 'genial lov'd return'.

GLAMOUR

THIS beautiful word has been bludgeoned to death by modern showmanship, which has attached it to every young lady who contributes a face to the film or a limb to the chorus. It is an English importation from Scotland where it had long signified magic with magical effect. I had fancied that it was pronounced 'glam-oor' until I found Burns rhyming it with grammar.

> Ye gipsy gangs that deal in glamour
> And you deep read in hell's black grammar.

Until quite recently glamour was reserved for conjuring tricks and was not bestowed, as now with such damnable iteration, on all aspiring to or professing 'it', 'umph' or 'sex-appeal', to use the modish titles of what used to be called plain loveliness. It was really Mr. David Devant who had true glamour in my boyhood, not Miss Gabrielle Ray. Jugglers and magicians were said to cast glamour, as it were dust, over the eyes of the public and even Tennyson used the word of wizardry. (It is noticeable that the word 'wizard' was recently a smart-slang term for anything attractive or excellent.) Now glamour and glamorous are tagged on, with infuriating frequency, to any kind of tinsel pleasure or personality. Chorus Girls, so dear to the Edwardians, have ceased to exist. They are all Glamour Girls now.

GLAUCOUS

THIS is simply a transliteration from the Greek and Latin and, as a rule, so close a classicism makes poor English. But here, surely, is an exception. Have we any single word which so well describes the usual tint of our national border and bulwark? 'Of a full green colour passing into greyish blue', says the O. E. D. Not the sea at its radiant best or white with anger, but in its normal hue. Day after day our shores are set about with glaucosity and no other word so comprehensively establishes the hue of our firths and channels in an average view. Cries Shelley's Panthea,

'Ere-while I slept
Under the glaucous caverns of old Ocean,

Often enough we have tried to sleep on top of them. To spend a week or more gazing at the glaucous wilderness can be very boring, and perhaps glaucous, with its ponderous surge of sound, does also suggest the heavy hours and heaving motion of a voyage prolonged.

GLEEK

WHY has gleek for jest, both verb and noun, so largely disappeared? It is curt and expressive. 'I have seen you gleeking and galling at the gentleman,' says Gower to Pistol, with reference to Fluellen. There is some punning point there because the episode includes the compulsion to eat a leek. But Shakespeare also used the word straightforwardly. 'I can gleek upon occasion', said Bottom to Titania. We might follow his example.

GRACE

How lucky our Dukes have been to inherit a title of such high privilege, for grace has long been blessed among English words, signifying beauty both of body and of matter. The divine Graces of the pagans were the bestowers of all forms of loveliness and of 'a laughing way in the teeth of the world'. Milton, banishing Melancholy, summoned the Graces.

> But come thou Goddess fair and free
> In heaven yclept Euphrosyne,
> And by men, heart-easing mirth,
> Whom lovely Venus at a birth
> With two Sister Graces more
> To ivy-crownéd Bacchus bore.

Christianity adopted the simple and serene word to mean the Divine Favour and the state of those enjoying it. Thence comes the meaning of favour generally. Shakespeare's Benedick puns on the two states of grace. 'Till all graces be in one woman, one woman shall not come in my grace.' Grace, as a favour or permission, lives on in University lingo. Next comes gratitude, at table or elsewhere. What a comprehensive word is this which first means the favour demanded and then the thankfulness of a recipient! Grace has drawn to itself all manner of fair visions and implications. It must not be abused by overwork.

GREENTH

England is everlastingly praised for its greenery, though it is grey for more months than it is green. Certainly our spring and summer landscape offers countless varieties of green, for which the writer has sadly few terms. How he envies the painter when confronted with the spring-time subtleties of young larch, beech, and willow! Indeed, almost every tree runs to a different shade of what Horace Walpole called 'greenth'. Rejoicing to be home, after travel, and beside his darling Thames, he wrote,

> I do nothing but plume and clean myself and enjoy the verdure and silent waves. Neatness and greenth are so essential in my opinion to the country that in France, where I see nothing but chalk and dirty peasants, I seem in a terrestrial purgatory that is neither town nor country. The face of England is so beautiful that I do not believe Tempe or Arcadia were half so rural; for both lying in hot climates must have wanted the turf of our lawns.

Most Hellenic travellers will agree that he is wholly right about Arcadia and Tempe. English grass would seem a blessed miracle to a Greek peasant, sheep, or goat, especially in the Peloponnese. Greenth, Walpole's own coinage, is not beautiful, but somehow expresses the lush growth of a river valley better than does the cooler and more pleasant-sounding greenery. The English writer, as I said, is sorely limited in means to describe green things. The Latinities, verdant and virid, are chilly and formal.

HALCYON

THE Halcyon was supposed to nest on the sea-surface and to put a spell on the winds and waves, completely calming them in order that the nest might survive. This legend is especially connected with the waters round Sicily.

Alcyone was the daughter of Aeolus the wind-god and threw herself into the sea when a storm killed her husband. As a response to this sharp, daughterly reproach the gods turned the couple into kingfishers, who nested on the sea. Aeolus, now repentant, kept the waters tranquil for their breeding season. As Shelley observed,

The halcyons brood around the foamless isles,
The treacherous ocean has forsworn its wiles.

In any case, it is an exquisite word, passing on from tranquil weather to all benign and peaceful things. But Shakespeare thought of another aspect of kingfishers, when he mentioned the 'halcyon beaks' of servile, smiling rogues, which honest Kent so disliked to look upon. Halcyon here simply implies a long and sharp feature: in that case, we are all acquainted with a halcyon beak or two, but these are not necessarily limited to knaves and toadies.

HEBETUDE

HEBETUDE, both meaning by classical derivation and suggesting with its sound a dull heaviness, is now rare. It was used by A. E. Housman in his dismissal of inferior Latinists and Housman was never the kind of scholar to display nervous hesitation in the criticism of his fellow-classics. He brought 'hebetude' crashing down upon their skulls as though it were a lexicon itself. I regret its rarity, for it has a fine, ponderous expressiveness. Another classical rarity, concinnity, might well be restored to common use along with hebetude. It happens to be almost its opposite in meaning, since it signifies the skilful harmonizing of parts in thought and speech and so implies elegance of style. The first Lord Birkenhead, himself a relentless hammer of all hebetude, employed concinnity as a word and often displayed that quality in his quick forging of a sharp and shining phrase.

HESPERIDES

MANKIND from the earliest has looked westward for salvation: that is odd since the dawn, the obvious symbol of a new and better day, is not there. But the notion of Atlantis, of Blessed Isles, of a happy land beyond the evening star has been remarkably constant. America, by becoming the refuge of the pilgrim and the persecuted, the restless and the exile, naturally gave modern man new cause to favour the Hesperidean myth. The words Hesperus and Hesperides are themselves magnetic to the pens of poets and I can never see either without inclining to the old sentimental dream of some Paradise on the westering verge of great Oceanus.

> Love's tongue proves dainty Bacchus gross in taste:
> For valour, is not love a Hercules,
> Still climbing trees in the Hesperides?
> Subtle as sphinx; as sweet and musical
> As bright Apollo's lute, strung with his hair?
> And when love speaks, the voice of all the gods
> Makes heaven drowsy with the harmony.

Thus young Shakespeare's young Biron, flown with conceits and profligate of words. Those who like a vocabulary to be both inventive and irridescent can dip and dip again in *Love's Labour's Lost* and still come up with fresh discovery.

HOMELY

THE Englishman in America is warned not to call young women homely since there it means ugly instead of natural and simple. It is a charitably evasive usage which we might recover. I say 'recover' because, as usual, America has kept the original meaning which we have lost. The Pilgrim Fathers took 'homely', meaning unbeautiful, in their humble lexicon. Milton makes that certain. When Comus has given the lady his nicely-sounding plea for nudism,

> Beauty is nature's brag and must be shown

he continues,

> It is for homely features to keep home,
> They had their name thence; course complexions
> And cheeks of sorry grain will serve to ply

The sampler, and to teize the huswife's wooll.
What need a vermeil-tinctured lip for that
Love-darting eyes, or tresses like the Morn?

We need not accept the monster's belief that lip-stick lifts girls above the domesticities, but we English may well repatriate the ancient use of 'homely' which America has preserved to its profit.

HONEY

HONEY is a fair word of curious fortune. As an endearment it lingers more in America than in England, where it is most common in the form of 'hinny', a popular usage for darling in the North-East. (Hinny, in the live-stock lists, means the offspring of a she-ass by a stallion!) The favour shown to honey depends naturally on the sweetness of an epoch's tooth. Ours, whose taste is for the austere and stark and acid, would regard 'honey-tongued' as an adjective of contempt if applied to a contemporary poet. Yet, to the Tudor mind, this was the highest praise. It is noteworthy that the earliest contemporary allusions to Shakespeare nearly all relate him, with rapture, to the honey-pot. Spenser's

> But that same gentle Spirit from whose pen
> Large streames of honnie and sweete Nectar flowe

may or may not refer to Shakespeare, but it exemplifies the use of honey as a word of tribute. The same applies to Chettle's rebuke on a poet's silence at Elizabeth's death, a rebuke perhaps intended for William.

> Nor doth the silver-tongued Melicert
> Drop from his honied Muse one sable teare.

Meres (1598) was more specific. 'The sweete, wittie soule of Ovid lies in mellifluous and honey-tongued Shakespeare, witnes his Venus and Adonis, his Lucrece, his sugred Sonnets among his private friends.'

In the same year Richard Barnfield wrote

> And Shakespeare thou, whose hony-flowing Vaine
> (Pleasing the World) thy Praises doth obtaine.

In 1599 John Weever cried,

> Honie-tongued Shakespeare, when I saw thine issue
> I swore Apollo got them and no other.

In the 'Parnassus' Cambridge plays he is 'Sweet Mr. Shakespeare' and later on the 'nectared vein' is continually stressed. In Shakespeare's own work honey is often used, as noun and adjective, for exquisite things. But nowadays we hardly think of the author of *Hamlet* in terms of the honey-pot. For those who want an even more dulcet term of praise there is 'rodomel', which means the juice of rose-leaves mixed with honey and sings its way very happily into a line of the lusher poetry.

HORDE

THE history of horde is typical of the way in which we work words to death. It came to us from the Near East and first meant simply a nomad tribe with no suggestion of ferocity. Then it proceeded to imply savagery and next a large number of savages. Now horde is commonly, very commonly, employed to describe the enemy, suggesting both his myriads and his bestiality. Civil Servants, according to the Press, habitually move in hordes. 'A horde of highly-paid officials' is the modern variant of the Dickensian Barnacles. Since the war the Nazis have habitually been massing (only one's own side mobilizes) in hordes (only one's own side has millions of well-trained troops). One of the most striking instances of this usage in my recent experience was an article hopefully describing the millions of men in the Russian armies, who would far outnumber the Germans. None the less the latter were still described as moving in 'hordes' as though they were doing something particularly odious in being thus numerous — but not

71

quite so numerous as their enemies. Our allies, of course, had armies, not hordes.

HORRID

THE decline of horrid is lamentable. It should carry the idea of something bristling and frightful with a spiky menace and not merely be a mild term for nastiness. Vergil's 'Bella, horrida bella' sets spears and swords flashing in the air and does not refer only to the discomforts and incivilities of war. Milton is always exactly classical in his employment of such words. The Elder Brother in 'Comus', in the famous speech on Chastity, says that the owner of that virtue can traverse without harm 'Infamous hills' (i.e. unknown country) and pass

> where very Desolation dwells
> By grots and caverns shagged with horrid shades

unmenaced by goblin or 'swart faery of the mire'. Shakespeare, writing earlier than Milton, is none the less often closer to us in his usage. So it happens with horrid, which he applies vigorously to ghosts, night, thunder, speech, and hent. Hent, by the way, means to seize, or, as a noun, a seizing or design.

Horrible has suffered equal decline. When Cowper, musing on 'The Solitude of Alexander Selkirk', remarked

> Better dwell in the midst of alarms
> Than reign in this horrible place,

he meant something far more frightening than his adjective now implies. The same thing has happened in his next verse, which is made wellnigh ridiculous by the change of meaning in 'shocking'.

> The beasts that roam over the plain
> My form with indifference see;
> They are so unacquainted with man,
> Their tameness is shocking to me.

While on the subject of epithets in mutilation or decay, let me quote this recent advertisement of a popular musical play: 'Terrific cast of 50.' That was meant to attract, not deter. Poor terrific!

HORTULAN

THIS adjective to signify of or pertaining to gardens is pure Latin and was used in the seventeenth and eighteenth centuries with some propriety, since the Palladian style of architecture was then the stately vogue and carried with its Italian splendours Italian notions of landscape-gardening. How elaborate those notions were can be seen from the syllabus to an intended book of John Evelyn's called *Elysium Britannicum*. Here are some of his projected chapters as cited by Miss Eleanour Sinclair Rohde and Mr. Eric Parker, most eager of hortulan anthologists.

'5. Of Knots, Parterres, Compartments, Borders, and Embossments. — 6. Of Walks, Terraces, Carpets, and Alleys, Bowling-greens, Malls, their materials and proportions. — 7. Of Groves, Labyrinths, Daedales, Cabinets, Cradles, Pavilions, Galleries, Close-walks, and other Relievos. — 8. Of Transplanting. — 9. Of Fountains, Cascades, Rivulets, Piscinas, and Water-Works. — 10. Of Rocks, Grots, Cryptas, Mounts, Precipices, Porticos, Vendiducts. — 11. Of Statues, Columns, Dials, Perspectives, Pots, Vases, and other ornaments. — 12. Of Artificial Echos, Music, and Hydraulic motions. — 13. Of Aviaries, Apiaries, Vivaries, Insects. — 14. Of Orangeries, and Conservatories of Rare Plants. — 15. Of Verdures, Perennial-Greens, and perpetual Springs. — 16. Of Coronary Gardens, Flowers, and rare Plants, how they are to be propagated, governed, and improved; together with a Catalogue of the choicest Trees, Shrubs, and Flowers, and how the Gardener is to keep his Register. — 17. Of the Philosophico-Medical Garden'.

'There's richness for you', as Mr. Squeers said of another matter. What, by the way, goes on in 'Philosophico-Medical' pleasaunces? Nowadays one can only think of an Open Air or Hortulan Brains Trust led by James Bridie and Oliver St. John Gogarty.

IMBRUE

HANDS stained with blood seem much more gory when imbrued. Pistol, sword in reluctant hand, made the word forever melodrama when he cried, in burlesque of his rival-mummers, 'What, shall we have incision? Shall we imbrue?' Bacchus, in Anglo-classical poetry, is continually imbrued with juice of the grape.

> And little rills of crimson wine imbrued
> His plump white arms and shoulders, enough white
> For Venus' pearly bite.

This is certainly not the happiest of Keats (no genius was more liable to bathos than his), but imbrued gives it what quality it has.

INCHOATE

AN imposing word and one almost as generally misused as fruition. Fruition's passage from meaning enjoyment in Marlowe to meaning fulfilment in modern political speeches and leading articles was caused by the simple fact that it began with the letters 'fruit'. The abuse of 'inchoate', which is properly applied to a thing just begun, is caused by a careless confusion with 'chaos'. The altered position of the vowels does not deter people from this muddle and politicians will announce that 'The Government's plans have now become utterly inchoate' which is to say that a boy has become a baby. 'Inchoate', is a good, resounding Latin word meaning incipient and was properly used by the judicious Hooker when he contrasted the inchoation of spiritual grace with its consummation.

INDIFFERENT

WORDS always seem to come down in the world and I have sought in vain for one that has risen in esteem, that is to say a word whose meaning has gone from slight to serious or indifferent to important. I mention indifferent because that is an example of the general process of decay. To Sir Philip Sidney it meant impartial and was an adjective of warmest praise when bestowed on justice. His description of sleep

The indifferent judge between the high and low

is a tribute. To a modern it might merely suggest a judge who did not know his business. Shakespeare used indifferent in both senses (Sir Andrew says that his leg 'does indifferent well in a flame-coloured stock') and sometimes, characteristically, he blends the meanings. What exactly does Hamlet intend by 'I am myself indifferent honest'? Moderately honest or completely impartial? Respectable is a similar word which has suffered parallel devaluation. It was once an epithet of genuine praise. To call a general a respectable soldier was to say that all looked up to his abilities. Now it implies that nobody looks up to him at all. Respectable is slightly kinder than indifferent, but it is not welcomed. David Garrick would have liked to be called a respectable actor by a critic: now an actor thus described would feel himself aggrieved. The gradual segregation of respectability for a rather dull kind of piety has worked some of the damage. It is strange how shy is man of having virtue thrust upon him.

INFINITE

INFINITE is not in itself an attractive word, but it occurs in some of the most powerful passages of English poetry. This, as F. L. Lucas points out in his admirable edition of John Webster's plays, is due to Renaissance absorption in the enormous mystery of creation. The conception of size, of boundless and eternal things, was a splendour in their minds. The idea of the colossal allured those fiery particles who built English poetry by marrying the vernacular to the new learning and Latinity from the East. The Hitlerite cry of him who was to be Richard III,

To undertake the death of all the world,

is the very voice of an ambition which will have nothing but the universal. It sounds like Marlowe, who constantly utters this same passion for the endless and the absolute. Webster plays continually with infinity. It occurs in a tribute of devotion.

> Had I infinite worlds
> They were too little for thee.

It spreads its misty magic over this marvellous farewell to life.

> I am i' the way to study a long silence;
> To prate were idle, I remember nothing;
> There's nothing of so infinite vexation
> As man's own thoughts.

(The first line is surely the perfect last line of a dying actor.) Infinite is often on the lips of Hamlet and both describes and voices the fascination and the longings of Cleopatra. She cries to Antony,

> O infinite virtue, come'st thou smiling from
> The world's great snare uncaught?

and, at the end, we know

> She hath pursued conclusions infinite
> Of easy ways to die.

Death and black cypress and minds forlornly ranging 'beyond the infinite of thought' are the background of Elizabethan fifth acts. Almost a mean word to the ear is infinite, but it keeps majestic company.

INGENIOUS

THIS good word should be restored to its ancient and honourable estate, whereby it implies possession of intellect or genius and not just a species of inventive cunning. To the men of the Renaissance Italy was essentially 'Ingenious Italy'. Carelessness has also muddled this word with ingenuous, which means nobly-born and then honest, straightforward. Shakespeare was in error over this. Timon's 'Ingeniously, I speak' should obviously be 'Ingenuously'. (Perhaps Shakespeare was right and his printers wrong.) However, the error became so general that our word 'ingenuity', which ought to mean straightforwardness, is now always used for a light kind of cleverness, as though it were the noun of the adjective 'ingenious'. There is a case here for some tidying.

JINK

JINKS, like dudgeon previously noted, are now always high. Jink, verb or noun, is a Scots word and a lively one for a lively process. Escaping Scotsmen jink their creditors, the jink being a quick side-step. If the word is not used of footballers, it should be, for jinking is an exact term for the elusive footwork and swerve of a great runner with the ball. 'Our billie's gien us a' the jink', wrote Burns of one who had flitted overseas. Apparently at the card-table jinking means 'winning a game of spoil-five, twenty-five, or forty-five'. This sport is beyond my ken.

So, says Oxford, jinks pass on to signify 'various frolics at drinking parties'. And there, as we have seen, height appears to be the inseparable quality of jinks. These matters of measurement are queer. High jinks go with low company.

Jinking during the war was a term much used in the Royal Air Force for dodging anti-aircraft fire by rapid moves this way and that.

JUGULATE

MAY we admit words which are only attractive if misused? We frowned on the mistaken fruition and praised its proper application. Perhaps, for once, we may reverse that process. Jugulate ought to mean 'cut the throat of', in which case it is a direct, rather ugly, Latinized, surgical term. But Thackeray, very happily, applied it to a lady's singing which he much disliked. He was obviously thinking in terms of Nash's ditty of avian spring-song with its refrain of 'Cuckoo, jug-jug, pu-we, to-witta-woo'. Thackeray's confusion has certainly given us an aptly descriptive word. We have all of us encountered sopranos for whom jugulation is a proper term.

JUNCTURE

THIS is an ugly Latinism, but interesting. It means, of course, a meeting or union, but modern usage has reserved junction for that and now quite commonly applies juncture to a moment of time. First important events converged so that it was reasonable to talk of a 'critical juncture'. The phrase was striking and, like so many striking phrases, became an overworked cliché. Every careless writer began to use 'At this juncture' when he simply meant 'then'. I was reminded of this by finding the word used by Gilbert White of Selborne in a passage where it could refer both to a moment of time and an act of union. He was writing of the mating of swifts and claimed that swifts 'tread, or copulate, on the wing'. (Tread is a technical and descriptive term of avian amours.) The swift, he explained with that stately stride of his prose which is like good, supple walking,

> is almost continually on the wing; and as it never settles on the ground, on trees, or roofs, would seldom find opportunity for amorous rites, was it not enabled to indulge them in the air. If any person would watch these birds of a fine morning in May, as they are sailing round at a great height from the ground, he would see, every now and then, one drop on the back of another, and both of them sink down together for many fathoms with a loud piercing shriek. This I take to be the juncture when the business of generation is carrying on.
>
> As the swift eats, drinks, collects materials for its nest, and, as it seems, propagates on the wing; it appears to live more in the air than any other bird, and to perform all functions there save those of sleeping and incubation.

Juncture is rarely used with such aptitude to both its meanings.

KITTLE

KITTLE means tickle, possibly by confusion of the two sounds, both of which are based on the light noise of the action itself. So one kittled the strings of a violin. Curiously both verbs are used in the same way as adjectives, meaning difficult or risky. We all know that women are 'kittle cattle' and golfers, with any sense of language, know the terrors of greens that are kittle. Tickle, which now seems much more delicate than ticklish because the latter has been so much used of purely physical reactions, occurs in Sir Walter Raleigh's great poem 'The Lie'.

> Tell wit how much it wrangles
>> In tickle points of nyceness,
> Tell wisedome she entangles
>> Her selfe in over wiseness,
> And when they doe reply
>> Straight give them both the lie.

It was good legal English of the Elizabethans to 'stand upon a tickle point'.

LEATHERY

LEATHER is a poor word for a substance that can be so handsome. Leather ought to burnish our poetry far more than it does. But our Horseback Halls, so much less articulate and so much more frequent than our Heartbreak Houses, have never sufficiently voiced their own beauties. It has always been the metals that made the music and the glitter; the swords, not the saddles, romantically gleam. So leathery things are usually left to prose or the paint-box of Mr. Munnings. As if there were no lyrics lurking in a stable! There are, of course, and Mr. John Betjeman fetches them out, as in his lines on Upper Lambourne.

> Leathery limbs of Upper Lambourne,
>> Leathery skin from sun and wind,
> Leathery breeches, spreading stables,
>> Shining saddles left behind,
> To the down the string of horses
>> Moving out of sight and mind.

There is a large piece of England in the several stanzas of that shining poem.

LEWD

A QUEER, revolting, and therefore apt little word is lewd. It originally meant a layman, unclerical, and therefore unread. From that it came to signify vulgar and base in general and was rapidly annexed for a single species of evil. Lewd, by Shakespeare's time, is nearly always used of sexual unpleasantness. The Biblical translators, with their 'lewd fellows of the baser sort', may not have been thinking only of the lecherous, but the horrid little word was being strongly tilted in that direction and has remained so. Once meaning the ignorant it is now applied rather to the precocity which knows too much. In a subsequent note it will be observed how the English words for strong and stubborn all seem to begin with 'st'. A similar curious thing occurs in the case of sexual debauchery. Here 'l' is the favoured initial. Lewd, lecherous, libidinous, loose, lustful — they make a loathsome addition to the tranquil propriety of love. Another which might have been added to this rakish company is luxury, since that to the Elizabethans meant sexual indulgence and not the appurtenances of a costly hotel. Now luxury has come up in the world and is applied rather to caviare than to chambering. (When did the phrase 'lap of luxury' first appear and had it a sexual significance then?) A cinema 'de luxe' (or 'de loo' as the really refined have been known to call it) now only suggests pile carpets, fountains with goldfish and more nutritive fountains of ice cream, padded 'fotiles', and usherettes in pyjamas. To Shakespeare it would have meant a picture-house with a brothel attached. 'Fye on lust and luxury' sing the fairies pinching Falstaff at the close of *The Merry Wives of Windsor*. This does not suggest that the Garter Hotel, Windsor, was the Grand Babylon of its day, but merely that Sir John had been behaving as a nasty old man: in short, as Mistress Page observed, he was 'a lewdster'.

LOVE

'FROM weak grade of Teutonic root leub' and so linked with the Indo-European lubido. English has softened this simple and inclusive word which covers all yearning from strongest passion to tenderest affection, and then wanders off to mean a game of cards or 'no score' at lawn-tennis. It is sometimes claimed that the Tudor poets, who so enchantingly used it, pronounced it as north-country folk do still, luv. Either way, it does well. To fall in love is a fair phrase, as simple as the actual process and as pleasant. The strange thing about the vocabulary of passion is the inadequacy of the words for love's fulfilling. The commonest in use is a mean and ugly monosyllable which is not fit even to be an oath, while the correct and printable are heavy and dull. Copulate and cohabit sound as little attractive as a laboratory or legal process. Fornicate, for less legitimate pleasures, is a most unlovely word which comes out of the brothel. The Biblical 'Chambering and wantoning' has a less deterrent sound and does at least suggest enjoyment. The lowest depth of pitiful insufficiency in language was reached by a young man whom I heard using sex as a verb of the active mood. So we come back gladly to the brief, comprehensive, and fair-sounding love.

MADRIGAL

LET the scholars argue over the ultimate origin of this lovely alien. The O. E. D. traces it back through Italy to the Greek word for a fold and says 'a pastoral song'. Morrison Boyd in his *Elizabethan Music*, following E. H. Fellowes, affirms, as seems more probable, that it simply means 'a composition in the mother tongue'. We can leave the etymology to the specialists. It is more generally important that the Renaissance wafted the madrigal to England where it flourished exceedingly under such masters as Byrd, Downham, Farnaby, Gibbons, Morley and other leaders of that enchanting choir. 'A madrigal was a secular composition for unaccompanied voices (two to eight) each singing a separate part.' Five voices were

common and common too was a theme of love. Gilbert and
Sullivan have made us think of the madrigal as 'merry', but the
Elizabethan's addiction to melancholy admitted sighs and groans
and 'dumps' to this form of writing. Madrigal, because of its
exquisite sound, naturally passed into general poetic usage as a
synonym for all sweetness of sound. Marlowe's Passionate Shepherd
calling,

> Come live with me and be my love
> And we will all the pleasures prove

invites to a session

> By shallow rivers, to whose falls
> Melodious birds sing madrigals.

After that madrigals go ringing down the aisles of English poetry
and might be said to ring the bells of heaven too, when Henley
called the Wren spires of London's city 'madrigals in stone'.

MAGAZINE

A MAGAZINE comes, by way of France, out of Araby. It has in
its time meant any kind of store from a dairy (magazine of milk and
butter, Defoe), to an arsenal. Charles Cotton, in a gay little song
defying winter, described his resources for the campaign.

> There, under ground, a magazine
> Of sovran juice is cellar'd in:
> Liquor that will the siege maintain,
> Should Phoebus ne'er return again.

James Thomson inquired of the winds,

> Where are your stores, ye powerful beings, say,
> Where your aerial magazines reserved
> To swell the brooding terrors of the storm?

In the later eighteenth century the word added to its general utility by taking on its now common literary meaning. By 'Magazine of Taste' you might expect to find described one of the glossier and more expensive fashion-journals. But'this magnificent phrase was, in fact, the title of a dining-room utensil popular a century ago. This was a super-cruet, containing all possible condiments, 'zests' and sauces, and carried the proud, proprietary title of 'Dr. Kitchener's Magazine of Taste'. To remark 'May I trouble you, Sir Eustace, for the Magazine?' did not imply a churlish desire to read at table, but only an interest in added savours.

MANSE AND MANSION

MANSION once meant, according to its Latin origin, any 'remaining-place', a country as well as a house. Then it developed a special meaning on the medieval stage, whose 'mansions' were the separate sections or apartments signifying different spheres of heaven, hell, and earth. The famous but strange-seeming line, 'In My Father's house are many mansions', is explained by this usage. The Scottish form 'manse' is a beautiful word and though, as applied to the minister's dwelling, it has often been a Bleak House in puritanical fact, it comes most softly and sweetly to the ear. The English poets might have seized it. Instead they have realized the rhythmical value and slightly celestial implications of the longer word. Housman began his hymn 'For My Funeral' with,

> O thou that from thy mansion,
> Through time and place to roam,
> Dost send abroad thy children
> And then dost call them home.

Emily Dickinson, vividly creative in her use of words, had 'Summer's nimble mansion'. It is indeed a pity that the Victorian 'real estate men' snatched and assassinated mansion when they started to build what we call 'flats' and Americans 'apartments'.

MARGARINE

YES, margarine, with the 'g' hard, is a beautiful word and much the same as Margaret, for both come out of Greece and mean pearl or pearly. Unfortunately for margarine it has been usurped to signify legally 'any substitute for butter made from oleomargarine' and can be used for all substances made in imitation of butter and offered for sale. The stuff was once an oily horror and that has damned a fair word in a foul mess. A revengeful public degraded margarine to 'marge'. But science has so far bettered margarine as to make it often preferable to a dubious butter and so we owe the word some compensation. Butter is a good, fat word, but unlovely. 'He asked for butter and she brought forth milk. She brought forth butter in a lordly dish.' Margarine has far more delicacy and, if we could only refer it back to its jewelled origins, might take its place in poetry. With its pearly connotation and with 'g' kept hard, it could certainly stand in limpid Tennysonian numbers.

> The sky was azure, flecked with margarine,

or

> Fair Margaret in silk of margarine

might have resounded well in a revival of Victorian modes. But the laboratory and the grocer have put an end to all that.

MEAGRE

MEAGRE began by signifying a thin person and proceeded later to describe the diet likely to make him so. In Chaucer the man is meagre, in Lamb the banquet. As applied to an invalid the adjective can have a pallid, haunting vividness. Milton has

> Blue, meager hag or stubborn unlaid ghost.

Again, there is

> Thou shalt see the field-mouse peep
> Meagre from its celléd sleep.

Thus Keats on the tim'rous beastie. The most poignant usage of meagre that I know occurs in Shakespeare's *King John* during Queen Constance's superb lament for the doomed Prince Arthur.

> There was not such a gracious creature born.
> But now will canker sorrow eat my bud,
> And chase the native beauty from his cheek,
> And he will look as hollow as a ghost,
> As dim and meagre as an ague's fit;
> And so he'll die;

The Queen then goes on to the majestic cry,

> Grief fills the room up of my absent child,
> Lies in his bed, walks up and down with me,
> Puts on his pretty looks, repeats his words,
> Remembers me of all his gracious parts,
> Stuffs out his vacant garments with his form;
> Then have I reason to be fond of grief.

In connection with these lines one has to remember that *King John* was written, fairly certainly, late in 1596. In August 1596 Shakespeare's only son, Hamnet, died in Stratford-on-Avon, aged eleven. We do not know the cause, but that the boy looked at the end

> As dim and meagre as an ague's fit

is all too likely. If ever a poet wrote after personal loss and from a riven heart, surely it was here.

MEW

WHY have we let slip a word so apt for all sorts of confinement and restriction?

> For aye to be in shady cloister mew'd,
> To live a barren sister all your life,
> Chanting faint hymns to the cold, fruitless moon,

is Theseus' well-known threat to Hermia. The brief, expressive, melancholy word fits beautifully into all such pictures of the cloister without a hearth. Mewing, originally, meant penning up a falcon while it moulted, or setting a fowl apart for fattening. But it was lifted for larger matters of human imprisonment, as Juliet was 'mew'd up to her heaviness'. It is rather a sad comment on the rigours of Elizabethan life that with their mewing and cribbing and cabining they have so rich a vocabulary for so bleak a subject.

MICHING

MICHING is skulking, hiding, or thieving. Perhaps Herrick had both shades of meaning in mind when he wrote

> A cat
> I keep, that plays about my house,
> Grown fat
> With eating many a miching mouse.

Hamlet's 'Miching mallecho' is usually interpreted as secret mischief.

'Shall the blessed sun of heaven prove a micher and eat blackberries?' asked Falstaff, thinking rather of trespass.

The same poem of Herrick's, by the way, has a curious verb for the fruitful hen.

> A hen
> I keep, which, creeking day by day,
> Tells when
> She goes her long white egg to lay.

Herrick, like Clare, two centuries later, is a great minter of words. Out of his treasury tumble ancient and modern pieces. His 'Once a virgin flosculet', for example, is a very classical bud, but Herrick sometimes sets Latin moving on tip-toe instead of using the heavy Roman tread.

MOM

THIS is a joke-word and possibly has no business here. Certainly no dictionary has knowledge of it. But it could be very usefully employed, especially to 'de-gas' a certain type of intellectual blimpishness (for surely there can be blimps of cerebration as of the reverse) and so I offer it for adoption. I owe it to the dramatist, John Van Druten, who some years ago passed it on to me as an 'Initial' Word, composed of the first letters of Mind Over Matter. Far be it from me to dethrone the brain from its proper sovereignty over body: what Mom signifies is not a due regard for reason, but all the Thought that is High with a capital 'H' and all the Mindedness that is Right with a capital 'R'. It curtly summarizes the tiresome people who believe that they are mystics simply because they are mystified and claim to be on a higher plane than most of us because their minds are in a far greater mess. They appear to choose words by their length and opinions by their muddle. To say of these that they are 'terribly Mom' is often as just as it is expressive.

MONSTER

A MONSTER, from being a divine portent, came to mean anything unnatural. It is not necessarily large. Indeed, the word seems unusually vivid when preceded by the adjective 'little'. Monster as a noun-epithet for anything vast is a usage of modern journalism, which has to keep on the high note and pretend that any big gathering is a 'monster-meeting'. The adjective monstrous has been worked to death, but the substantive has still virtue in it. The Loch Ness Monster, for example, seemed to me much more impressive and frightening than any Dragon or Apparition of Loch Ness. The word can be most effectively used as any contrast to reality. The old dramatists had graceful epilogues instead of the limping after-curtain speech whose wearisome distribution of 'credits' is a curse of 'first-nights' in our time. One of the best of such tributes by an author to his colleagues is that at the end of

Webster's *The White Devil*, whose prologue, incidentally, puts Shakespeare in his place as one of many approved and not as the genius 'out-topping knowledge' of later opinion. Here is the epilogue:

> For the action of the play (i.e. acting) 'twas generally well done and I dare affirme, with joint testimony of some of their own quality, (for the true imitation of life without striving to make nature a monster) the best that ever became them; whereof, as I make a generall acknowledgement, so in particular I must remember the well-approved industry of my friend Maister Perkins and confesse the worth of his action did Crowne both the beginning and the end.

The dramatists of that time were ever nervous lest the actor, deserting nature, should play the monster. But Webster certainly gave the play-boys encouragement. For some of his characters are pretty near to being monsters themselves — as well as having 'monstrous fine' things to say.

MUSHROOM

Moss is a good soft word for a good soft thing. (It were much better if London's hill of the Mosswell had not been hardened into our ugly Muswell) and Mushroom is one of its products, most charming in its early form 'mush-rump'. It is queer to discover that our use of mushroom for an upstart is as old as the sixteenth century. Then one would have expected it to refer only to a tasty fungus growing among fairy circles.

There is always a suggestion of magic about mushrooms, so swift and so nocturnal in their coming. 'Sleeker than night-swollen mushrooms' are the heifers in 'Endymion'. It is right that Shakespeare's magician, Prospero, should be the only one of his characters to mention mushrooms. One imagines Rosalind's Arden and Oberon's Athens to be full of them. But Shakespearean mushrooms grow only where Ariel has trod.

NAPPY

Liquors, like cloth, have their nap. So nappy is a foamy beer, stuff with a head to it. It is mainly thought of as Scottish now, since Burns had it often on his lips.

> While we sit sousing at the nappy,
> And gettin' foo and unco' happy.

Later in 'Tam o' Shanter' the beer has become 'swats', another good toss-pot word.

> Fast by an ingle, bleezing finely,
> Wi' reaming swats, that drank divinely.

But the nappy is good Tudor English too. Campion, writing in the courtiers' conventional but not always convincing praise of the cottar's Saturday night, sang of his Jack and Joan,

> Well can they judge of nappy ale
> And tell at large a winter's tale.

Shakespeare makes no use of it, but the word foams freely about the tankards and verses of his time.

NESH

Nesh, for tender and susceptible (especially to hard climate) lingers on in country dialect. It is the kind of simple and vivid word which one might expect to be rediscovered by a probing genius, like Cecil Sharp, along with English folk songs and dances in mid-America whither it had been carried in some pilgrim's pack. It used also to have a contemptuous significance, hinting at poltroonery. 'Sitting ower t' fire makes a body nesh', says the northern farmer. But it is essentially a tender-sounding word and should be tenderly restored to the service of tender people and of delicate things.

NOSEGAY

'THERE be some flowers make a delicious Tussie-Mussie or Nosegay both for sight and smell.' Thus John Parkinson, a herbalist of the early seventeenth century. Tussie-Mussie was too good to be lost, but lost it seems to have been. The charming simplicity of nosegay remains, though nostrils are certainly less sensitive to fine aromas owing to smoking. (Tobacco does more to weaken sense of smell than sense of taste.) Nosegay was fairly common in Tudor English, whose lovers 'said it with flowers' and with other things.

> With bracelets of thy hair, rings, gawds, conceits,
> Knacks, trifles, nosegays, sweetmeats —

There are the Shakespearean tokens and tribute of adoration. Shakespeare applied 'posy' only to verse — it is simply a shortening of poesy — and this usage is now extinct. But posy, as a bunch of flowers instead of as a bunch of flower-like words, was familiar to Marlowe and posies have gone on rhyming with roses ever since he wedded them.

OBSEQUIOUS AND OFFICIOUS

A LONG list might be made of terms which have gone down hill. Both these words, for example, have somehow acquired a bad name. Both rightly mean dutiful, but obsequious was degraded to mean over-humble and so fawning, while officious was employed for over-busy and so fussy and meddlesome. Both are to be found in their state of innocence in the poetry of the seventeenth century. George Wither, for example, sang,

> When, with a serious musing I behold,
> The grateful and obsequious Marygold,
> How duly, every morning, she displays
> Her open breast, when Titan spreads his rays,

while Marvell, moved by silver in darkness as Wither by the bloom of gold in day, cried,

> Ye glow-worms, whose officious flame
> To wandering mowers shows the way,
> That in the night have lost their aim
> And after foolish fires do stray,
> Your courteous lights in vain you waste . . .

Milton called the stars 'Bright luminaries Officious' and Dryden frequently used officious to signify serviceable. In his Panegyric on the Coronation of Charles II he wrote,

> Now charged with blessings while you seek repose
> Officious slumbers haste your eyes to close.

It would be an obsequious and officious action to restore these good words to their former state of honour.

ODDLING

THE O. E. D. knows nothing of oddling, a word which pleases me by its double suggestion of the lonely and the queer. (Ben Jonson's odling, which probably means cozening, is another matter altogether.) Oddling seems to be the perfect word for certain types mainly to be discovered of old in winter-time, sitting in seaside hotels when patrons are few and prices low, or watching February seas from the shelter on the deserted esplanade. I first met it in John Clare's lines, as sombrely beautiful as woods in December, called 'Emmonsail's Heath in Winter'. He uses it of crows in the plural and one pictures a brace of peevish solitaries whom spring may render more mutually sympathetic.

> I love to see the old heath's withered brake
> Mingle its crimpled leaves with furze and ling,
> While the old heron from the lonely lake
> Starts slow and flaps his melancholy wing,
> And oddling crows in idle motions swing
> On the half rotten ashtree's topmost twig,
> Beside whose trunk the gipsy makes his bed.

A few lines later he has 'and coy bumbarrels twenty in a drove'. Mr. H. J. Massingham's editorial note in *Poems about Birds* explains 'bumbarrel' as a long-tailed tit, a rustic beauty of a word for an all too rare and beautiful species. Clare, that embodiment of East Midland earth, a piece of heathland animate, spills words in handsome plenty as he wanders across his simple fields and wastes.

OOZE

AN ugly word, but expressive. Nowadays it suggests slime and sluggish brown water or a slow trickle of some probably unpleasant fluid. But Shakespeare used it several times of the sea, mainly of thick water on the bottom, and Shelley followed him when he described the submarine forest of seaweed as,

> The sea blooms and the oozy woods which wear
> The sapless foliage of the ocean.

Dryden said of Father Thames 'Deep in his ooze he sought his sedgy bed', thus distinguishing between the water (ooze) and the muddy bottom. Ariel was wont to 'tread the ooze of the salt deep' and one thinks of that sprite treading only a cleanly moisture. Pericles, in an almost certainly Shakespearean passage of the play called after him, talks of throwing a coffin in the sea and here calls the sea 'ooze'. Perhaps ooze is now damned and muddied o'er beyond redemption. But, before I leave the word, I would like to give it my salute by suggesting a Shakespearean emendation which would lift ooze on to a peak of poetry. What did Macbeth mean when he cried,

> This my hand will rather
> The multitudinous seas incarnadine,
> Making the green one red?

Two theories are advanced. One, the least likely, that he meant making the Green One (i.e. the sea) red. Two, that 'one red' stands for 'all red'. But does either sound in the least like Tudor English? Are there parallels for such handling of the words? I suggest,

Making the green ooze red.

The printer's error in setting one instead of ooze is a much smaller one than many in the First Folio. Ooze here is not, I admit, altogether euphonious. But, with ooze as a noun, the sense is good, and you may take it alternatively as a verb, since Shakespeare employs it so. Either way the usage is truly Shakespearean. Let me confess that I have never found any support for this verbal hazard of mine. But I still believe in it.

OVER-GRIEVING

THE combination of 'v' and 'r' is often both melodious and powerful. The word grief, simple and common, is itself a gem, far more effective on the lips than pain or woe, and well-matched with sorrow, where again the 'r' is playing its emotional tricks. Grief is one of the words which almost make a line of poetry before the poet has begun. Listen to it in James Logie Robertson's masterpiece of accurate moderation concerning the Scottish climate. (It should be explained for the benefit of the English that 'aye' means always.)

> It's no aye rainin' on the misty Achils,
> It's no aye white wi' winter on Nigour;
> The winds are no sae mony sorrowing Rachels,
> That grieve, and o' their grief will no' gie owre.

There is a kind of unintentional humour (far from dry) about lines one and two. The Scotsman is having no poetic licence with the rainfall on the way to Gleneagles. No false claims for him. It will really stop raining sometime. Lines three and four have the music of the stormy hills. Trust the 'w's, 'r's and 'v's for that. The title of this Scottish variant on the Horatian 'non semper imbres' is 'Hughie seeks to console a Brother Shepherd, over-grieving for the loss of his Son'. 'Over-grieving', with its play of 'r's and 'v's, is excellent. There is good use of climatic grief in Browning's

What I love best in all the world
Is a castle, precipice-encurled,
In the heart of the wind-grieved Apennine.

Wind-grieved for heights is as good as 'wuthering'.

OVERWEEN

OVERWEEN now smacks of history-book English. 'The king, in
his overweening pride', etc. In these days it is always pride that
overweens, but there were times when people did their own
overweening, that is to say looked and carried themselves arro-
gantly, and the word might well be restored to the sense in which
Aubrey used it of Gwin, the Earl of Oxford's secretary.

> A better instance of a squeamish, disobligeing, slighting,
> insolent, proud fellow perhaps can't be found. . . . No reason
> satisfies him but he overweenes, and cutts some sower faces
> that would turn the milke in a fair ladie's breast.

There was no quicker portrait-painter than Aubrey. He could
make a word do a page's work.

PARADISE

PARADISE is simply a transliteration of the Greek word for a
park. Parks are still, to many town children, paradisal and park in
Scotland is still the meadow-land of a croft or farm. That bleak
and dusty horror, a car-park, has presumably destroyed the short
word's attraction, but the longer Paradise, though sometimes
sicklied with the worst kind of unction that religiosity distils, is a
grand word upon the lips. The letter 'r' is so often a comforter, in
the old sense of that word which I have already recorded and always
enjoy. The last line of a sonnet is safe with the roll of paradise in
its rhythm and rhyme. Siegfried Sassoon's

Remembrance of all beauty that has been
And stillness from the pools of Paradise,

suggests its magic. I was early taught by a man who had endured
a long and crippling illness. To him, at last able to sit in his garden,
the simple lines of Gray were truth indeed.

See the wretch that long has tost
On the thorny bed of pain,
At length repair his vigour lost
And breathe and walk again:
The meanest floweret of the vale,
The simplest note that swells the gale,
The common sun, the air, the skies,
To him are opening Paradise.

The sentiment is not trite to those who have suffered. I have not
forgotten the light in his eye as he spoke the verse and the surging
relish of Paradise upon his tongue. The Catholic martyr, Robert
Southwell, in the beautiful lines beginning

Christ's thorne is sharpe, no head His garland weares

used imparadise as a verb.

Sweet volumes, stoared with learning fit for saints,
Where blissful quires imparadise the mind.

Could there be a finer description of what is sometimes called by
Auctioneers a 'Gentleman's Library'?

PAVAN

PAVAN is the peacock-dance, a grave and stately measure, elabor-
ately costumed, another gift to England of the Renaissance.
The 'smash-hit' of early seventeenth century music was John
Dowland's pavan 'Lachrymae' with its modishly melancholic
numbers.

Hark you shadows that in darkness dwell,
   Learn tò contemn light,
Happy, happy they that in hell
   Feel not the world's despite.

Those Jacobean 'blues' were certainly deeper and darker than ours —
and more dignified. Also their popular tunes had a longer life.
The popularity of 'Lachrymae' was still a play-house jest in 1624,
although Dowland had published it in 1605. It appeared thus:

> Lachrymae or Seaven Teares, Figured in Seaven Passionate
> Pavans with Divers Other Pavans, Galiards, and Almands, set
> forth for the Lutes, Viols, or Violons, in five parts.

A Galiard was a brisk dance, the epithet galiard (more commonly
galliard) still being in use as an equivalent to gallant. Sir Toby asked
Sir Andrew why he did not go to church in a galliard and come
home in a coranto. Almand or Almaine was, of course, a German
step. Robert Dowland in his 'Varietie of Lute-Lessons' listed
'Fantasies, Pavins, Galliards, Almains, Corantoes, and Volts'. The
two last were the running and the leaping dance. Says the Duke of
Bourbon in *Henry V*,

> They bid us to the English dancing-schools
> And teach lavoltas high and swift corantos.

Shakespeare is here assuming too much for his own country and
even playing at annexation. It was Italy that taught England both
to show a leg and charm the ear, and most musical was the
vocabulary of her instruction.

PAVILION

THE English cricketers did well to annex this butterfly term for
their premises, whether those be a humble shanty by a village field
or the august, metropolitan temple of the M.C.C. It is now a
graceful, green-and-white sort of word and rides easily in a world of
flannels and smooth turf. But the poets in the past have linked

pavilions with more martial and majestic things. The Hymnal has claimed this canopy for heaven and praised 'Our Shield and Defender, the Ancient of Days, Pavilioned in Splendour and girded with Praise'. Shakespeare, whenever he imagined a tented field was prodigal of 'brave pavilions' and naturally Cleopatra, first meeting Antony, was couched in a pavilion on that glittering and scented barge which 'burned upon the river'. All good makers of a lyric have seized on the word's musical possibilities and Francis Thompson sang 'the red pavilions of the heart'.

PEEK

PEEKING, for peering or spying, is another of the old English words which have retained their vitality in America, where a popular magazine can be called *Peek* to suggest its powers of scrutiny. The title would, I think, merely mystify the average customer at a London bookstall. That is a pity, for it is a nicely descriptive word and well suggests a sharp eye above a peering nose. I found it vividly employed in *A True Narrative and Relation of His Majesty's Miraculous Escape from Worcester in September, 1651.* Charles II, 'on the run', was hiding in the oak at Boscobel, guarded by the faithful family of Penderel. 'William and his wife Joan were ever peeking up and down.' Peep, which survives in common use, once served for celestial vision (cf. Vaughan's 'So some strange thoughts transcend our wonted themes, And into glory peep') and now is applied to small and gentle glimpses. The hard 'k' in peek is excellent for a tougher kind of observation and patrol-work. Peeping Toms should really be peekers. Keeking is common Scots for the same kind of thing, from Allan Ramsay to the crofters' lingo of to-day.

PERDU

PERDU, one lost or at least one of whom hope is mainly abandoned, was an ironic Elizabethan term for a soldier with a stiff place to hold.

Then it came to mean any kind of sentinel, without suggestion that the task was extremely hazardous. To Fuller shepherds are 'perdues in defence of their flocks' and the word crops up prettily in the lyrics of the seventeenth century. Cordelia applied it to old Lear's exposure.

> Was this a face
> To be opposed against the warring winds,
> To stand against the dread, deep-bolted thunder,
> In the most terrible and nimble stroke
> Of quick, cross lightning? To watch — poor perdu! —
> With this thin helm?

and Suckling has it in a parody of Shakespeare's early and sensuous vein. He is describing, in the manner of 'Lucrece', a lady couched.

> Out of the bed the other fair hand was
>   On a green satin quilt, whose perfect white
> Looked like a daisy in a field of grass
>   And showed like unmelt snow unto the sight:
> There lay the pretty perdue, safe to keep,
> The rest of the body that lay fast asleep.

Perdu seems now to be lost to the English language, to which it was a graceful immigrant. One of its modern equivalents in desperate gallantry is the 'Tail-End Charlie' who volunteers to be rear-gunner in a bombing aeroplane.

PEREGRINE

THIS term for a traveller or alien has almost dropped out. It is now limited to the peregrine falcon, who is not an alien, but certainly peregrinates the air with a compelling beauty and swooping magnificence of wing. Peregrinate is both Tudor verb and Tudor epithet. Shakespeare's schoolmaster, Holofernes, thus describes the Spaniard, Armado:

his humour is lofty, his discourse peremptory, his tongue

filed, his eye ambitious, his gait majestical, and his general
behaviour vain, ridiculous, and thrasonical. He is too picked,
too spruce, too affected, too odd, as it were, too peregrinate,
as I may call it,

to which the curate, Sir Nathaniel, adds 'A most singular and choice
epithet'.

Holofernes was a pedant and to use now, in his method, such fine-
sounding and polysyllabic terms as thrasonical and peregrinate
might savour of pretentiousness. But the shorter 'peregrine' is a
handsome word and would be a courteous welcome to a stranger.

PICKTHANK

I came across pickthank in Sir Thomas Browne, who wrote of
'pickthank delators', i.e. fawning informers. A pickthank fellow is
one who would steal your gratitude and a very good term it is. I
was the more surprised to find so blunt a piece of Saxon in Sir
Thomas, whose lexicon was mainly compounded of a grand
Latinity. From Rome he took his delator; from his own London
came pickthank. Shakespeare's Prince Hal has it too: he complains
of the 'smiling pickthanks and base newsmongers'. Biron in *Love's
Labour's Lost* comes very near to it with his disdain of

Some carry-tale, some please-man, some slight zany.
Some mumble-news, some trencher-knight, some Dick.

How feeble our modern 'yes-man' seems beside this roll-call of
the sycophants. Sir Walter Scott also used pickthank with effect in
dialogue.

PINCHBECK AND NOSTRUM

Politics afford a particular haunt for clichés. As an example of
the epithet that survives in a moribund state and only in one connection is 'pinchbeck', which scarcely ever appears nowadays without a
following 'Napoleon'. But how many of the scribes who have

dismissed Hitler or Mussolini or any upstart fellow who happens to sit on the wrong political bench as a 'pinchbeck Napoleon' could explain the term? Pinchbeck, as a matter of fact, is a town in Lincolnshire, and so gave a place-name to one Christopher Pinchbeck, a watchmaker who was skilled in the use of a certain alloy of copper and zinc which had the look of gold. Hence 'pinchbeck' comes to be used for 'false', and was so applied by Thackeray to a lady's golden tresses. But now there is only one kind of pinchbeck — namely, the Napoleonic — and its special habitat is righteous, democratic indignation.

The same kind of leader-writer, in the days of party politics, had the astonishing habit of referring to any measure put forward by the other fellows as a 'nostrum'. The word once meant a curative recipe or medicine, but it is a long time since anybody asked his chemist to give him a nostrum for catarrh. In politics a nostrum is always quackish and contemptible, which is absurd for a word meaning only 'our'. Surely if a measure is to be dismissed with disgust, the dismissing party should not thus appear to claim its ownership: 'a paltry vestrum' would make far better sense.

PLOY

WHILE lexicography relates the common 'employ', by way of the French, to the Latin *implicare*, the brief 'ploy' is set down as 'origin unknown'. Well, foundling or not, it is a good child, still flourishing north of Trent and Tweed for a hobby, occupation, adventure, or, when used of the mind, a fancy. So taken it is happily found in this quatrain of Mr. Macdiarmid's.

> Wheesht, wheesht, my foolish hert,
>   For weel ye ken
> I widna hae ye stert
>   Auld ploys again.

Ploys can be sinister. This I came across in Mr. Neil Gunn's tale of

North-East Scotland in the early nineteenth century, *The Silver Darlings*. Describing the licence of the old landowners, he writes,

> The minor lairds could, on occasion, exercise a lurid authority
> over a defenceless tenantry,

and he then talks of 'the shocking ploys' of these mean tyrants in relation to sexual matters.

Still, ugly as such ploys may have been, the word is attractive. Words are my personal ploy.

POW

THE dictionaries turn away from pow. Southern England will not acknowledge it. Burns made it familiar.

> But now your brow is bald, John,
>   Your locks are like the snow,
> But blessings on your frosty pow,
>   John Anderson, my Jo.

Again, of a limping and bent old man he wrote that he hirples

> Wi' his teethless gab and his auld beld pow.

But it is not just a Scotticism. In Mr. T. Thompson's robust and racy sketches and dialogues of Lancashire life there is often a gathering at the barber's. 'To pow' a man here is to cut his hair, and a nice, crisp term for it too. Pow-wow, for a putting of heads together in counsel and debate might come from this, but does not. It is one of the Red Man's gifts to his White conqueror. It is odd that, while the Redskin is usually pictured as a serene and silent chieftain, wrapped in tobacco-smoke and silence, one of our most graphic words for a talk should be his. Palaver, another good one, comes from Africa.

PRAGMATICAL

WORDS often go from good to worse: pragmatical has had one of these downhill slides. First it was practical: then busy; then over-busy. It has a good classical weight for the description of an inter-fering creature. With it Pepys truncheoned a too zealous constable encountered on a vinous and vagrant occasion.

> Home in a coach round by the wall; where we met so many stops by the watches, that it cost us much time and some trouble, and more money, to every watch to them to drink; this being encreased by the trouble the prentices did lately give the City, so that the militia and watches are very strict at this time; and we had like to have met with a stop for all night at the constable's watch at Mooregate by a pragmatical constable; but we came well home at about two in the morning.

Plainly, a difficult night. Wars and their permits and restrictions offer great chances to the busybody. The too pragmatical patriot is a common nuisance to his country.

PRIGGER

MUCH has been written about the richness of thieves' cant in Victorian times. There are, for example, such tributes to the nine-teenth century lingo of the craft as Mr. W. L. Hanchant's *The Newgate Garland or Flowers of Hemp*, which is full of pretty terms. But for me the Tudor pamphleteers are supreme practitioners in description of the coney-catching tribe. Robert Greene, for ex-'ample, could roll out a grand list of knavish nomenclature, with words as curt as they are expressive. 'And lastly look for a bead-roll or catalogue of all the names of the foists, nips, lifts, and priggers about London.' That quartette does indeed cram the town's rich thievery up. Fagin's world is here complete — and anticipated by two hundred and fifty years.

PUDGE

A PUDGE is a stout and puffy man. It is also a muddy puddle and good either way. John Clare liked pudge and the epithet pudgy, for his winter-landscapes. Among his Asylum Poems (this one so sanely observant and serene!) is,

> Little trotty wagtail, you nimble all about,
> And in the dimpling water-pudge you waddle in and out.

Nimble, as a verb, is nice.

PURSY

FROM quite old times pursy has been connected with the money-purse and meant purse-proud or wealthy. Also, because the strings of the purse are often drawn tight, it came to mean anything closely gathered: a pursy skin meant a tight, puckered covering for the face. But there is another pursy, a vigorous and expressive epithet, a corruption of pursive, meaning panting or broken-winded. Quarles sang of solitary folk in 'solemn groves'

> Where they sit and pant
> And breathe their pursy souls,
> Where neither grief consumes nor griping want
> Afflicts, nor sullen care controls.

I wonder whether Shakespeare may have had both senses in mind when he wrote, 'For in the fatness of these pursy times'.

The unfinancial, wheezing pursy is cousin to the French *poussif*. It reminds me of a drive in one of the antiquated landaus which survive in the Royal Deer Park, now public, at Klampenborg outside Copenhagen. (From this admirable piece of country motor-cars are excluded.) As we trotted agreeably along through the beech-groves a small boy with me asked the coachman what his horse's name was. 'Pouster' came the reply, that being the Danish for 'wheezer'. It might have been Pursy, which is really the same word and was a fairly accurate name in this case. Has poor Pouster become sausage-meat by now? If so, may he lie heavy on some pursy German's paunch.

PYRAMID

PYRAMIDS, more impressive by bulk than by design, bring a Greek name out of Egypt and, so doing, have appealed to the poets with most sense of an imposing sound. Milton deemed 'my Shakespeare's reliques' well enough famed without benefit of 'star-y pointing Pyramid', and Shakespeare himself had liked the word well. When

> palaces and pyramids do slope
> Their heads to their foundations

was Macbeth's idea of chaos come again. Cleopatra naturally mixed pyramids with her 'immortal longings'. Her defiance of the triumphant Augustus makes use of the four-syllabled plural which gave a rich roll to an iambic line.

> Shall they hoist me up,
> And show me to the shouting varletry
> Of censuring Rome? Rather a ditch in Egypt
> Be gentle grave unto me! rather on Nilus' mud
> Lay me stark nak'd, and let the water-flies
> Blow me into abhorring! rather make
> My country's high pyramides my gibbet,
> And hang me up in chains.

In our time the Pyramides have been a form of fireworks, which are often imaginatively titled toys (see my note on 'Tourbillion'), and the word has also denoted a variety of billiards. Furthermore it is also used for geometrical figures. But fie, as the Lady said in the Old Comedy, let us not be mathematical.

QUEASY

THIS is one of the fascinating words with an active and a passive meaning. It suggests both troublesome and troubled. The times, being queasy in fact, make men queasy of mind. A troubled mind may be the more exacting and so queasy comes to designate the fastidious. Probably its most frequent sense to-day is that of restlessness, inability to digest, gastric or mental tenderness. What helps to make it so expressive for us is its seeming collision of queer and uneasy. A queasy stomach is a phrase which proclaims itself. Queasy in Shakespeare may mean either disgusted ('queasy with his insolence'), fastidious, or sickly. Benedick had 'a quick wit and a queasy stomach'. With a transference of meaning from fastidious to feeble it can be most effectively given a slight turn of sneer. Those who in American slang 'are yellow and can't take it' are dismissible as queasy.

RANTIPOLE AND ROUSTABOUT

MR. OSBERT SITWELL, in the admirable book on Brighton, which he wrote with Miss Margaret Barton, quoted a ballad of 1815, signed 'Peter Pindar', called 'Royal Rantipoles, or The Humours of Brighton'. Rantipole implies a mixture of the romp and the rake, which suited the Regent well enough. 'Peter Pindar's' lyrical description of life at the Pavilion and of a royal game of 'Blind Man's Bluff', with the Prince laying hands upon the ladies, is distinctly rantipolitan.

It must be said of that age that its grossness was not in all things tyrannical. The Royal Rantipole had liberal impulses and gave freedom to burlesque: witness the licence which permitted the publication of this impudent Pindaric ode. Straying on so fine a word as roustabout one would naturally take it to be of the same family and reference as rantipole. Not at all. It is the American for a handyman. None the less, I suggest that 'Royal Roustabouts' would have been just as apt a name for 'Peter Pindar's' poem about the parlour-games of Prinny and his friends.

THERE is nearly always something rather likeably odd about the words ending in double 'e'. One feels that a raree-show must be a good one, its rareties genuinely scarce, its freaks freakish beyond a peradventure, and its showmanship terrific. Grandees came from Castile and there was no doubt about their grandeur, just as there can be no second thoughts about the viciousness of a debauchee. Raree, like debauchee, has become too rare nowadays. Of rare Ben Jonson it could be added that his masques and plays present a double raree-show, one of fantastic characters and humours, the other of the English language. A later type of notable exhibition was the galanty-show or shadow-pantomime. The term is too rich a one to be limited to so jejune a matter as shadow-play and silhouette. All the history of fops and pretenders, of bucks and macaronis and possibly of genuine heroes too, is surely a galanty-show.

RATHE

I HAVE seen 'rathe' dismissed as obsolete. It is a calamity, if it be so. For it is a strong and simple word for all speedy and vehement things.

> I am the hunte which rathe and early ryse.

Then it acquired a special reference to flowers and fruits which are lured on by early sun and gallantly, perhaps rashly, anticipate their hour, like Milton's 'rathe primrose'. It is odd that Shakespeare, with his grand sweep of vocabulary, should have missed 'rathe'. It was perfect for his daffodils that 'come before the swallow dares'.

REAM

IN the note on Nappy the word 'reaming' occurred. It is Scottish and northern and much happier, with its creamy suggestion, than the meagre frothy. Drinking songs tend to be monotonous and boring. Eulogies of beer, after we have flavoured such old favourites

as 'Bring us in good ale' and 'Back and sides go bare', become rather
tedious. The best descriptions of beer come from the land of whisky.
Alexander Hume, for example (1557-1602), in his sun-drenched poem
'Of the Day Estivall', deals thus with Scotland's summer-thirst:

> The Caller wine in cave is sought,
>   Men's brothing breasts to cool;
> The water cauld and clear is brought,
>   And sallets steept in ule.
> Some plucks the honey-plum and pear,
>   The cherry and the pêche:
> Some likes the reamand London beer
>   The body to refresh.

London beer, presumably, was a Trade Title. It is hardly to be
supposed that sixteenth-century Scotland took London's liquor on
so long a journey. Robert Fergusson in 'The Farmer's Ingle', on
which Burns drew closely for 'The Cotter's Saturday Night', writes:

> O' nappy liquor owre a bleezin' fire:
>   Sair wark and poortith downa weel be joined;
> Wi' butter'd bannocks now the girdle reeks,
>   I' the far nook the bowie briskly reams.

Poortith is poverty, the bowie a bowl or tub. Sair work and poortith have not yet been disjoined. But the nappy and 'the swats' still
ream for consolation.

RENEGE

RENEGE means to desert, or renounce. Sometimes it is spelt reneague.
It was a Tudor word, used of religious recantation and still surviving
apparently in the Scottish slang of crooks, for so James Bridie, the
dramatist, has employed it in his dialogue. I was surprised and glad
to find it there, for I thought this nicely descriptive word had not
been much heard since Shakespeare said of the love-shackled
Antony,

> his captain's heart,
> Which in the scuffles of great fights hath burst
> The buckles on his breast, reneges all temper,
> And is become the bellows and the fan
> To cool a gipsy's lust.

Lear's Kent has it too in his railing at the varlet Oswald, whom he groups with the smiling rogues who

> Renege, affirm, and turn their halcyon beaks
> With every gale and vary of their masters,
> Knowing naught, like dogs, but following.

Halcyon beaks is exciting and halcyon has already been put in the honours list. Mr. Arthur Ransome tells me of a boatman at Barrow who bade him not renege, i.e. abandon an audacious plan of navigation.

RUBIOUS

THE ruby has ceased to be a fashionable gem and Ruby as a Christian name is now rare. But the word has the richness which the letter 'R' so often confers, as Fitzgerald was well aware.

> But still the Vine her ancient Ruby yields.

The second noun does powerfully suggest a splendour on the palate and a glow in the mind. All who have ever lost their heart to Shakespeare's Viola — that is all who ever read *Twelfth Night* — remember the delicate cherry of her mouth,

> Diana's lip
> Is not more smooth and rubious.

The jewel has here turned gentle and this 'rubious' seems very far removed from the crude scarlet slash favoured in the make-up of so many a contemporary miss.

mask to 'heel the high lavolt' (Italians both), and thence to the Spanish saraband, which, whatever its optical charms, is also a glorious noise. Bottom offered Theseus an epilogue or a bergamask after the play of Pyramus and Thisbe, but both were prudently declined. The English saraband was born in the year of Shakespeare's death.

> And the strains of the sarabande
> More lively than a madrigal,
> Go hand in hand
> Like the river and its waterfall,

sings Mr. Sacheverell Sitwell of public dancings by the Rio Grande. So once in Whitehall the lordly masquers of the Stuart court trod this euphonious measure.

SCAMBLE

WHY on earth has this excellent and convenient verb been allowed to sink into the dictionary's 'Obs. and Arch.', the graveyard, so often, of the just? Scamble seems to have been all things to all men. By scambling money you squandered it. Or by scambling money up you hoarded money up. To scamble a meal was the same as our 'knocking up' and a scambler was the visitor whom you had to oblige with this process, often so much more laborious than one expects. A scambler is a really good word for the person who looks in a little before supper. To scamble was also to wander or lounge and so to be a kind of strolling wastrel and knave. Antonio, of *Much Ado About Nothing*, uses it in an angry dismissal of smart, swaggering knaves:

> What, man! I know them, yea,
> And what they weigh, even to the utmost scruple —
> Scambling, out-facing, fashion-mongering boys,
> That lie and cog and flout, deprave and slander . .

From this the passage is obvious to the fine dismissive phrase for mental vapouring, 'skimble-skamble stuff'.

SCRUNTY

SCRUNTY is Scottish and you can form your own idea of what it means simply by looking at it and muttering the two syllables. It occurs in the tale of bad Robin-a-Ree, a ballad admired and quoted by Charlotte Brontë's Caroline Helstone.

> Oh! ance I lived happily by yon bonny burn —
>   The warld was in love wi' me;
> But now I maun sit 'neath the cauld drift and mourn
>   And curse black Robin-a-Ree!
>
> Then whudder awa', thou bitter biting blast,
>   And sough through the scrunty tree,
> And smoor me up in the snaw fu' fast,
>   And ne'er let the sun me see!

Whudder, sough, scrunty and smoor, all in three lines! The Scots have rarely been great artists in music, but as ballad-makers they were immense and in the making of words they showed a rare genius for the look and the cadence and the flavour of the thing, be it bonnie and blithe or scrunty merely.

SECRETARY

HOW often does the user of the word secretarial think of it in terms of deep confidence? Indeed, the fact that we have to employ the phrase 'confidential secretary' shows how far the original meaning has disappeared. (Really, one might as well talk about a culinary cook.) The Secretary of State was the man who held the secrets of the nation and any secretary's first business was rather to keep his mouth shut and ears open than to write and file letters. Hence secretary was applied to any conniver at privacies, especially to darkness. In an anonymous seventeenth century poem of passion, drawing obviously on Latin sources, I came across the word in that connection.

> Let us begin while daylight springs in heaven
> And kiss till night descends into the even,
> And when that modest secretary, night,
> Discovers all but thy heaven-beaming light
> We will begin revels of hidden love
> In that sweet orb where silent pleasures move.

Shakespeare only uses secretary in its modern, official sense, perhaps because he already had so many exquisite metaphors for night's concealment.

SEEL AND SEELY

EVERYBODY knows Macbeth's invitation to the dark.

> Come seeling night,
> Scarf up the tender eye of pitiful day.

Most people probably take seeling to be a Tudor spelling of sealing. But it is a different verb, derived, like many Tudor terms, from falconry. Seeling was a part of the taming and training process and meant tying up the birds' eyelids with a thread. So Antony employed the metaphor.

> But when we in our viciousness grow hard —
> Oh misery on't — the wise gods seel our eyes:
> In our own filth drop our clear judgments: make us
> Adore our errors: laugh at us, while we strut
> To our confusion.

Seely is an odd word: it has nothing to do with the falconer's seeling, but is not quite the same as silly, since it first meant well-omened and lucky. Then, by way of piety, it came to imply simplicity and so to be united with silly, of which more in its proper place. Ben Jonson in his verses in the Shakespearean First Folio wrote of 'Seeliest ignorance'. He probably meant simple and had no thought of the verb seel and its darkness.

SILLY

SILLY has become a term of contempt, but to the men of Shakespeare's time it implied an honourable form of simplicity. 'Like to the seely fly, to the dear light I fly', sang Davison. The poets of that epoch habitually contrasted the uneasy glory of a courtier's life with the homespun safety of the peasant's cot. When Campion warned the 'courtly dames and knights' that

> Yet, for all your pomp and train,
> Securer lives the silly swain,

he was not deeming his Jack and Joan to be fools. The meaning had not changed when Burns wrote of the silly walls of the field-mouse's nest. Shakespeare also used silly in this sense and it was applied to sheep to describe their innocence rather than their lack of brain. In the beautiful passage in *Henry VI*, Part III, where the young King Henry muses on the happier life of the 'homely swain', a passage manifestly prophetic of the superb monologues of *Richard II*, the King exclaims,

> Ah, what a life were this! how sweet! how lovely!
> Gives not the hawthorn-bush a sweeter shade
> To shepherds, looking on their silly sheep,
> Than doth a rich embroider'd canopy
> To kings that fear their subjects' treachery?
> O, yes, it doth; a thousand-fold it doth.
> And to conclude, — the shepherd's homely curds,
> His cold thin drink out of his leather bottle,
> His wonted sleep under a fresh tree's shade,
> All which secure and sweetly he enjoys,
> Is far beyond a prince's delicates,
> His viands sparkling in a golden cup,
> His body couched in a curious bed,
> When care, mistrust, and treason wait on him.

The whole passage is worth citing in a note of this kind because of its further and nice usage of delicates and curious.

SMIRK

SMIRK is a good old word for neat and trim, cousin to smikker which is a casualty in England but still, in a similar form, is the ordinary word for pretty in Denmark. We can hardly now dissociate smirk from a knowing, leering glance and to find a 'Smirk Butler' in Herrick is no doubt particularly pleasing because of its hint of a Davus, even of a Jeeves. The Smirk Butler appears in the parson's robustly sensuous Nuptiall Song or Epithalamie on Sir Clipseby Crew and his lady ('To bed, to bed, kind Turtles') and is described as eager to express his wit in the arrangement of napery and even as striving to catch her ladyship's eye. I have a feeling that Sir Clipseby may have found it necessary to be rid of the fellow before long and to find a rather less smirk successor. What did Herrick mean exactly by 'smirking wine'? Smiling, bubbling? Here is the passage.

> If smirking wine be wanting here,
> There's that which drowns all care, stout beere.

Wycherley used smirk with the odious sense that we attach to it, attributing to one of his characters 'the canonical smirk and filthy clammy palm of a chaplain'.

SNIDE AND SNOOP

THESE two words are mainly used in America and deserve to go on the list of England's necessary imports. Snide for bogus or dishonest has some record of English usage, but it is far commoner in America, where it is a living and expressive term. I have noticed it several times in the works of Mr. George Jean Nathan, who is not as a rule addicted to archaism. His 'snide lawyers' are just the men to employ some snooping creatures. Snoop, of a Dutch origin, is a superb word for poking and prying and hiding and spying. Like snide, it seems only to have visited England. Both migrants should be henceforth impounded and naturalized.

SOCIAL

POOR social! It has fallen on bleak times and now is almost invariably tagged to a 'problem' or a 'service'. This friendly and liquorish word has become Blue Bookish and as dry as a Report on Stitchery Instruction in Girls' Clubs. Moreover, the older and happier meaning has also been applied to such oppressive occasions. 'A social evening', 'A social function'. Does any heart beat at the phrase, does any eye sparkle? What would Burns have made of these celebrations? Yet social was a great word of his, as of his century, and was usually applied to the happiest of moods and of refreshments.

> So may through Albion's farthest ken
>   To social flowing glasses
> The grace be 'Athole's honest men
>   And Athole's bonnie lasses'.

In the Epistle to James Smith, with its defence of 'the hairum-scarum, ram-stam boys, The rattling squad', there is ample praise of 'Cheerfu' tankards foamin' And social noise'.

The social cup should come again to ease our weariness with social problems.

SPANIEL

THE use of 'spaniel' as a verb is typical of Shakespeare's flash of phrase. With what a prodigal collision of metaphors does he describe the desertion of Antony that followed the treachery of Cleopatra! First he cries out that she

> Like a right gipsy hath at fast and loose
> Beguiled me to the very heart of loss.

Then he adds,

>   The hearts
> That spaniel'd me at heels, to whom I gave
> Their wishes, do discandy, melt their sweets
> On blossoming Caesar and this pine is barked
> That overtopped them all.

Spaniels are the only dogs about which Shakespeare is frequently particular. The hounds in general he knows, the 'shoughs, water-rugs, and demi-wolves' and, of course, the mastiffs of the baiting-pit and bull-ring, his theatre's neighbours at Paris Garden. But of terriers he says nothing. Spaniel he employs as noun, adjective, and verb, making it the symbol of affectionate humility. His spaniel is sometimes seen as basely fawning, perhaps, but also as the happy and likeable tail-wagger. I surmise a genial grovelling of spaniels at New Place and one of this species as the earliest Bardolater or worshipper of Mr. W. S. The verb is delightful, and I am happy, here as ever, to spaniel on Shakespeare's use of words.

SQUANDER

OUR limiting of squander to financial matters has narrowed the usage of a vivid word. Squander was first an intransitive verb and meant to be scattered. Flocks squandered. Then it became more active and meant to disperse. When Shylock calls Antonio's argosies 'squandered abroad' he means locally dispersed and is not thinking of monetary wastage. So with Jaques.

> The wise man's folly is anatomized
> Even by the squandering glances of the fool.

Edmund Blunden, whose use of words is always fascinating, employs squander with aptness in his beautiful poem 'The Alms-women'.
With

> At Quincey's moat the squandering village ends,

he begins his picture of the old village women:

> All things they have in common, being so poor,
> And this one fear, Death's shadow, at the door.
> Each sundown makes them mournful, each sunrise
> Brings back the brightness in their failing eyes.

Squandering is so exactly right for the end of an English village as it fades off into its little chaos of orchards and of cabbage-patch, of shippons and tool-sheds and tumble-down steadings of all kind.

STADDLE

A SERVICEABLE old word for a support or crutch or a staff of any kind. If you grow weary of reading about 'Pillars of Society', it is because we have forgotten our Staddles of the State. Mr. Churchill proved himself at the dangerous hour to be every inch a Staddle. The word is metaphorically taken from forestry in which a staddle is a tree left standing when others are thinned out. Thomas Fuller, discussing the means of raising good infantry as well as wealthy cavaliers, wrote,

> Wherefore, to make good infantry, it requireth men bred, not in a servile or indigent fashion, but in some free and plentiful manner. Wisely, therefore, did that knowing prince, King Henry the Seventh, provide laws for the increase of his yeomanry, that his kingdom should not be like to coppice-woods, where, the staddles being left too thick, all runs to bushes and briers, and there is little clean underwood.

The word's usage has dwindled, but the doctrine holds.

STALWART

EARLIER I mentioned the politicians' delight in cliché. The British parties have developed their inseparable adjectives. The old and bold of Liberalism are always described as 'Stalwarts', while Tories are always Stout. Labour favours Staunch.

Stalwart is my favourite of these. It is, in fact, a form of the older, 'stalworth', which means worthy of a place or seat and is thus an excellent word for a politician. (Stalwart accordingly is really equivalent to the phrase 'A representative man', which helped to carry Mr. Veneering into Parliament for the Borough of Pocket

Breaches, with his friends enthusiastically 'rallying round' and with that incomparable duo of toadies, Messrs. Boots and Brewer, told to 'take cabs and go about' as the very essence of the rallying process.) But nowadays 'stalwart' has a strong hint of chesty, 'chin-up' men who never doubt that clouds will break. I can clearly visualize a 'Liberal Stalwart' or a 'Stout Tory'. The staunch Labourite remains cloudier. Why, by the way, do many of our terms for endurance begin with 'st'? Not only are men of stamina stalwart, stout, and staunch, but they are strong, stubborn, strenuous, sturdy, and steadfast stickers-to-the-end.

STOLCHY

STOLCHY, meaning trampled into mire, I found in Edmund Blunden, Suffolk's singer and the worthy editor of John Clare, both being bards so earthy and ethereal at once.

> When groping farms are lanterned up
> And stolchy ploughlands hid in grief,
> And glimmering by-roads catch the drop
> That weeps from sprawling twig and leaf . . .

This, I take it the East Anglian, form of the word is much better than the more general 'stoach' and 'stoachy'. Kipling wrote of fields 'stoached with sliding hoof-marks'. But the 'l' is sovereign. It powerfully stiffens the mire and expresses all the squelch and struggle of a walk across November clay.

When I once used the word 'stolchy' a correspondent reminded me of the Scottish and Northern English 'clarty' which appears to mean much the same thing. But clarty, to me, has a clear, sharp, frosty tang, which is very different. Clarty would be a grand word for a day of sun, rime, and east wind.

STOUR

THE English have kept the finely-sounding stour only for their rivers. Otherwise it has been left to the Scots. It meant battle and also any sort of struggle or stress: from that it came to denote tumult and the dust of combat. Altogether it is a nicely expressive word, effectively used by Spenser for whom it was English enough, but then relegated to the North where it abides in what is left of Scots. It has the deep note of doom and is a grand word for a stern occasion, as Dunbar knew well. In his *Lament for the Makars* he says of the 'tyrand' Death,

> He takis the campion[1] in the stour,
> The captain closit in the tour,
> The lady in bour full of bewtie:

And Burns, in one of his most memorable songs, cried from the heart,

> How blithely wad I bide the stoure,
> A weary slave frae sun to sun,
> Could I the rich reward secure,
> The lovely Mary Morison.

How mean the English 'stir' seems after that! Scottish realism has used the dusty side of it with effect. John Muir, the grave-digger in *Cloud Howe*, Lewis Grassic Gibbon's wonderful study of small-town life in the Mearns, talks of mankind going down to 'stour and stink' in the end.

THRILL

JOURNALISM, as I have already noted, seizes on the short word, seizes and soon works it to death. 'Thrill' has been one of its most unhappy victims. Originally it meant a shiver down the back and the adjective thrilling was applied to things shiversome on the grand scale. In Shakespeare thrill is tremendous. 'I have a faint cold fear thrills through my veins.' We should shudder at that. In Claudio's magnificent speech on the terrors of death thrilling, now tagged to any tawdry event or stage-surprise, magnificently takes its place.

[1] Champion.

Ay, but to die, and go we know not where;
To lie in cold obstruction, and to rot;
This sensible warm motion to become
A kneaded clod; and the delighted spirit
To bathe in fiery floods or to reside
In thrilling regions of thick-ribbed ice,
To be imprison'd in the viewless winds,
And blown with restless violence round about
The pendent world;

Thrilling there comes in like a whip-lash of East wind — or did to an Elizabethan. When Charlotte Brontë wrote of 'thrilling pains in her back' she meant agony. Thrilling has retained its dignity and power in some modern poetry. In Kipling's Sussex,

Here through the strong and shadeless days
The tinkling silence thrills.

This splendidly mingles the sheep-bells and the stab of sun upon the treeless chalk. In Laurence Binyon's famous poem 'For the Fallen'

Solemn the drums thrill: Death, august and royal,
Sings sorrow up into immortal spheres.

But the 'boosters' of the Entertainment Industry, as well as the hard-pressed sub-editors seeking a short word for excitement, have effectively murdered thrill by now and are pathetically striving to revive it with emphatic prefix. I recently read a puff of a film with 'A Thousand Super-Thrills'. As if that helped!

TOPIARY

THE topiary art is that of trimming hedges and bushes into fantastic shape. The Tudor gardeners were topiarists of distinction and one would expect the eighteenth century to have enjoyed the formalities of the craft. But Addison and Pope denounced topiary in gardens, Pope announcing heavily that 'all art consists in the imitation and study of nature', which seems to be a sweeping misstatement. Pope went on to quote (or invent) ludicrously from the catalogues of topiary in his time.

> Adam and Eve in Yew. Adam a little shattered by the fall of the tree of knowledge in the great storm: Eve and the Serpent very flourishing,

and

> Divers eminent modern poets, in bays, somewhat blighted, to be disposed of, a pennyworth.

The truth surely is that topiary in gardens suits houses and estates of a certain period. Round a great Tudor mansion the peacock should stand in yew as well as strutting in full feather.

TOSY

TOSY and cosh both mean snug and are very happily used by John Galt in his *Annals of the Parish*. His Rev. Mr. Balwhidder complains of the tea-drinking that has come into Ayrshire (1762), but reminds himself that it does less harm than the 'Conek' (cognac) with which previous beverages had been laced.

> There is no meeting now in the summer evenings, as I remember often happened in my younger days, with decent ladies coming home with red faces, tosy and cosh, from a posset-masking.

Could there be better adjectives to suggest a modest alcoholic after-glow? One thinks of the 'decent ladies' very affable with the Minister and then reduced to tittering and even to less than decent conversation when Mr. Balwhidder had passed by.

Cosh, by the way, was the name of one of John Aubrey's sources of information. That glorious gossip, after relating some neat or scandalous episode, would note, 'This I had of old Major Cosh'. The Major suggests one of the ripest of the seventeenth-century talkers. He was doubtless almost always tosy.

TOURBILLION

ANYTHING which goes round and round, especially a firework which gyrates. A good word, surely, for the literary or dramatic critic. Is not Bernard Shaw the unquenchable tourbillion of the theatre, is not H. G. Wells the restless tourbillion of the Left? G. K. Chesterton was certainly the gyrating firework of the Faith, the Catherine Wheel of orthodoxy, in his day. The old descriptions of firework displays are always delightful. When Stratford-on-Avon celebrated the birthday of Shakespeare in 1830, a Mr. Robert Southby, of the Royal Gardens, Vauxhall, London, did his best to set the Avon on fire with his unparalleled array of 'Pyramids, Batteries, Saucissons, Mines, and Tourbillions'. So let us have fewer stale metaphors from the hard-worked rocket and some fresh ones from these glories of a nineteenth-century nocturne, the tourbillion especially.

TOURMALINE

THIS substance, which sounds like something sensual in Swinburne, is, in fact, 'a brittle pyro-electric mineral' and 'a complex silicoborate with a vitreous lustre': also 'a specimen or gem of this mineral'. Why then include it in a book of estimable words? Because it is the kind of jewel that used to flash in the vocabulary of aspiring poets and is doing so again. It occurs along with agate, sphene, jacinth, topaz, sardonyx, and feldspar, in a poem on Euterpe by a very young and rather mineralogical minstrel, Mr. A. G. Lambert, who shared a volume called *Silver Gold* with his colleague, Mr. A. J. Neame, while both were attending Cheltenham College.[1] The latter bard was as much excited by Echo as Mr. Lambert was by Euterpe.

> Her tiara is garnet and bright tourmaline,
> With glittering facets of chrysoberyl light.

[1] Cheltenham's previous output of minstrels was limited to Adam Lindsay Gordon, a vigorous Australian rhymer with a strong equestrian interest. Mr. Day Lewis was for a while, I believe, a master in the Junior School.

For some years the English Muse has been robbed of these sonorous and romantic gems and decorated with the metaphor of fuse-box and flash-point, algebra and internal combustion engines. Here is some rescue of poetry from petrol and power-stations. Once more the English Muse may have rings on her fingers and bells on her toes and tourmaline may decorate both.

TRAFFIC

TRAFFIC, like horde previously noted, is a dog with a bad name. Why should it always be applied, in its trading sense, to shameful practices or articles deemed to be sinister and degrading? It was not always so. When Shakespeare talked of 'the two hours traffic of our stage' he was not implying dirty fun or censorable themes. Michael Drayton, honouring Shakespeare, claimed for him the ownership of

> As strong conception and as cleere a rage
> As any one that trafiqu'd with the stage.

(A clear rage is surely a most striking phrase for the kind of genius who, like Shakespeare, can lose his heart in his work and also keep his head.) But nowadays traffic is the word always chosen by the man who would abuse and even prohibit his neighbour's profession. To the fanatical teetotaller there is no such thing as 'having a glass of beer', which many citizens innocently imagine themselves to be doing. No, they are 'partaking of alcoholic stimulants purveyed by the Liquor Traffic'. This talk of the Liquor Traffic — monstrous phrase which includes the rarest claret with the roughest bath-tub gin — puts wine on a level with cocaine. Drugs, of course, are always the matter of a Traffic. I should like to rescue poor Traffic and reinstate it in good repute. Why not talk of the rose-traffic in Covent Garden or of the traffic in Holy Writ carried on by the British and Foreign Bible Society?

TREPAN

TREPAN now chiefly signifies a surgical instrument for cutting out pieces of bone, especially from the skull, and the act of so cutting. But to our ancestors it was a snare and the user of a snare and a very forcible word it was. Seventeenth and eighteenth century invective is resonant with 'Rogues and Trepans'. I have advocated the renewal of the word 'Cog' for cheating and cozening and with it I would have trepan. Burns applied it to the gay seducer in 'The Jolly Beggars',

> The ladies' hearts he did trepan
> My gallant, braw John Highlandman.

The surgeons must not have so good a thing to themselves.

UMBER

ALL through winter Britain abounds in exquisite tints. Blake's 'green and pleasant land' has become brown and russet. The bare, ruin'd choirs have their sombre splendour of tint as well as of form. But the writer who endeavours to paint this glory in words finds himself with a galling scarcity of satisfactory epithets of colour. Dun is a dull word and sepia smacks of the paint-box rather than of the vivid beauty of woods in winter. I have a liking for umber, which may or may not be connected with the Latin word for shade. That connection has long been lost: to Shakespeare umber was a pigment for staining things and disguising the complexion. ('And with a kind of umber smirch my face.') Now it has come to signify brown in general and its depth of sound suggests a like depth of colour-tone. For Housman,

> Wenlock Edge was umbered
> And bright was Abdon Burf
> And warm between them slumbered
> The smooth green miles of turf.

The adjective not only delights the ear: it helps to drench the stanza with the more sombre pigments of our coloured counties. Umber, I am told, is one name for a grayling, which by its swift, underwater movement acquires the dark look of a shadow.

UMBRAGE

WHY not restore to umbrage its proper meaning of shadow? Now it seems always to bear its later sense of disfavour and, there too, it is in disfavour, or at least in mockery. Who talks of 'taking umbrage' except as a joke? But umbrage, in its true significance, is a good, black, shadowy term for suggesting a dense covering of leafy or needled branches.

Milton's

> When highest woods impenetrable
> To star or sunlight spread their umbrage broad

drives into the dark heart of silvan gloom. Hamlet used umbrage for the shadow of a man and any word in Hamlet's vocabulary has a prescriptive right to endurance. For adjectives there are umbratile and umbrageous, umbrous and umbrose. Umbrageous is the most common. Carlyle's Teufelsdrockh, that ingenious and impassioned spinner of words, moved on 'umbrageous lawns'. Umbratile will not do now. It too unhappily suggests the pert trade name of a patent waterproof hat. Umbrageous might also be a telescoping of umbrage with outrageous and is not right for quiet, shady places. Umbrose hints at a man called Ambrose in a pet. Umbrous is best. Meanwhile we have to recover umbrage from its status of a slightly comic alternative to 'dudgeon' and put it back among green thoughts beneath the trees.

UNCONSCIONABLE

IN the note on 'barkable' allusion was made to the various employments of the termination -able. Unconscionable is an example of the oddest use. It is the equivalent of unconscientious. Why it took its present form is difficult to see. Does it mean something that conscience cannot cope with, or is it simply the fine, dismissive sound which has shaped it thus queerly? The eighteenth century drama is full of unconscionable dogs and rogues, for the epithet comes soundingly upon the angry lips of Sir Olivers and Sir Anthonys. From unconscientious it came to mean perverse or preposterous or extreme, as in the familiar royal apology for being 'an unconscionable time a-dying'. And most effective it is there.

VALE

A COMMON word, indeed, for I am not thinking of the bisyllabic 'vale', Latin for farewell, beautiful as that is too. How much more appropriate to its object is the now rather poetic vale than the usual valley! For vale is broad and flowing like the northern dale, while valley is a mean, scampering little word. Wordsworth, who was much less of a mountaineer than of a dalesman, made constant melody of dale and vale, far more than of fell and ghyll. He loved their feeling of expanse with gentleness. The Highlanders have permitted one Lake (instead of Loch) and one Vale (instead of Strath, glen being reserved for the steep and narrow defiles). The single Highland Vale is that of Atholl, down whose broad loveliness the Tummell gallops to meet the Tay. Strath Atholl would have been difficult and ugly. So the Highlanders wisely accepted the English Vale and the Vale of Atholl remains the perfect name for the green and tranquil levels between the surge of Grampians East and West.

VENUST

I HAVE never thought that the Latin word Venus, whether pronounced in the English manner or as Waynoose, was musically adequate to its subject. Yet the old adjective 'venust', used by the Scots makars, has always pleased me. How did they pronounce it? 'Venoust', I suppose, in which case it becomes a pretty addition to the language of love. The Latinism of the Scots poets of the latter part of the sixteenth century, so magnificent in the use of their native words, is sometimes oppressive. Is 'The Day Estivall', as Hume called it, preferable to 'The Summer Day'? But when a lover woos his

> tender babe venust

one immediately accepts her as adorable and regrets that the English dictionaries now pass the word by. Alexander Scott's use of it occurs in the lovely as well as alliterative verse,

> My bird, bonnie ane,
> My tender babe venust,
> My luve, my life alane,
> My liking and my lust.

Certainly this poem is a frank one, but not heavily so. The word lust, now possessing an ugly as well as an adipose tissue, has put on weight with the years, and to Scott was far closer to the German notion of a 'lustig' or merry state of mind.

WAG

WHILE staying with a farmer-friend in the Oxfordshire Cotswolds I asked him about local dialect words. He told me that Old Tom, his labourer, called his son his 'wag'. Wag, for a boy, with no implication of facetiousness, is Tudor English. Thomas Fuller wrote that 'Queen Elizabeth, coming into a Grammar School, made this extemporary verse,

> 'Persius a Crab-staffe, Bawdy Martial,
> Ovid a fine Wag'.

It now seems less than brilliant. By wag the Queen meant not a jester, but a brisk, gay fellow. When Shakespearean characters call each other 'Good wag' or 'Sweet wag' they are not necessarily implying that the youngster is an intending comedian. Imogen, when going into breeches, is advised by Pisanio to 'change her niceness into a waggish courage', i.e. the courage of a lad. But the idea of playfulness has begun to break in.

As waggish boys in game themselves forswear

says Helena. The modern notion of a wag, as a fellow of any age who eternally strives after quips and puns, is quite different. Old Tom when he calls his son 'my wag' may mean that his lad is a lively one, but does not wish to suggest word-play and facetiousness. Incidentally, Tom lives within twenty miles of Stratford-on-Avon. Robert Burns employed 'wag' for the 'bad lad' of the village, as we say. These lines must have been noted in Ayrshire at the time and are not forgotten now.

> Lament him, Mauchline husbands a',
>   He often did assist ye;
> For had ye staid whole weeks awa',
>   Your wives they ne'er had missed ye.

> Ye Mauchline bairns, as on ye pass
>   To school in bands the gither,
> O, tread ye lightly on his grass,
>   Perhaps he was your father.

They are headed 'Epitaph on a Wag in Mauchline
Garrick, in writing one of his Shakespearean odes, spoke of his hero as the 'Warwickshire wag'. For him it was equivalent to lad.

WAMBLE AND WIMPLE

THERE are many vivid words for unsteady things beginning with 'w'. What more vivid than 'a wambling stomach', for a disturbed one? Pistol's paunch must have wambled much 'when qualmy at the smell of leak'. All shaky, tottering things, from the stomach to the State, have been effectively criticized as wambling. Wimple, as a verb (not as the noun which denotes a copious form of head-dress) is a gentler term and means to meander. That last word, itself an aptly sounding one, comes from the river Meander in Asia Minor. Wimple is mainly Scottish. Burns loved 'a wimpling burn' and so might anybody.

WAN

DIM has been given inclusion. Shall wan remain behind? A beautiful word for all pale, lack-lustre things, it throws a shadow wherever it strikes. What better entry than that first line of King Henry IV, now wearing the murdered Richard's crown?

> So shaken as we are, so wan with care,

But, apart from the everlastingly wan stars of romance and the wan maids more lovesick than any of Castle Bunthorne, my chief reason for bringing in this frail monosyllable is desire to cite the exquisite use of it in the Scottish ballad of Fair Annie, which begins with what is surely the cruellest stanza in all such doleful story.

> It's narrow, narrow, mak your bed,
> And learn to lie your lane;
> For I'm gaun owre the sea, Fair Annie,
> A braw bride to bring hame.
> Wi' her I will get gowd and gear,
> Wi' you I ne'er gat nane.

When the 'braw bride' was brought in:

> Fair Annie served the lang tables
> Wi' the white bread and the wine;
> But ay she drank the wan water
> To keep her colour fine.

The wan water! There is a splash of magic in that. The impact is physical and unforgettable.

WANDER

WANDER is a simple and a common word, one of those whose beauty and expressiveness are overlooked just because of their familiarity. But say it to yourself as though you had never seen or heard of it before. It has far more of loneliness and bewilderment in the sound of it than have our Latin words for the same thing, errant or vagrant or even vagabond. (This last is the best of the three.) What an exquisite line is Wordsworth's

> I wandered lonely as a cloud.

No 'staying in solitude' could approach its emotional tone. The sound of wandering to me suggests enormous spaces and cold, unfeeling vacancies, perhaps because it occurs so majestically in those amazing lines in the Epistle of St. Jude in which certain ungodly and lascivious men are withered with a ferocity of cold damnation as relentless as a night of Russian winter.

> These are the spots in your feasts of charity, when they feast with you, feeding themselves without fear: clouds they are, without water, carried about of winds: trees whose fruit withereth, without fruits, twice dead, plucked up by the roots: raging waves of the sea, foaming out their own shame: wandering stars, to whom is reserved the blackness of darkness for ever.

Incomparable climax with its trisyllabic trinity, 'the blackness of darkness for ever'! War-time nights taught us the full menace of that unrelenting phrase. But the chill of 'wandering stars' had previously done its work.

WATCHET

WATCHET, for several tints of blue, is dismissed by the dictionaries as 'Obs. or arch.'. But Lamb used it of the uniforms worn by the boys in Christ's Hospital and it came naturally to John Clare, who did not die till 1862.

> But now the evening curdles dank and gray,
> Changing her watchet hue for sombre weed;
> And moping owls, to close the lids of day,
> On drowsy wing proceed;

While chickering crickets, tremulous and long,
Light's farewell inly heed,
And give it parting song.

Chickering, more usually chicking, is used of clocks and seeds rattling in pods. Watchet must have survived in the cottages which Clare knew long after lexicography had written it off. Perhaps it still does. Presumably Watchet on the coast of Exmoor refers to the colour of the Bristol Channel in sunlight. This from a friendly fisherman, 'The dark watchet is one of the most famous of Yorkshire trout-flies and imitates the iron-blue dun. Its wings are made of the darkish blue feather from a tom-tit's tail.'

WILDERNESS

G. K. CHESTERTON once observed that so simple a line from the nursery as 'Over the hills and far away' is one of the most beautiful in all English poetry. The analyst will probably be right in assigning its magic to the roll of the 'r's and the final plaintive force of the 'w'. The same combination of 'r' and 'w' has the same poignancy in wilderness and bewilder. The latter word has lost its original conception of losing a person or being lost in a desolate place; bewilderments are now problems and puzzles of the mind. Few, if any, moderns, having strayed in the wilds, would describe themselves as bewildered, but wilderness has retained its territorial meaning as well as its mournful loveliness of sound. None knew the tricks of the poet's trade better than Fitzgerald (of *Omar*) and his

Wilderness were Paradise enow

played memorably on the 'w's and 'r's. The young Shakespeare of 'Titus Andronicus' called Rome 'a wilderness of tigers', thus anticipating his better known 'wilderness of monkeys'. This last well describes a scamper of 'film-fans' to touch the garment of some well-featured nit-wit. Yet wilderness, an exquisite word, is really too good for anything but a desirable desert.

WILLOW

No stranger, certainly, but deserving an obeisance. Ever since the Jewish exile hung his harp thereon, ever since it was the parasol of Behemoth ('The shady trees cover him with their shadow: the willows of the brook compass him about'), it has been as much the poet's joy as the symbol of mourning and of melancholy. It both weeps and bewitches. 'Sing, willow, willow, willow.' Always it sings. Why does Viola cry 'Make me a willow cabin at your gate' when any other timber would do as well, and no doubt better, to provide the building material for patient adoration? Try the line with some other tree or timber, 'Make me an oaken cabin at your gate'. The spell vanishes. There is usually some magic about the letter 'w' when carefully employed. (I have alluded to the emotional difference between farewell and good-bye.) Alter 'Oh withered is the garland of the war' into 'Oh faded is the garland of the fight' and all is lost. Most lovely letter. Willow is its beneficiary, and deserves to.be, so lovely is the tree, in all its forms, not least the Salyx Babylonica, the weeping willow.

WOODBINE

In the note on Margarine I spoke of the ruin brought by science and commerce to a word of pearly origin and charm. An interesting but melancholy roll might be called of words which have suffered a similar fate: marmalade, which ought in accuracy to be the essence of quinces, and the fragrant woodbine would be at the top of the list. Woodbine has now gone up in smoke. But it has a melting beauty if we can put the tobacconist out of mind. The dictionaries usually equate woodbine with honeysuckle, but to Shakespeare these two were man and wife: not one person. Everybody knows about Oberon's thymy bank 'quite over-canopied with lush woodbine', but there is an even lovelier reference in the same play:

> So doth the woodbine the sweet honeysuckle
> Gently entwist: the female ivy so
> Enrings the barky fingers of the elm.

What a master of unostentatious alliteration was Shakespeare! The magic of these lines owes so much to the subtle interplay of e's and f's, of g's and r's.

WORTHY

THE adjective is unexciting, but the noun 'a worthy' has a good history. At one time it referred exclusively to an agreed and neatly balanced team of nine ancient heroes. There were three Jews, Joshua, David, and Judas Maccabaeus, three Gentiles, Hector, Alexander, and Julius Caesar, and three Christians, Arthur, Charlemagne, and Geoffrey of Bouillon. The admission of the last rather suggests the final and despairing choice of a cricket secretary, who is still in difficulties about raising a side at 1 p.m. on Saturday and is 'fairly in the Bouillon', as Mr. Wodehouse's Mr. Wooster so often remarks. But there seem to have been permissible variations. For example, when the clowns in *Love's Labour's Lost* present the Nine Worthies in mummery for the courtiers' entertainment, some of the above have dropped out and Hercules and Pompey have 'muscled in' to the honorific list.

Worthy next became the title of any man of note. It did not imply any ethical respectability. There is a nice Victorian volume of county lore called *The Worthies of Bucks*. One of the most ancient of these was the British King Cymbeline, who might be described as the earliest-known tenant of Chequers, since the fine, barrowed crest behind the Premier's seat is called Cymbeline's Mount and the village below has remained for ever Kimble. A much later and most 'desartless' worthy of these beechwoods was Sir Francis Dashwood. This landed Georgian playboy confessed that all numbers over four figures were to him impenetrable territory, but he was elevated (in the Age of Reason) to be Chancellor of the Exchequer, despite his bland assurance that any Budget of his would be received with ridicule. He was right. It was. So the Worthy retired to the more congenial activities of the Hellfire Club and to a private life of agreeable depravity.

WRITHEN AND WRITHLED

IN Kipling's poem on 'Sussex' in *The Five Nations*, we are told with as much melody as truth,

> No tender-hearted garden crowns,
> No bosomed woods adorn
> Our blunt, bow-headed whale-backed Downs
> But gnarled and writhen thorn.

Kipling's 'writhen' trees upon the Sussex hills are vivid to the eye, toughly invading and interrupting the smoothness of that curving line which Belloc deemed 'so noble and so bare'. Shakespeare, or whoever wrote *Henry VI*, Part I, had the same kind of twisty thing in mind when he used the word 'writhled'. But he applied it to a smaller matter.

> It cannot be this weak and writhled shrimp
> Should strike such terror to his enemies.

Were shrimps on sale in the fish-shops of his London so that he could note their writhled nature in a street stroll, or had he met the article alive and writhling while on a sea-side jaunt? But sea-side jaunts were unusual then. Shakespeare's marine contacts are strange and worth investigation.

YARE AND YERK

OUR Tudor revivalists ply us with warming-pans and half-timbered suburban villas, Ye Olde Gifte Shoppes, and God-wottery garden ornaments. Why not attend to the vocabulary, from which so many good and genuine Tudorisms are allowed to vanish? There is nothing bogus about yerk. It means, in the first place, to pull tight threads or laces, as a Ouida heroine might have yerked her corsets while her Guardsman did the same for his boots. But by Ouida's time the nice little, tight little word had disappeared. Its second meaning was to thrust or strike. Iago thought to have yerk'd Brabantio under the ribs and at Agincourt the wounded steeds of the French knights were seen to

> Fret fetlock deep in gore and with wild rage
> Yerk out their armed heels at their dead masters,
> Killing them twice.

Yerkers may be said to have done the job yarely. Yare for quick or nimble is another Tudor loss. Cleopatra, robed, crowned, and marble-constant to her death-wish, bade her attendant Iras be yare in giving her the asp and then yerked the venomous worm into her bosom. True, Shakespeare did not use the word yerk here, but yare has its immortal place in the greatest scene, as I believe, that Shakespeare ever wrote. For me there is nothing in English poetry to equal the last two acts of *Antony and Cleopatra*: in them the most ordinary words are yerked into glory or raised to a higher power, as mathematicians may say. In this book I have dealt mainly with words curious and beautiful in themselves. But genius in writing is an infinite capacity for making dim words shine and for giving to a commonplace collection of syllables new meaning and new magic.

INDEX

A WORD IN YOUR EAR

JUST ANOTHER WORD

AUTHOR'S NOTE

THIS sequel to *A Word in Your Ear* would never have been written had it not been for the encouragement which I unexpectedly received. I had put the first book together as a war-time distraction for myself and I had scarcely hoped that many people would, at such a time or even at any time, share my interest in the shape and sound of words. But the response has been wide and cordial and I have learned, from the range and volume of my correspondence, that large numbers of people are fanciers and collectors of words and wisely regard this English language of ours, with its multiple origins and charming diversity of accent and idiom, as a free and limitless playground for the curious mind. To be enthusiastic is not difficult, but to be so enthusiastic as to take pen and paper and discharge letters into the void is remarkable. Some of the many letters which have reached me came from Service camps and stations (one even arrived from a prisoners' camp in Germany) where the business of settling down to write must have been particularly tiresome. I need hardly say that I am under a particular obligation to such correspondents.

I add a list of those who have been good enough to send me thanks, criticisms, and suggestions. If any who have done so are omitted, I hand them my apology along with this incomplete acknowledgment. (If names are wrongly spelt, the owners must thank their own handwriting.) This second book owes much to those who have so kindly added their contributions to my first attempt. Where I have availed myself of counsel and information in order to fill another volume, I offer to these generous givers all my gratitude — and none of my royalties.

My correspondents are for the most part, like myself, amateurs in etymology. They follow their fancy in local lingo, domestic invention, or terms amusingly telescoped and confused, like Sancti-moody for sanctimonious. I have certainly no pretensions to enter the honourable list of sages and scholars to whom the study and enjoyment of English owes so much, men such as Henry Bradley,

Logan Pearsall Smith, and Ernest Weekley. On their research, as on that of the great lexicographers, I have drawn: but my purpose, as before, has been to anthologize, to make a garland of words that seem to merit picking, and to explain, in a quite personal way, the reasons for my choice. The idea has been to make a book of pleasures rather than a schedule of instruction.

On the whole, I have avoided purely dialect words, though some of the Scottish terms included may scarcely seem to the English to be other than local. Many correspondents have sent me lists of racy and full-flavoured words once and often still heard round the myriad parish pumps of Britain. But were I to include all these, there would be no end to it. I have preferred, therefore, the dialect words which are also to be found in literature and have some sort of Dictionary Status. This rule has not been rigidly kept, for, as I said, these are the sports of an amateur and, as such, tinged with a reasonable amount of anarchism in the performance. Originally I drew on my own reading and this time I have been favoured with suggestions from the reading of others. But reading, not vernacular gossip, is the base of it. Occasionally I have included or alluded to dialect words hardly ever seen in print. But in general I have preferred the language which has at least some sanction of lexicography, beyond that of a handbook of local terms and usages.

The greatest bulk of letters concerned some words which, though I wrote of them as rare or antique, are in fact thriving to-day in certain parts of the country. Renege, for example, and cog and mich. Scots, Northerners, Irish, and Welsh have all assured me that such terms are full of life, renege in the card-room and cogging and miching in the school-house. Shakespeare would have known what was meant by a miching (truant) schoolboy who cogged (cheated) at lessons and reneged (backed down) when challenged to a fight. In Southern England few people know these terms, but elsewhere they have currency, the truth being that English words, like the Celtic races before them, have been driven Westward and have lingered most in high and lonely places. Thus Yorkshire English, being long sheltered in the dales by the steep dividing fells, is much closer to Chaucer's than is that of the Home Counties, while the

6

English spoken in Wales and Ireland (as well as in Inverness) is often more authentically English than anything to be heard nowadays in Hampstead or even in Hogsnorton.

Watchet, meaning blue, was attributed to local dyes and local pottery. I leave the final verdict to Exmoor folk. 'Browned off' appears to be an old Service term and is probably related to the treatment of gun-barrels. At least that is as good an explanation as any.

To my correctors I gladly admit that I should have recognized the pansy in Spenser's 'prettie paunce'; his 'chevisaunce' finds no agreed interpretation. Chervil is a strong favourite. My approval of Shakespeare's

> A mole cinque-spotted, like the crimson drops
> I' the bottom of a cowslip

has roused considerable criticism. The drops, it is said, are not crimson at all, but brownish. Well, it being, as I write, precocious April and the cowslips abounding at the bottom of my garden, I have ample opportunity to investigate the matter. The drops, I should say, are of a reddy-brown colour, possibly what the ornithologists mean by their rufous. They certainly have a red element. We can derive from this, as we please,

(1) That Shakespeare was using poetic licence to 'lay colour on a bit'. But he was certainly correct in his counting of the five and must have been looking a cowslip in the face.

(2) That cowslips, unlike the leopard, can change their spots and have lost colour, at least in their drops, in the last three and a half centuries.

(3) That Shakespeare's notion of crimson was less gaudy than ours.

What is unquestionable, a point on which I shall never renege, is that the passage from Iachimo's speech on the sleeping Imogen is as lovely as any bank of April flowers: and there enough.

My beneficiaries, to whom I once more tender my thanks, are as follows. Will those whom accident or carelessness has omitted forgive me? The list, in any case, is drawn up only until mid-April, 1943.

7

Miss Gladys Allen
Miss Kathleen Arnold
Miss F. Berryman
Mrs. A. M. Clark
Miss Alice M. Coates
Miss V. Coldstream
Miss Clare Drummond-Hay
Mrs. Monica Ewer
Miss Judith Foljambe
Mrs. Phyllis Goldingham
Miss Mabel Goss
Miss Phyllis M. Giles
Miss Elizabeth Hawes
Mrs. Anne Handley
Mrs. G. Hanmer
Mrs. C. M. Hudson
Miss Margaret Mellor
Mrs. Pauline Peard
Miss Dorothy Una Ratcliffe
Miss Jane Rennie
Miss Y. E. Skipwith
Miss G. B. Stern
Miss Dorothy Margaret Stuart
Miss Mary Morison Webster
Mrs. Mary Withey

Lord Keynes
Lord Macmillan

H. de Bels Adam
James Agate
Vincent Alford
A. O. Baxter
A. G. Bayliss
John Beavan
Dr. Martin Berry
John Betjeman

E. H. Blakeney
A. W. Boyd
Bertram Carter
C. S. Chapman
Air Vice-Marshal Cowtan
H. Ian Danby
Alan Dent
L. Edgcumbe
C. A. Fordyce
R. W. Frew
Philip Godlee
Lt. J. C. Goldingham
J. E. Goudge
Lt. Hilton Greenwood
Lionel Hale
C.Q.M.S. V. F. Hancock
David Heggie
Colonel H. W. Hill
Driver P. G. Horn
W. A. Jesper
Dr. Thomas Jones
M. Kermode
C. S. Lewis
Robert Lynd
Desmond MacCarthy
Lt. P. Macdonald
J. W. McFeeters
J. A. Mackereth
P. Maloney
H. J. Massingham
John Mavrogordato
O. E. Miles
James Milne
Lt. John Moore
Major Orr-Ewing
Dennis Peck

J. R. Peddie
Arthur Ran
Arthur Ransome
E. J. Rea
D. Mackay Reside
J. Harvey Robson
Osbert Sitwell
E. Scot Skirving

M. H. Smith
F. Stancourt
G. E. Stevenson
G. W. Stonier
B. E. Sutton
Dr. Hugh Thursfield
R. Williamson
H. C. Withers

I owe a further debt to Miss Gladys Allen for her secretarial help, not least in the deciphering of my correspondents' scripts. My own is bad: but some have been worse. To my colleague Mr. J. C. Trewin I am under great obligation for his kindly and acute aid as a proof-reader and counsellor.

PREFACE

In the preface to my previous volume I commented on the curious fact that, while the space for printing words grew smaller under stress of war-economies and deprivations, the words chosen for use seemed to grow continually larger. During the past year this process has certainly not grown less and, whenever I pick up my wisp of a war-time newspaper, I find that the terms and phrases are more cumbrous than ever. What Political Correspondent, for example, would write simply, 'Those who know say that things get worse'? Such a sentence, with its bare monosyllables, would stand no chance to-day. It would certainly become, 'In the opinion of authoritative circles at the higher levels it is considered that the situation is showing an increasing tendency to deteriorate.' That is not a parody: it is pure transcript. Nor is it only in the political and diplomatic commentaries that one finds this addiction to wordy, windy statements. Every Government Department has its favourite formulae of this kind and sometimes one word is a strong favourite with all at once.

The present darling of the Departments — and Fleet Street echoes gladly the boom of Departmental verbosity — is Rehabilitation, a word originally applied to the restoration of a degraded man's rank and privileges. By the middle of the nineteenth century it was occasionally used to mean restoration of other kinds. Suddenly it has become the administrators' pet. A year or two ago nothing was mended, renewed or restored. Everything had to be reconditioned. Now reconditioning has been supplanted by rehabilitation, which has the merit of being one syllable longer. Districts and regions as well as people and things are now to be rehabilitated; the blessed word 'goes' officially with everything from houses to invalids. I can see no reason why the Ministry of Health should not still seek to heal people instead of rehabilitating them. But heal — poor old Biblical monosyllable! Will the next translation of the Bible be allowed to heal the sick? No, it will have to rehabilitate those who are suffering from psycho-physical maladjustment.

Waste of print and paper apart, does this lust for jargon do any harm? I think it does. It helps to clog speech and writing and thus to make a slow, weak ooze of words instead of the keen and forceful jet which human expression ought to be. That the use of long complicated words instead of simple short ones is tedious is one nuisance; but that it is inefficient is a far greater plague. The more people wrap their thoughts in this wadding, the more they reach down these ready-made packets of wordy cotton-wool, the less surely do they drive into the minds of their readers and listeners.

What appals me to-day is the inability of supposedly well-taught people to convey their meaning quickly and forcibly in language. Educational authorities are often just as bad as anybody else and the academic *élite* of the Professorial chairs are guilty of piling long words into long sentences in which the meaning is suffocated. Editorial experience has over and over again brought home to me that educated people, who may have something really important to say, care very little about their way of saying it.

Imagine a highly trained man charged with drawing up a Report on which he believes that important action must be taken. It is obvious that he must convince his readers as well as inform them. Or he may be stating a case for some Department, some sect, some movement, some policy. Does he often pause to consider the means of this persuasion as well as the matter of it? In other branches of life he would take great trouble about his instrument. The craftsman is proud and careful of his tools: the surgeon does not operate with an old razor-blade; the sportsman fusses happily and long over the choice of rod, gun, club or racquet. But the man who is working in words, unless he is a professional author (and not always then), is singularly neglectful of his implements. He does not realize that, in many cases, the fewer the words the more forcible their impact. He does not stop to think that others may not stop to read. Does he reflect that his first sentence, his first paragraph, must arouse attention, state the issue, and generally strike at our sympathy? Rarely indeed.

Time and time again I have been faced with letters, reports, pleas and suchlike in which the first page contains a mere cranking up of the engine: it gets nowhere. People who want to make a point about aerial policy in 1943 go rambling back to 1917. Not only do they go swimming into the ocean of world history: they do not even do so with knowledge of that exercise, but roll and puff and flounder in a foam of words. At last they reach the point and it may be a sound one, which deserves to be widely and strongly urged. But, because they have not considered the tools and the technique of explaining and commending it, the point seems far less important than it should. When every mechanic is carefully watching his tools, it is preposterous that workers in thought, with speech as its engine, should be so careless about words and sentences.

One knows the temptations. Long words sound imposing — or seem to do so. So in come the deteriorating situations, the reconditionings and the rehabilitations. A man does not want to be too precise for reasons of security. So arrive the authoritative circles and the well-informed quarters, which, after all, only mean, as a rule, the Press Officer of a Government Department. Moreover it is not easy, especially for a tired or a busy man, to avoid clichés. They are savers of time and trouble. It is hard work to think out afresh the words which you may most effectively use in each sentence. So why not fetch one of the well-known packets off the shelf? When I look at my leading article, there they all are. Still plans 'bid fair to come to fruition'. Still 'new avenues are opened' for diplomatic exploration; still 'the proposals are couched in friendly terms'. Does the leader-writer, when bidden to sup with neighbours, explain to his wife that 'the proposal is couched in friendly terms', that 'dietary conditions at The Laurels show no signs of deterioration', that he does not believe the soup, at any rate, will be 'in short supply'? Does he 'counsel acceptance' of the invitation? No, he says 'We'd better go'. But he could never write thus.

Yet to compose with the cumbrous reach-me-downs, while it saves bother, must surely blunt the effect. More and more do I find myself put into a coma by English of this sort. I have had to read so much of it. It becomes like the noise you do not notice, such as the roar of traffic in the townsman's ear. And what could be worse for the man with a message than a method of giving it which starts by dulling the attention and ends by defeating it

12

altogether? Yet how many message-bearers ever give their vocabulary the slightest attention? How many stop to think whether a shorter, fresher word, a shorter, sharper sentence might not catch the drowsy reader before he drops off to sleep altogether? It has to be remembered that most people in offices, even in war-time when economy of words and paper should be paramount, are surfeited with minutes, drafts, reports, and publications of every kind. All the more reason for brevity and pungency in writing. Very rarely do we have it.

There seems to be considerable interest in the speaking of English. If you pick up a local paper, even in war-time, you will note, perhaps with surprise, the number of people who advertise their powers as teachers of elocution and presumably manage to make a living thereby. In order to sustain so large a profession, there must be a steady flow of students eager to use words better.

What are their motives? Some are aiming at the politician's or the preacher's office; others wish to improve their pronunciation and forms of speech for professional and commercial reasons; others, again, may be resenting a local accent and are eager, perhaps foolishly, to be rid of it. A section may believe that they were intended by destiny to entertain their fellows and are 'taking elocution' as a first step to delivering recitations and even to progressing from the amateur platform to the professional stage. Recitation of ballads or rhymed narratives is, to my taste, as dreadful an infliction as the devilish ingenuity of man can devise. But the general taste apparently welcomes this species of diversion. At 'Socials' there is much recitation, which the audiences receive undismayed or even with genuine approval. It may be Shakespeare or Shelley, Kipling or Robert Service, Far Western or East Indian in its setting: on, in all variety, it goes. When I once performed (rashly and wrongly) as a judge at one of the great Music and Drama Festivals, which used to be organized by seaside resorts in order to fill the lodgings and boarding-houses in the off-period between Easter and Whitsun, I was overwhelmed by the sheer quantity of this type of spouting. Day after day, Keats and Shakespeare were rained at me from breakfast to supper. Much of the delivery was competent; but why, oh, why?

The odd thing is that we apply ourselves with such tenacity to memorizing and repeating the words of other people and take so little interest in the choice and ordering of words for ourselves. Yet that, which used to be known as the art of rhetoric, is naturally precedent to the art of elocution and was by the ancients regarded as an essential element of a polite and ample education. The British idea is that you learn to address an audience by trial and error; the audience endures that you may improve; the physical elocution you may study with a teacher, but the craft of planning a sentence or a period in order to achieve the maximum effect by arousing the emotions to which orators commonly appeal — pity, indignation and so on — is scarcely ever professionally taught or privately practised. People scribble down an outline of what they are going to say, make a few notes, or leave it wholly to chance. Indeed, to perform as a master of rhetoric would by most be regarded as bad form. The enunciation and the use of the vocal implement can permissibly be studied: to consider the emotional value of words and groupings of words, of pauses, rhythms, sentence-endings, and so on, is no longer part of the citizen's equipment for life. Public-speaking is learned by trying it on the public. Our universities abound in young people arguing, debating, and agitating. But there are no Professors of Rhetoric now. (Edinburgh, truly classic city in spirit as in architecture, is faithful to the old tradition and links the name of Rhetoric with that of English Literature in its Chair of the latter, but such acknowledgment of what was once the chief accomplishment of an educated man is exceptional.) We no longer give instruction in that art of stating a case which the Romans and Greeks believed to be indispensable. The beginners either pick up a facility on the stump or they never pick it up at all.

Indeed, the very word rhetoric is now suspect. It suggests a cold formality or an intention to deceive. But it was once not only a laudable but a much-coveted form of ability. There is some excuse for its decay, because writing has so largely supplanted speaking as the chief medium of information and persuasion. Even when the microphone restored the spoken word to power, it restored it far more as conversation than as oratory. Very few people can triumphantly throw an oration upon the air. Mr. Churchill is a notable exception to the general rule. But most prefer the Roosevelt manner, the fireside chat. For the great majority of broadcasters experience prescribes the value of an easy colloquial approach to their widely separated millions of listeners. At least it is the generally accepted theory of specialists in radio that a carefully natural talk will be far more effective than a carefully contrived oration. Accordingly broadcasting, which might have restored the art of rhetoric to its old position, has done nothing of the kind.

Radio has brought back to some extent the art of speaking verse, but the poems read into the microphone, like those declaimed at Music and Drama Festivals, are usually of some age. The poet of to-day does not as a rule write for the voice and the ear: he writes to be published and read. So here again there is less encouragement to study the emotional significance of certain letters and arrangements of letters, of certain syllables and rhythms, their sequences and inter-actions. That was what the minstrel as well as the rhetorician once did. But now these graces are not wanted.

It does not require much reading of contemporary verse to realize that there is scarcely any liking, and certainly no love, for words as such. There are sometimes painters who are little interested in paint. They use the stuff to convey something, their notion of significant forms and of arresting patterns and groupings of forms. The poets of to-day seem to be in the same position. Words to them are so much raw material and are no more valued for themselves than are the bricks which go to make a house. Such a poet has a concept or an image to express and he uses the words to put this on paper. That words can be far more than mere bits of raw material for sentences has more usually been the view of the artist; poetry, to many, has seemed to consist of 'words raised to a higher power'. That is to say, the emotional vibration proceeding from the words was perfectly harmonized with the emotion or the idea to be expressed. So the selection and alignment of words, with reference to their musical value and their significance in power and poignance, was a natural part of poetry, just as it was the essence of rhetoric. But that attitude to poetry is temporarily out of fashion.

The new austerity disdains such sensuous trifling. To please the ear is not a task to be considered either by the young person blundering into public speech or by the intending singer writhing in the tangled wires of speech which are now the common form of poetry. My last book, an anthology of words, of which this is the sequel, was based on a perhaps too sentimental affection for words. It stressed their oddity and shapeliness, their humour, their music, and their power to haunt the memory and mature in the subconscious mind, like wines in the cellarage. To my pleasure this drew a very great number of letters, comments and suggestions from people of all types and professions; the interest in words is much wider than some suppose; a few poets now growing senior also assisted me. I did not expect to hear from the up-to-date bards; and I was right.

This is easily undetstandable. Beauty, for the time being, and especially beauty of words, is out of fashion. The history of poetry is a series of actions and reactions. The first man to break with workaday prose invents or discovers new, rich words and revels in the sound and shape of them. The professional bard or minstrel is born. Homer has arrived. Soon these words become familiar and over-worked and the patterns which he and his followers have made with them seem tired and conventional. With these patterns readily available it becomes too easy to be a poet. All you have to do is to turn on the tap and let the old terms and tags and tunes flow on. Then the young mind rebels against the tyranny of such traditions and deliberately chooses new and simple words, possibly even ugly words, harsh of sound, in order to escape from the bondage of the old rhetoric and the too familiar music.

Thus in Greek poetic drama, Euripides rebelled against the thunders of Aeschylus and the witty discussion of that revolt in *The Frogs* of Aristophanes sums up the eternally recurring conflict of an old conventional magniloquence with a new and austere realism. A similar break took place when the Elizabethans rebelled against the formal word-patterning of Lyly known as Euphuism and, most notably, when the English Romantics broke absolutely with the methods and vocabulary of Pope and his school. An

16

English student who first reads Gilbert Murray's translation of *The Frogs* and then Wordsworth's preface to *Lyrical Ballads* will get a quick view of the unceasing battle between the old, fine-sounding formulae and the new, more natural diction. Wordsworth felt that poetry could only renew itself by going to the mountains, the farms and the villages, not for scenery only but for vocabulary. The eighteenth-century type of versification had become as lifeless as a machine: its lingo and its rhymes, once termed heroic, seemed only to be a dull obstruction of the young idea.

It has happened again in our own time. The Victorian poets made a kind of verbal music, which was easy, fluent and pleasing. The danger of this was exemplified by Swinburne whose magnificent use of language applied to the powerful emotions of youth became later on a mere trick of metrical verbosity. This he continued to execute at full and formidable length when he really had nothing to say. In the same way Tennysonian iambics, which are the vehicle of some glorious poetry, could degenerate into a facile outpouring of honeyed speech, and the Laureate's successors, especially Stephen Phillips, who had an immense but 'bubble' reputation in the first decade of this century, kept raiding the hive with ruinous facility. Readers of Mr. Agate's *Ego* will find in an early volume of that contentious series some mention of a wager between him and me about the possibility of gushing out Phillipsian iambics *ad lib*. I think that I proved my point in performance. Any literate person should be able, after soaking himself for a few hours, in Swinburne or Tennyson, to turn out something indistinguishable from the work of these masters when writing without plenary inspiration. The thing is just verbal juggling. The so-called Georgian poets, indeed most minor British minstrels of the early twentieth century, were obviously handicapped as well as helped by the old vocabulary and its turns of sound. They too fluently proved that, if you know the tricks of the trade, it is no trouble to sing a song of sixpence even though you have little or no thought or feeling to justify your breaking into song at all.

Hence the inevitable reaction against the old rhythms and the old terminology. Rupert Brooke, whose popularity was so bitterly resented by the rebels, was intelligible, graceful and euphonious; accordingly the rebels seemed almost eager to be gawky and cacophonous as well as complicated. Poetry became allusive and elusive in one direction (e.g. Eliot and Pound), conversational in another (e.g. Auden), or just a tortuous mass of strained symbols, of bad grammar, and of worse noises (e.g. half the contributors to any anthology of nineteen-thirtyish verse). The last thing desired by these minor poets was to be recited or quoted or sung in the bath. Well, they have had their wish: they aren't.

This self-denial, which declines the 'taffeta phrases, silken terms precise', is rooted, let us admit, in a species of integrity. 'Let us keep language and poetry spare and active' is the cry, 'and not depend on the easy, ear-tickling methods which any child can learn.' What could be worse for poetry than to acquire a special jargon or Poetese? Words must signify meanings, not cosset the senses. From this the zealots of austerity proceed to rule out altogether the pursuit of beauty in language and to dismiss as 'mushy' (the term, I think, is Mr. George Orwell's) specially 'poetic' terms, e.g. such a word as loveliness. There, surely, the monkish attitude to language becomes absurd. It may be silly to imitate the lush vocabulary and ear-enchanting rhythms of Swinburne, lest we suffer from a sensuous surfeit, but to begin ruling out certain words altogether is as idle as ruling butter off the dietary because butter can be nauseous when laid on too often and too thick.

This austerity campaign, in any case, appears to have gone its niggard way and to be petering out. It now seems definitely 'prewar', a nineteen-thirtyish mood. I have seen a fair number of poems sent in for consideration by young men and women in the Forces: many of them have returned to the familiar rhythms and to an almost Tennysonian diction. They are easy and agreeable to read. They may not be great, but they are not gibberish. So action and reaction move again.

What fascinates me — and what does not in the least interest the nineteen-thirtyish composers of tangled-wire poetry and of the jerky, unrhythmical prose then in fashion — is the power of verbal arrangement and the sound of certain syllables to enhance meaning.

18

If you can, by making special patterns with letters and words, please the ear, affect the feelings, and generally drive home your point, surely the artist should not be frightened out of doing so by the charge of playing tricks. Trickery, after all, is only a rude name for what is politely called technique. Great acting is far more a matter of technical acquirements than of deep feeling. So the adverse critics disparage an actor because of his tricks and mannerisms while the favourable critics are holding forth about his technical perfection. Great speaking and great writing have always had their tricks, though it is doubtful to what extent the speakers and writers were conscious of their own devices. Take the case, for instance, of Ciceronian rhetoric. Did the Roman orator end so many of his periods on purpose with the run of syllables similar to those occurring in *esse vĭdĕātŭr*? Or was it just subconscious habit based on a feeling that this particular sequence of noises had a solemn and effective emotional impact? The similar question could be asked of the historian Gibbon, who ended so many of his exquisitely constructed sentences with an 'of' clause. 'Of a Roman Emperor', 'Of a mighty nation'. Such terminations abound in his mighty prose. They are a trick: but they are an effective trick. One feels the sentence rising like a wave; then it curls over at its crest and powerfully descends upon the ear. Charles Dickens, presumably, was unconscious of the amount of blank verse which he put into his prose when dealing with poignant subjects: his death-scenes abound in iambics, because he intuitively realized the emotional suasion of this metrical pattern. Little Nell dies in decasyllables. And not Dickens only. Numerous writers have slipped into this metrical pattern without knowing it when they were seeking to drive at the heart.

If the manner of building a clause or sentence can thus powerfully touch the hearer's or the reader's sensibility, what of the words themselves? Here too is a most engaging subject for inquiry. It is a natural process to pause, when reading either silently or aloud, and ask oneself why certain lines or arrangements of letters and syllables exercise such dominion over the attention and the affections. This leads to the study of alliteration, not in its crude simplicity ('Round and round the rugged rocks the ragged rascal ran'), but in the subtle alternations and interlacings which are its finest manifestation. Next comes the consideration of certain letters which seem to possess a special power to communicate sensation. These have been some of the motives prompting me to reflect upon words and assisting me to find continual pleasure in that unexhausting pastime.

It is generally admitted that Shakespeare was supreme in his invention of phrase and mastery of verbal music. He alliterated constantly and subtly. How far was the process conscious? Did he deliberately work tricks of the word-spinners' trade? He must have been a rapid writer to combine so much composition with his acting and managerial duties and his conduct of investments in Stratford and London; indeed Ben Jonson says as much. Therefore we can hardly suppose that his interlaced alliterations were the deliberate product of careful cogitation. When he made Cleopatra cry over her Antony's dead body

> The Crown o' th' earth doth melt. My Lord!
> Oh withered is the garland of the war.
> The soldier's pole is fallen: young boys and girls
> Are level now with men; the odds is gone.
> And there is nothing left remarkable
> Beneath the visiting Moon,

he probably did not stay, in the surge of a supreme inspiration, to calculate the tricks he was playing. But we can examine them now.

We note first the roll of r's and, if we consider these things at all, we know that r has an infectious, vibrating quality and is excellent in all words of mourning. Sorrow, grief, tears, bereave — how much more apt to depth of mood they are than pain and anguish! Then comes the union of r's and w's, and that is tremendous. W is always a helpful letter in an emotional setting; we weep or cry waly in our woe. Garland, too, is an irresistible word.

> Oh withered is the garland of the war

is, to me, one of the most superbly doleful lines ever written. But supposing Shakespeare had written

> Oh faded is the flower of the fight.

The alliteration is stronger and more obvious. The sense is identical. But the effect is trifling. Grief has dwindled to a mere grievance. What was a masterpiece of brief lamentation has become only a whine of complaint. What a difference lies between the stirring word 'war' and the mean little word 'fight'. The component letters are the cause of it. Happy warrior or happy soldier? The former, of course. W and r together always win.

Then follows the stream of l's, seven of them within six metrical feet, the succession being renewed in 'left remarkable'. So one liquid following another works its magic. That sort of analysis can be applied anywhere in Shakespeare at his best. Always the same fact emerges about his genius, a triumphant awareness of the right letter and series of letters.

> Give me my Robe, put on my Crown. I have
> Immortal longings in me.

Again the r's and l's. Indeed the words mortal and immortal, because of that union, never fail to touch the sensibility, a fact of which Swinburne was, perhaps excessively, aware when he wrote,

> Pale, beyond porch and portal,
> Crowned with calm leaves, she stands
> Who gathers all things mortal
> With cold, immortal hands.

Substitute human and inhuman for mortal and immortal and the lines perish.

> Thou hast conquered, O pale Galilean: the
> world has grown grey from thy breath.

Once more the l's and r's, with a trio of g's to help, give powerful aid to the splendid rhythm of the line.

Writers naturally vary in their use of such artifice. The austere Wordsworth has little of it; the sensitive and sensuous Housman a

great deal. The latter used constant interlacing of letters, how far
with deliberation, how far by impulse, none can say.

> On the idle hill of summer
>   Sleepy with the flow of streams
> Far I hear the steady drummer
>   Drumming like a noise in dreams.

The texture of d–s–m is a lovely piece of design: so is the s–d–r
scheme, with b added in

> Wake: the silver dusk returning
>   Up the beach of darkness brims,
> And the ship of sunrise burning
>   Strands upon the eastern rims.

It is not my business to write a treatise on the varieties of alliteration
and emotional qualities of the various letters and arrangements of
letters. All I wish to do is to remind readers and writers that these
qualities are there and that the choice of one word rather than
another may alter the whole weight and influence of a poem or of a
passage in prose.

That brings me back to my original point, the curious carelessness
of our time about what was once called rhetoric, the art of stating
your case. How often do our propagandists — a class continually
increasing in numbers and activity — stop to consider the values of
words? It is astonishing to me that people whose profession is to
persuade or whose passion is to win converts to a cause should be
so careless of their tools and so well content to employ long, tired
terms and clichés instead of seeking fresh, brief and apt ones, terms
whose value in sound is so easily discoverable. Public men, with
policies to urge, continue to drool and drone on platforms and in
print with no discoverable awareness that they are killing their own
case by the dull and ponderous language they employ.

Yet the models are everywhere and easily available. There are
two exemplars in the use of words. There is the poet who, by
instinct, understands the relative value of arrangements of letters
and sounds and can make his syllables quiver and sting, lull and

22

enchant, according to his mood. There is also the master of simple prose, often a man of action rather than a writer, who can state simply what has occurred or what he means and wants and, by so doing, out-reach in power of expression the employers of a pretentious verbosity. The majesty of monosyllables is for ever maintained.

> These are the times that try men's souls . . . We fight not to enslave, but to set a country free and to make room upon the earth for honest men to live in.

Thirty-two words: only four of them reach two syllables and none of those is a long or heavy word. Yet this writing of Tom Paine's has abiding power and persuasion: matched with such triumphant terseness, the background eloquence of modern warfare seems as petty as it is prolix. (I am, of course, excepting a few masters of the brief and cogent word, Mr. Churchill in particular.) Soldiers and sailors can often do it still. None ever reported a victory better than did the American, Oliver Hazard Perry —

> We have met the enemy and they are ours.

Imagine that in modern officialese. 'After effecting contact', it would begin, and then ramble wearily onwards.

Surely these things deserve the care of all who are trying to reach the minds and hearts of their fellows. But can we foresee the next flood of official reports and documents turning back to monosyllables? Will their authors seek simply to mend houses or end poverty? No, they will assuredly rehabilitate residential premises and terminate financial insecurity. And they will no less surely soothe into the deep sleep of a Whitehall summer afternoon those very readers whom they sought to challenge and arouse as well as to instruct. The Departmental Ditty of to-day is a lullaby: how sad that it should have all the power of the poppy with so little of its grace!

AKIMBO

Sir Thomas Urquhart, the Cromarty Rabelaisian, writes in *The Jewel* of the Admirable Crichton's mummeries: 'he rants and vapours it with gingling spurs and arms a-kenbol. Like a Don Diego he strouts it.' A-kenbol has become akimbo. It has also been a-gambo or a-kenbold or, earlier still, in ken-bowe. The origin of the word baffles the learned. One pursues it to Iceland, where keng-boginn might mean bent staple-wise. Another thinks the Middle English cambok or crooked-stick is the guide. Akimbo has settled down as the proper, if inexplicable word, for the arms-on-hips position commonly adopted by masterful ladies in the music-hall, Pantomime Dames, and others who address the world and deliver sharp commentary on men and matters.

'She got terribly akimbo' became a species of Mayfair slang for what was earlier called 'high horse'. I have also heard it used by stage people for over-acting. 'So and so was a bit akimbo to-night'. Urquhart's Crichton seems to have been 'a-kenbol' in this sense too.

BEHAVIOUR

Behaviour used to signify good manners, even virtuous living. Now it has to be preceded by an adjective. When Defoe wrote of 'aversion to behaviour' he signified a dislike for proper conduct. We have kept the old sense in 'Behave yourself', but, when we ask 'How did so-and-so behave?' we are implying the possibility of a faulty bearing or conduct, which the eighteenth century would not easily have linked with the complimentary term behaviour. 'To know behaviour' was to be a gentleman, possibly such a Natural Gentleman as Joseph Watson, the centenarian game-keeper of Lyme. Concerning this lusty, thirsty, and decent veteran I made a misquotation in my previous book and, thanks to the good offices of the *Stockport Advertiser*, I can now quote the complete text of his epitaph, which seems to me a model of measured rhythms and aromatic prose.

Burried at Disley, in Cheshire, June 2nd, 1753, Mr. Joseph Watson, in the 105th year of his age; he was born at Mosley Common, in the Parish of Leigh, in the county of Lancaster, and married his wife from Eccles, in the said county; they were a happy couple for 72 years. She died in the 94th year of her age. He was Park Keeper to the late Peter Legh, Esq., of Lyme, and his father, 64 years. He did show the Red Deer to most of the nobility and gentry in this part of the kingdom to a general satisfaction of all who ever saw them, for he had driven and commanded them at his pleasure, as if they had been common horned cattle. In the reign of Queen Anne, Squire Legh was at Macclesfield, in company with a number of gentlemen, amongst whom was Sir Rodger Mason, who was then one of the Members for the said county: they being merry and free, Squire Legh said his keeper should drive 12 brace of Staggs to the Forest of Windsor, a present to the Queen, so Sir Rodger opposed it with a wager of 500 guineas, that neither his keeper nor any other person could drive 12 brace of Staggs from Lyme Park to Windsor Forest, on any occasion. So Squire Legh accepted the wager, and immediately sent a messenger to Lyme, for his keeper, who directly came to his master, who told him that he must immediately prepare himself to drive 12 brace of Staggs to Windsor Forest for a wager of 500 guineas. So he gave the Squire, his master, this answer, that he would, at his command, drive him 12 brace of Staggs to Windsor Forest, or to any other part of the kingdom, by his Worship's direction, or he would lose his life and fortune; he accordingly undertook and accomplished this astonishing performance, which is not to be adequated in the annals of the most ancient history. He was a man of low stature, not bulky, of a fresh complexion, pleasant countenance, and drank one gallon of malt liquor one day with another, for about 60 years of his time, and at the latter end of his time he drank plentiful, which was agreeable to his constitution and a comfort to himself. He was a very mild tempered man, he knew behaviour, and was cheerful company, and was allowed by all who knew him to be as fine a keeper as any in England. In the 103rd year of his age, he was at the hunting and the killing of a Buck, much to the astonishment of George Warren, in his park at Poynton, and performed that diversion with astonishment. It was the fifth generation of the Warren family he had performed that diversion in his time at Poynton Park.

The syntax of the last sentence needs amending. The use of 'with astonishment' for astonishing the others is interesting. So, too, is the employment of 'adequated' for 'matched'. 'He knew behaviour' is superbly simple and perfect in its place.

BINGE

'A R E you full of binge?' General Montgomery is said to have asked of his men, meaning what others would call 'pep'. And so, I discover, did Mr. H. A. Vachell use it, 'This binges me up'. What a curious history 'binge' has had, for, only a few years ago, it was the equivalent of a 'blind' and to be full of binge would indicate a very jaundiced look and total lack of animation! 'Going on a binge' had dropped out by 1942. The original binge was a bow or curtsy or a verb meaning to bow or curtsy, more common in Scottish than in English usage. That really suits the sound of the word well. The adjective 'bingey' is North Country for sour applied to milk. Mrs. Gaskell used it of 'a taint worse than sourness'. This links up with binge as excessive revel and its acid consequence, but certainly not with the glorious and tip-toe jauntiness of the Montgomerian binge.

BLINK

B L I N K has had a curious history. People using it seem never to have been quite sure whether they intended a pleasant twinkle of the eyes or a hideous stare. Shakespeare stamped the idea of ugliness upon it when he applied it to an idiot. When Pyramus says to the 'sweet and lovely Wall',

Show me thy chink to blink through with mine eyne

26

the suggestion is neutral. Blink is here merely look. But when Aragon opens the silver casket and finds 'the portrait of a blinking idiot' the adjective can only apply to a horrible and vacant stare or twitching of the eyes. Helena in *All's Well* speaks of

> a world
> Of pretty, fond, adoptious Christendoms
> That blinking Cupid gossips.

The whole sentence is obscure. And what exactly does blinking signify here? Cupid was traditionally blind.

In Scotland blink was habitually used in a favourable way. 'On him she blinket bonnilie'. Stars blink graciously in ballads and Burns observes in 'Blythe Was She',

> The evening sun was ne'er sae sweet
> As was the blink in Phemie's e'e.

I have never forgotten a passage which I came across when studying the history of sea-bathing. In the eighteenth century this habit was practised grimly by invalids in pursuit of health, an end not always achieved. (Supposedly hygienic immersion in Solway Firth was one cause of Robert Burns's early death.) The Scots also drank sea-water in their zeal for salubrity.

In the records of *Johnny Gibb of Gushetneuk*, quoted in my note on 'Dulse', Maister Saun'ers drinks a pint of sea-water and says to Jock, 'Noo, laddie, I'm easy physicket. I'll need no more: but an ordinar' dose for a stoot healthy man's aboot half as muckle again as I've ta'en.' Jock, after complaining that 'it'll gar me spew', was told that a 'gweed waucht [good draught] would redd his stomach'.

The English incident that stayed in my mind was the astonishing entry of the sea at Brighton in November by some young ladies intending to strengthen themselves. This hardihood was practised, moreover, at night. 'By the pale blink of the moon' was the phrase. That was in the 1780's. 'Blink of the moon' is charming and reminds one of the Scottish usage of blink, not the Shakespearean. But such a blink is no companion, surely, for a winter dip.

Now blinking has become in London slang a dreary word of

dislike and dispraise. Almost anything unfavourably viewed can be 'blinking'. Does this derive from the fact that Shakespeare had so powerfully joined the adjective with idiocy? It is an odd, and rather melancholy, tribute to the power of poetry if that is so.

BOON

I T is very easy to be mistaken about the author of this passage:

> Of Gehol's matchless gardens, for delight
> Of the Tartarian dynasty composed
> (Beyond that mighty wall, not fabulous,
> China's stupendous mound) by patient toil
> Of myriads and boon Nature's lavish help.

It sounds most Miltonic, but is, in fact, Wordsworth, but Wordsworth very obviously under Milton's sway. For 'boon Nature', meaning kindly, occurs in *Paradise Lost* where she 'pours forth flowers profuse', and there too occurs the nice 'Heightened as with Wine, jocund and boon'. Nowadays boon is an adjective (it is the same as French *bon*) which seems always to go with companions. Jocundity used also to be implied. 'A boon Bacchanalian skinker' became a boonfellow in Meredith. In childhood's history-books the less creditable kings used to have boon companions, whom, later in life, one gathered to be more perverse than jocund. It was hard on boon to be so much linked with the Gavestonian class of comrade. Boon as a noun, meaning prayer or the gift rewarding prayer, has been overworked. But boon, the epithet for kindly and bountiful things, deserves revival.

BUSY

B U S Y is an Old English word which has come into a state of grace in our new English civilization. In making this ascent from disrepute it reflects man's opinions about the nature of work. It is only since the Reformation that the idea of labour as a social obligation has afflicted mankind. Previously toil was the curse of

Adam, not his duty or his opportunity. Wise gentry got slaves or serfs to work for them while they followed the wars, the arts, and the ladies. Then came this all-conquering notion of honourable toil, a Puritan conception, which has endured; nowadays to proclaim yourself above all claims of drudgery and a careless fleeter of the time is to be regarded with disfavour even by the lordly ones. Consequently to assert that one is busy is now to make a claim to virtuous living; but busy at one time was frequently used with an unkind suggestion of meddling and officiousness. It was implied that only a fool, a knave, or a mischief-maker would busy himself. Oberon talks of the meddling monkey and the busy ape, while Emilia, in *Othello*, cries:

> I will be hanged if some eternal villain
> Some busy and insinuating rogue
> Some cogging, cozening slave, to get some office,
> Hath not devised this slander.

Again, Hamlet, having stabbed the eavesdropping Polonius and dismissed him as a 'wretched, rash, intruding fool', adds:

> Thou find'st to be too busy is some danger.

Busy here obviously means over-busy by our standards. We preserve the usage in talking of a busy-body.

Henry Vaughan sang to

> Dear Night, this world's defect,
> The stop to Busie Fools, Care's check and curb.

Busy was a favourite word of John Donne. Did the daylight interfere with his amours? Then would he protest,

> Busy old fool, unruly Sun,
> Why dost thou thus
> Through windows and through curtains call on us?
> Must to thy motions lovers' seasons run?
> Saucy pedantic wretch, go chide
> Late school-boys or sour prentices,
> Go tell court-huntsmen that the king will ride,
> Call country ants to harvest offices.

In that frankest of poems, his Elegy xx — odd that a future Dean of St. Paul's should have given us the most pagan and precise acclamation of sensual raptures — he bids his beloved,

> Unpin that spangled breast-plate which you wear
> That th' eyes of busy fools may be stopped there.

The hour of Judgment occurs for Donne 'at the last busy day'. He obviously hated business. He saw no goodness in occupation. But the Puritans and the Business Men have altered all that. No longer does the busy ape or lecher set the meddlesome example. The busy bee has become our tutor in morality. Yet the old notion of busy lives still in the slang of thieves and criminals. For them a detective or a policeman is 'a busy'. Raging against their enemy in the cell, they may in fact be echoing English poetry and cursing with the language of Shakespeare and of Donne.

BUXOM

ONLY wenches are allowed to be buxom nowadays and by that one implies a ruddy cheek and sturdy limb. Buxom, however, if a carnal solidity be the suggestion, is one of those words which has turned a somersault. It is of the same root as the verb 'to bow', and first meant tractable, gracious, obliging, flexible, and yielding. It was the discovery in *Piers Plowman* that 'in cloistre cometh no man . . . but all is Buxomnesse there and Bokes' which made me look into the chronicles of this now burly piece of language. Buxomnesse for Langland was obviously a gentle graciousness, but by Shakespeare's time it had become the epithet of merry and valorous people. In Gower's prologue to *Pericles* — the prologue being fairly obviously not Shakespeare — a fair young lady was

> So buxom, blithe, and full of face
> As heaven had lent her all his grace,

which suggests a comely gaiety. (What exactly did 'full of face' mean then? Fat or full of expression? We may assume the latter.)
Milton's 'buxom, blithe, and debonair' surely means gracious,

not solid. Certainly he reverts to the old meaning of 'yielding' with
an added hint of balm in this passage from *Paradise Lost*:

> Where Thou and Death
> Shall dwell at ease and up and down unseen
> Wing silently the buxom air embalmed
> With odours.

It nearly always happens that when Milton and Shakespeare use a
word of changing meaning, Milton, though he wrote considerably
later than Shakespeare, keeps the early sense, while the dramatist
prefers the innovation.

There was nothing airy left about buxom by the time that Byron
came to it, commenting, in *Don Juan*, on the comparative chastity
of the Russian Army in a captured city. Some lapses there were,

> But on the whole their continence was great
> So that some disappointment there ensued.

For instance:

> Some voices of the buxom middle-aged
> Were also heard to wonder in the din
> (Widows of forty were these birds long caged)
> Wherefore the ravishing did not begin?

The jest has now become venerable. Only when reading this
passage did I realize that it was a century and a quarter old. And
doubtless Byron did not invent it.

CANTRIP

C A N T R I P , for a trick of witchery or piece of mischief, is mainly
Scottish, but found its way into Tennyson. Burns's 'Tam o'
Shanter' of course has cantrips, the poem being packed with all
such Satanic manifestations. Cantrip in the lighter sense of fun and
games I found in a novel by William Black. Does anybody read
William Black now? According to the London Library, there is
little raiding of the shelves which hold his ample range of romantic
Anglo-Caledonian fiction. Black's late Victorian Scotland was full

of English Stag-parties (in the sporting sense), Inverness capes, whiskers, deer-stalker caps, spatter-dashes, yachts, millions of money, John Brownish ghillies 'profusely bearded' and given to mournful piping at odd moments, and lovely Highland daughters of the native, proud, and impecunious lairds and chieftains. These always had blue eyes and enormous reserves of purity. Such an one was the heroine of his 'Wild Eelin', a Miss Macdonald of Kinvaig, much given to cantrips as well as to Jacobitism and works of charity. Her cantrips included swimming dangerous rivers and falling out of boats, which antics she practised when not taking tea and eggs to the aged and infirm of Glen Garva. Thus she gave admirable opportunities for gallantry to the Canadian millionaire (a Macdonald returned from exile) and the local journalist, both of whom equally worshipped the frolic Miss Eelin: the more cantrippery she displayed, the greater the devotion. (Tactfully she solved the problem of their rivalry by dying at about p. 450 as the result of a cantrip.) Black graced his novelettish plots with a Roman grandeur of style. His books are like tartan-covered sofas: one sinks easily into them. The cantrips of his Wild Highland lasses were a convention, but the mountains of which he wrote are real — save that it is hardly ever raining on them.

CATERAN

THE Highland cateran, an aptly-sounding word for the tough yokel, is the same as the Irish and Shakespearean kern or kerne. This latter marches across our stages and dramatic texts in frequent association with a gallow-glass, the couple sharing a line not only of *Macbeth* but of *Henry VI*, Part II. Shakespeare has a particularly lively set of epithets for kerns. They are crafty and they skip: they are uncivil, shag-haired, and rug-headed. The double allusion to the towsled curls of a cateran or kern suggests the spectacle of Irish prisoners brought to London or that journey to Scotland which some believe Shakespeare must have made. (Some of his craft and period certainly made 'a stroll of players' as far as Aberdeen.) Both cateran and gallow-glass are Gaelic words. The former comes from Caithairne, meaning peasantry. Its application to the roving cattle-thief came later. Rob Roy and his men lowered the once unblemished name of cateran. Indeed, I was reminded of the cateran by reacquaintance with Bailie Nicol Jarvie, who said of Rob:

> And then he's sic an auld-farran lang-headed chield as never took up the trade o' cateran in our time; mony a daft reik he has played — mair than wad fill a book, and a queer ane it would be — as gude as Robin Hood, or William Wallace — a' fu' o' venturesome deeds and escapes, sic as folks tell ower at a winter-ingle in the daft days.

Presumably Caithness is Caithairne-ness, the headland of the caterans — in the original and reputable sense of the word.

CATZERIE

C A T S O was Italianate-Tudor-English for a scamp. 'Nimble-spirited Catsos' play their tricks in Ben Jonson. The abstract noun is Marlowe's and occurs in a grand piece of description (*The Jew of Malta*, Act IV):

> He sent a shaggy, tatter'd, staring slave,
> That, when he speaks, draws out his grisly beard,
> And winds it twice or thrice about his ear;
> Whose face has been a grind-stone for men's swords;
>
> His hands are hack'd, some fingers cut quite off;
> Who, when he speaks, grunts like a hog, and looks
> Like one that is employ'd in catzery
> And cross-biting; . . .

The trick of extracting a beard and then looping it round the ear seems bizarre, but attractive.

Cross-biting is another term for swindling. Marlowe's contemporary, Robert Greene, writing on 'Coosnage', explained that sometimes 'a nip, which the common people call a cutpurse, hath a crossbite by some bribing officer'. He also spoke of 'the leger-demaines of nips, foists, conycatchers, and crosbiters'. Greene had a magnificent lexicon of knavery. But he seemed to miss catzerie.

S o m e Shakespeare texts print 'chopped hands' in Casca's description of the mob in *Julius Caesar* and also in Touchstone's description of Jane Small, the milk-maid. But chapped or chapt is surely correct. It is not a remarkable word for cracked or fissured, but it is masterfully used in the A.V. translation of Jeremiah, where it is applied to the split, baked earth of a drought:

> Because the ground is chapt, for there was no rain in the earth, the plowmen were ashamed, they covered their heads.
>
> Yes, the hind also calved in the field and forsook it, because there was no grass.
>
> And the wild asses did stand in the high places, they snuffed up the wind like dragons: their eyes did fail, because there was no grass.

Little as most of us know about dragons and wild asses, we shall admit that here is a magical fancy of the terror of the East, a world without rain, a universe chapt.

CHEESY

T h i s Victorian term for fine or showy seems to have vanished. 'Cheese it' has also disappeared with the old street cries, of which 'There's 'air' and 'I don't think' were unimpressive specimens. 'Cheese it' meant 'Give over' or 'Come off it' — but why?

Cheese has played a great part in our slang, but never with any consistency. For example, 'cheesy' meant fine, because 'the cheese' was the correct thing. Professor Ernest Weekley avers that cheese in this sense comes from the Hindustani 'chiz', and is one of our Anglo-Indian imports. But 'a cheese' has also been slang for a fool. The fact is that we have never quite made up our minds whether cheese is a splendid article or a common, even despicable, piece of country-life. To Calverley it was a symbol of simple excellence and beauty.

> The farmer's daughter hath soft brown hair
> (Butter and eggs and a pound of cheese)

And I met a ballad, I can't say where,
Which wholly consisted of lines like these.

'Bread and cheese and kisses' sang the older music-hall, naming them as types of thrifty pleasure. We have all met these songs with their dairy echoes and smack of the milk-shed. The English, wherever they went, took such rhymes and fancies in the vagrant's pack. This prayer, for example, comes from America:

> But I, when I undress me,
> Each night upon my knees
> Will ask the Lord to bless me
> With apple-pie and cheese.

Surely this charming supplication is an export, having been first taken overseas by a Yorkshireman, if it in fact be true that the admirable blending of the cheese and apple flavours be mainly native to that county.

Shakespeare, who perhaps had acquired the taste for highly spiced food then becoming fashionable in Tudor London, thanks to the voyagers among the Indies, East and West, and their treasured cargoes of pepper, cloves, and so forth, speaks somewhat slightingly of cheese. Was it the pride of the new-made 'cit', looking back to the simpler catering of Warwickshire, that inclined him to disdain 'the humour of bread and cheese' and make Hotspur say of the superlative bore:

> . . . I had rather live
> With cheese and garlic in a windmill far,
> Than feed on cates and have him talk to me?

Many of us would think a murmuring about 'toasted cheese' to be a sign of sanity. But King Lear thought upon this dish while in mental ruin.

Be that as it may, you can never delve far into the prose and poetry of the elemental English without finding a cheesy smell and savour. Is the moon made of green cheese? So our playful simplicity has continually inquired. Thin men, poor scraps of humanity, are likened to Banbury cheese, though why that cake-famous borough, lying among its rich, well-watered meadows, should yield so spare and mean an article is not explained.

The strangest meaning of cheese is a deep curtsy, to 'make cheeses', according to the O.E.D., being 'a schoolgirl's amusement, consisting in turning round rapidly and then suddenly sinking down so that the petticoats take something of the form of a cheese'. A Scottish correspondent bears this out as a usage of her childhood.

CLERISY

IF you read any article by Mr. G. M. Young, a leading authority on Victorian England as well as on many phases of public administration, it will be a good article: it is also very likely to contain the word 'clerisy'. This refers not to the body of clerics in the present ecclesiastical sense, but to the whole company of literate folk. The clerisy is really the well-educated section of the community. Emerson wrote 'The artist, the scholar, and in general the clerisy'. Mr. Young does well to preserve so useful a term. It is odd that it should have become a rarity. For the most part we now employ the alien and cumbrous intelligentsia.

CLIP

MRS. ALISON UTTLEY, commenting on the words in use in her childhood in the North of England, alludes to the survival of Shakespearean English among the fells. Her *Country Hoard* is a treasury of words as well as of memories.

When we were little we sat by the fire on buffets, which were low soft stools, stuffed and covered with carpet or felt. We were cossetted and clipped, which means petted and embraced. When anyone put their arms around another it was a clip. A term of endearment we heard in those early days was 'my chuck', and 'my chuckabiddy'. In *Henry V* the words occur 'Use lenity, sweet chuck'. A spoilt child was a mardy, a term of reproach that was intensely disliked by all.

I know nothing of mardy. Clip meaning embrace is as old as Chaucer and frequent in Tudor Drama.

> She shall be buried by her Antony.
> No grave upon the earth shall clip in it
> A pair so famous,

says Octavius over the body of Cleopatra. Antony himself, who called the dazzling Cleopatra his chuck (the gruff Enobarbus might well have called her a mardy), bade his soldiers,

> Enter the City, clip your wives, your friends,
> Tell them your feats, whilst they with joyful tears
> Wash the congealment from your wounds and kiss
> The honour'd gashes whole.

Macbeth called his lady 'Chuck' at a grim moment. Chuck is chicken, but Lady Macbeth ranked surely among the more formidable fowls.

CLOGDOGDO AND TITIVIL

WHAT is a clogdogdo? The O.E.D. knows that it occurs, but is not otherwise helpful, mentioning clog and dog, but carrying the puzzle no further. But Captain Otter, that admirable character in an admirable play, Ben Jonson's *The Silent Woman*, apparently knew a clogdogdo when he saw or heard one. Here are the Captain's views on holy wedlock:

> Wife? Buz! *Titivilitium*. There's no such thing in nature! I confess, gentlemen, I have a cook, a laundress, a house-drudge, that serves my turns and goes under that title. But he's an ass that will be so uxorious to tie his affections to one circle. Come, the name dulls appetite. Wives are nasty, sluttish animals . . . a wife is a scurvy clogdogdo, an unlucky thing, a very foresaid bear-whelp, without any good fashion or breeding, *mala bestia*!

Yet the lady in question was obviously of fashion, since Otter, not a consistent scold, next observed of his helpmeet:

A most vile face! She spends me forty pounds a year in mercury and hogs-bones. All her teeth were made in the Black-friars and both her eyebrows in the Strand and her hair in Silver Street. Every part of the town owns a piece of her. She takes herself asunder when she goes to bed into some twenty boxes and next morn is put together again like a great German clock.

A lively guide to the ways of London ladies in 1609. But what is a clogdogdo? I must leave it to my readers.

Titivilitium is the Plautine Latin for a trifle. It was Anglicized as 'titivil' which came later to mean any knave or tale-teller as well as a trivial piece of gossip. In Hall's *Chronicles* appear

Certain Catchepoules and Parasites, commonly called titivils and tale-bearers, who sow discord and dissension.

It is a pity that it faded away, for titivil is a finely descriptive term for a light form of tatler.

CLUBMAN

WHAT a strange impression of primitive gangsterism a foreigner must get when he reads in an English paper of 'a West-End clubman'! It will surprise him to learn that this seemingly violent term only denotes a gentleman usually to be found dozing in the leather arm-chairs of a Pall Mall or St. James's Street mansion. Clubman is one of those delightful words which now exist only in the minds of journalists. Nobody would say of any friend that he was a clubman, but, when a certain type of colonel or milord dies, he will inevitably be described in some papers as a 'well-known West-End clubman'.

Club, to denote a building, is a little over a hundred years old. In the seventeenth century it meant either a share of the expenses (Pepys, after 'dining merry', once found 'the club too great') or a gathering of persons. It was said of John Cleveland (1613-58) that 'He and Sam Butler etc. of Grayes Inne, had a club every night'.

CODGER

WHAT is an old codger? I have heard it suggested that it means a cogitating old man. But this picturesque idea of the Pensive Senior seems to have been derived from 'Ye Antient Society of Cogers', a learned debating club which used to meet in London. The dictionaries deny the word any such honourable connotation and give no reason for dropping the 'd'. (In any case wise Cogers should know better than to use the silly 'Ye'.) A Codger, at his best, is a whimsical old man, whose foible is that of Goldsmith's Mr. Hardcastle, an affection for all things antique. At his worst, codger is identical with cadger and means a mendicant. Nor was there always the association of age. In the eighteenth century a lad could be a codger if he were constantly asking his elders to increase his allowance or settle his bills. Thus both Charles Surface and Sir Oliver could have been called codgers in different senses.

Those modern Antients the Cogers used to meet in the Barley Mow Tavern in Salisbury Square, Fleet Street, beginning there in ...ie eighteen-sixties and moving to the Cock Tavern in 1921. The Barley Mow has been replaced by a modern inn which now carries the title of 'The Cogers'. The patrons are not, in my experience, codgerly in any of the less agreeable senses of the word.

CORONAL

HEARING,

> The gay Corin of the groves who lives
> For his own fancies, or to dance by the hour,
> In coronal, with Phyllis in the midst,

who would you say was the author? Does it happen in *The Winter's Tale* or is it somewhere in Milton or possibly Keats? As a matter of fact, it is in Wordsworth (*The Prelude*).

Coronal can be an adjective 'pertaining to the Crown', and so it has been applied equally to the rights of kings or hats of commoners. As a noun it means posy, wreath, or garland. There is nothing strange about it except that it seems to make music wherever it goes.

39

Star and coronal and bell
April underfoot renews
And the hope of man as well
Flowers among the morning dews.

So sang Housman, who knew the words that sing.

CRINKUM-CRANKUM

IN my previous volume I referred to the eighteenth-century use of crinkum-crankum for a curly, knobby, fussily over-decorated thing. But I now realize that it had earlier the meaning of false, poor stuff or naughtiness. This of Dr. Kettell, the President of Trinity, when John Aubrey went up to Oxford just before the Civil War.

> Mrs. Howe, of Grendon, sent him a present of hippocris and some fine cheese-cakes, by a plain country fellow, her servant. The Dr. tastes the wine: — 'What, sayd he, didst thou take this drinke out of a ditch?' And when he saw the cheese-cakes — 'What have we here? Crinkum-crankum?' The poor fellow stared on him and wondered at such a rough reception of such a handsome present: but the Dr. shortly made him amends with half-a-crown and a good dinner.

Hippocris or hippocras was a cordial made of wine with added spices. Chaucer speaks of it as a source of courage.

A kindly correspondent has also reminded me that crinkum-crankum occurs in an old folk-rhyme and means irregular conduct. The 'fallen woman' when penitent had to confess that she had lost her binkum-bankum owing to her crinkum-crankum.

CULPON

TO John Moore, part compiler of *The Angler's Week End Book* and author of much happily observant writing on the fruition of the English scene, I owe a list of Tudor fish-carving terms parallel to the similar list of bird-carving terms mentioned in my first volume. So before Malvolio had 'allayed' a pheasant, 'unlatched' a curlew, 'unbraced' a mallard, or 'unlaced' a coney, he had doubtless been no less exact and picturesque with the fish-slice in his hand. Here are the terms as set forth in *The Accomplisht Lady's Delight* (1719):

Barb a Lobster	Splat a Pike
Chine a Salmon	String a Lamprey
Culpon a Trout	Tame a Crab
Fin a Chevin	Tranch a Sturgeon
Scull a Tench	Transon an Eel
Side a Haddock	Tusk a Barbel
Splay a Bream	

Later terms of address to the fish course include 'frushing a chub' and 'gobbeting a trout' (1829).

This was all very well for the precise man, but would there really have been a riot among the Mohocks if one of the roaring boys had got things wrong and bidden the landlord tusk him a lobster or splat him an eel?

CULVERKEYS

ALSO to John Moore and the fisherman's poetry do I owe acquaintance with John Dennys, who wrote many good lines and at least one meet to be spoken by Oberon or Perdita. I refer to the end of this stanza about the fishermen's flowers:

> Among the Dazies and the Violets blew
> Red Hyacinth and yellow Daffodill,
> Purple Narcissus like the morning rayes
> Pale Ganderglas and azor Culverkays.

Culverkeys (or Culverkays) are supposed to be flowers reminding one of a bunch of keys; they were sometimes cowslips: here they seem to be bluebells. I do not myself see much point in the key-simile. Ganderglas (also gandergoose) is, when pale, apparently a light lilac-tinted variety of the purple orchid. Whatever the blooms may be, they make a lovely sound: that last line is of the kind one likes to murmur to oneself on a wet day of November in the Tottenham Court Road. It occurs to me that the piece might then be retitled in the Shelleyan-Golden Treasury manner as: 'Stanzas Muttered in Dejection Near Maple's'.

CUMMER

C u m m e r, a kinswoman in Scots, has an assortment of meanings. She is a god-mother; then a gossip; then any female. Burns writes of 'kittle kimmer', as others of 'kittle cattle', to signify the lady uncertain, coy and hard to please. Kimmer is a bed-fellow in the early Scots drinking-song 'Todlen Hame'.

> My kimmer and I lay down to sleep,
> And twa pint-stoups at our bed feet;
> And aye when we wakened we drank them dry:
> What think ye of my wee kimmer and I?

The word occurs also in the song:

> How do ye, kimmer,
>   And how do ye thrive —
> And how monie bairns ha'e ye?
> Kimmer, I ha'e five.

I was reminded of Cummer by the following curious description of Scottish rites consequent upon a birth. The goings-on, which were certainly lively and reflect oddly on the notion of the Scot as grave in his domesticity, were called a Cummer Party. The passage is taken from *The Diary of Elizabeth Mure* (1714-95). She was of Caldwell in south-west Scotland and is quoted by Mr. Fyfe in his *Scottish Diaries and Memoirs 1746-1843*, published by Eneas Mackay of Stirling.

> On the forth week after the lady's delivery she is sett on her bed on a low footstool; the bed is covered with some neat piece of sewed work or white sattin, with three pillows at her back covered with the same; she in full dress with a lapped

head-dress and a fan in her hand. Having informed her acquaintance what day she is to see Company, they all come and pay their respects to her, standing or walking a little throw the room (for there's no chairs). They drink a glass of wine and eat a bit of cake and then give place to others. Toward the end of the week all the friends were asked to what was called the Cummer's feast. This was a supper, where every gentleman brought a pint of wine to be drunk by him and his wife. The supper was a ham at the head and a pirimid of fowl at the bottom. This dish consisted of four or five ducks at bottom, hens above, partrages at tope. There was an eating posset in the middle of the table, with dryed fruits and sweetmeats at the sides. When they had finished their supper, the meat was removed, and in a moment everybody fled to the sweetmeats to pocket them. Upon which a scramble insued, chairs over-turned and every thing on the table; wrassalling and pulling at one another with the utmost noise. When all was quiet'd, they went to the stoups (for there was no bottles) of which the women had a good share. For tho it was a disgrace to be seen drunk, yet it was none to be a little intoxicate in good Com-pany. A few days after this the same company was asked to the Christening, which was allwise in the Church; all in high dress; a number of them young ladys, who were call'd maiden Cummers. One of them presented the Child to the Father. After the Cerrimony they dined and supped togither, and the night often concluded with a ball.

Reading this in war-time, one certainly realized the appeal of 'a pirimid of fowl'. What a pleasant collision of Euclid and gas-tronomy! The manners of the Scottish gentry in the time of Burns, 'wrassalling and pulling at one another' for sweetmeats after poultry, seem peculiar. Was there some special pagan privilege after a lying-in, as it were a posset to Lucina, with full liberty of rite and revel? Those who have denied the total penetration of Scottish life by Puritanism have here a passage on their side.

DANTER

A SCOTTISH ballad begins:

> To daunton me, to daunton me,
> O ken ye what it is will daunton me?
> There's cess and press and Presbytrie
> I think it will do meikle to daunton me.

(Cess and press are Scot and lot and Scot and lot are parochial assessments for the poor.)

Daunt (from Latin *domitare*) means abash, oppress or intimidate and daunton is presumably the same. This brings me to the odd word 'danter' sent me by a correspondent from Pembrokeshire. Among lads squaring up to start a fight, it was customary to tap the opponent on the shoulder and challenge him with the phrase 'There's your danter'. Presumably this danter was derived from daunt or taunt.

Curiously, just as I received this piece of information, a Lancashire friend happened, in a conversation on words, to tell of a similar queer phrase of boyhood fisticuffs. One pugnacious boy would tap another and say, 'There's your cagings'. Cagings must be a survival of the medieval 'gage', a pledge, usually a gauntlet, thrown down as a promise or invitation to the contest.

DARKLING

DARKLING began life as an adverb meaning 'in the dark'. 'Out went the candle and we were left darkling', says the Fool in *King Lear*.

'Wilt thou darkling leave me?' is Helena's protest to Demetrius. Cleopatra, as she beholds the dying Antony, cries to the heavens:

> Oh sun,
> Burn the great sphere thou mov'st in! Darkling stand
> The varying shore o' the world!

44

In Milton:

> the wakeful Bird
> Sings darkling and in shadiest covert hid
> Tunes her nocturnal note.

Keats also kept this, the correct, usage in his 'Ode to A Nightingale':

> Darkling I listen: and for many a time
> I have been half in love with easeful Death.

(This does not mean that he is going black in the face: merely that he is standing in the dark.) But before Keats's time darkling had come to be regarded as the participle of a verb 'to darkle'. (This error was natural enough. If day sparkled, why should not night darkle?) Ever since the beginning of the nineteenth century, all sorts of things from minds to moonless landscapes have darkled for the poet's benefit.

'When matter darkles or when spirit beams' is a line of Moore's and night often darkled for Byron. If you wish to be learned, you can call darkle a 'back-formation'. It is certainly useful and decorative. The same process can be seen in 'sidle', a verb 'back-formed' from the adverb 'side-ling' or 'side-long'. Old writers went 'side-ling'. Later on they sidled, as the nights darkled.

DELICATES

DELICATE was an adjective beloved and superbly used by Shakespeare, for whom stratagem or climate, cheek or carriage, prince, fiend or maiden, could all be so described. Our mistake has been to let go the noun, generally used in the plural, meaning rather more than our own delicacy. It could be, for the Tudor authors, either luxury or a honeyed mood. Shakespeare contrasted the shepherd's simple fare and peace of mind with

> the prince's delicates,
> His viands sparkling in a golden cup,
> His body couched in a curious bed.

45

Marlowe's Faustus exclaims:

> I'll have them fly to India for gold,
> Ransack the ocean for orient pearl,
> And search all corners of the new-found world
> For pleasant fruits and princely delicates.

(It is worth noting that 'ocean' was then a three-syllabled word. When did it become 'oshun'?)

Ben Jonson wrote of a lady's delicates as her sunny and charming demeanour:

> She should be allowed her passions
> So they were but used as fashions:
> Sometimes froward and then frowning,
> Sometimes sickish and then swowning,
> Every fit with change still crowning.
> Purely jealous I would have her,
> Then only constant when I crave her,
> 'Tis a virtue would not save her!
> Thus, nor her delicates would cloy me
> Nor her peevishness annoy me.

Froward, now something of an antique, means from-ward, opposite of to-ward, and therefore contrary. It has nothing to do with frowning in derivation, though often, as here, close to it in place.

DELIGHTSOME

DELICIOUS makes such a slushy sound to the ear that it is the more surprising that we have abandoned delightsome, a word that comes most musically in Dunbar's lines,

> Sweet rose of virtue and of gentilness,
>   Delytsum lily of every lustyness,
> Richest in bontie and in beautie cleare,
>   And every virtue that is wenit deare,
> Except onlie that ye are merciless.

would not Herrick's

> Charm me asleep and melt me so,
> With thy delicious numbers

be improved by delightsome?

Elizabeth Barrett Browning found melancholy capable of being delightsome and the adjective has the sanction of a minor prophet. The A.V. translation of Malachi has,

> And all nations shall call you blessed: for ye shall be a delight-
> some land, saith the Lord of Hosts.

It has a far prettier sound than delicious and I prefer it to our other common choice, delightful.

DIMPSY

SEVERAL West Country correspondents have advised me that dimpsy is still in use for twilight in their localities. I was more surprised to hear that the same is true of Lincolnshire, where duskling (pronounced 'doosling') is also in use. Our word 'dusk' follows the adjective dusky (for dark) and only came to be a noun and to mean the dark time at a later stage. Shakespeare, for instance, would not have understood what we mean by dusk. He would have called it the dusky hour. (Nor, incidentally, did he use twilight, a word dear to Milton):

> As when the Sun . . .
> In dim Eclips disastrous twilight sheds.

This use of disastrous will remind Shakespeareans of Horatio's lines in *Hamlet*:

> Disasters in the sun: and the moist star
> Upon whose influence Neptune's empire stands
> Was sick almost to doomsday with eclipse.

(Disaster originally meant something wrong with the stars and so an ill-starred occurrence.)

True twilight or dusk could hardly be thus disastrous, except amid the cursed necessities of war-time 'black-out' with its consequent tumbles, accidents, and losings of the way. Certainly so sweet a thing as dimpsy or duskling merits a kinder epithet.

While on this subject, I might point out that to dusk for to make dark is as old as Chaucer, while the verb is used intransitively with superb effect by A. E. Housman:

> I see the air benighted
>   And all the dusking dales,
> And lamps in England lighted
>   And evening wrecked in Wales.

While I write, lamps may only be lit behind curtains and the true magic of an autumn evening in the country is missing. No farm and cottage windows are throwing saffron beams into the gathering mist and where is the warm radiance behind those red curtains of the bar-parlour at The Barley Mow, which should call the lated traveller apace? Now all is black, but even blackness, with beer behind, has already enticed the punctual and thirsty regulars. One craves the glow again. The war-time dimpsy may have its own beauties of the dusking dales, but I would far prefer to meet the 'lamps in England lighted'.

DING

WE have kept ding in the sense of ring or sound, but lost it in the old sense of strike or smash. We ding matters into people's ears and ding-dong is a word whose brassy music does not soften or disappear. The Scots have kept the other ding. 'Ding the Cathedral doon' was the cry of the more violent Reformers. That ding was Miltonic but not Shakespearean. Other Elizabethans used it occasionally. I came across it in Kyd's *The Spanish Tragedy*,

> She, she herself disguised in armour's mask
> As Pallas was before proud Pergamus
> Brought in a fresh supply of Halbadiers
> Which paunch'd his horse and ding'd him to the ground.

Ding, no doubt, is too slight a word for the age which 'dings the Cathedral doon' with an 8000-pound bomb, but it well sounded the clash of steel on stone or other metal. The Highlanders, from Dunbar to Scott and Stevenson, were ever dinging each other. 'We'll ding the Campbells yet' was a sentiment from the north-west. 'Duns dings a'' was the voice of Scotland's self-confident south-east.

DULSE

THERE was a music-hall song which announced,

> As soon as I touched my sea-weed
> I knew it was going to be fine!

And fine it is with the words for sea-weed. What could sound sweeter than dulse? This, however, is not Latin at all but comes from Erse and Gaelic roots and means an edible sea-weed of our western coasts. 'Dulse and sandhoppers', boiled in milk, the sand-hoppers being small shrimps, was a favourite dish of Kintyre, while the sterner men of the north-east crunched dulse and shells raw. As an Aberdonian I have a fancy for studying the history of my county in that anonymous piece of pastoral-comical, 'Johnny Gibb of Gushetneuk or the Parish of Pyketillim'. When the parties went to take the waters (sea and spa) at Macduff, with 'the hardy dookers' sea-bathing and shiversomely relishing a distant view of dim Caith-ness hills across the Firth, Maister Saun'ers said of dulse to Jock Will: 'They're a vera halesome thing ta'en with the water'. He then exhibited and consumed raw 'a bunch of short, crisp dulse powdered about the root-ends with clusters of tiny shells of the mussel species'. As he crunched this prickly mess, he remarked that 'shells hae a poo'erful effeck o' the stammack'. Well, that is one way of setting things in motion. My forebears were hardy men.

Dulse sounds good enough. But what of Carrageen? Yet, when I found that described as 'sea-weed blanc-mange' I felt some loss of appetite. But apparently it is a Hebridean delicacy as well as a salve against chills. Carrageen must be largely iodine, but it sounds more romantic than that familiar antiseptic, while doing the same therapeutic work.

EAR-WIGGLE

OUR ear-wig (*forficula auricularia*) used to be the ear-wiggle, a more fitting title, since the creature was named after a supposed habit of wiggling or wriggling its way into people's ears. Ear-wigging has had a fair variety of meanings in English. Hunt and Pringle in *Service Slang* (1943) record ear-wiggers as head-phones and an ear-wigger as 'one who eavesdrops or butts in on other people's conversation'. This is old usage as well as new. One of the old ear-wigs or ear-wiggles was the man who sought the audience of the great in a fawning way. Joseph Hall, in his *Characters* (1608), wrote of 'The Porter of good tales who mends them in the carriage; whenever he walks with his friend, he swears to him that no man else is looked at; and that whomsoever he vouchsafes to look on and nod to is graced'. He finally describes this parasitic please-man as 'the ear-wig of the mighty'. The other type of human ear-wig was a pestering fellow, always hinting at or supplicating favours for himself and his cronies. Politicians in office were said to be ear-wigged by creatures of this kind. Crony, by the way, is an odd term, having nothing to do with crone. It is as old as Pepys and attributed to the Universities. An ear-wigging crony sounds like a sinister addition to a Senior Common Room.

ENGINE

A CURIOUS and changeful history befel this word until it became embowelled in 400 m.p.h. aeroplanes. How many, in our mechanic age, realize that this same engine is simply the Latin 'ingenium' and meant originally wit? Chaucer linked 'Memorie, engin, and intellect' together. After that it came to mean trickery, device, or implement. Hence the fisherman-author Richard Franck could write (1694) of river-poachers:

What are these, cannabals or murdering moss-troopers, to surprise fish by the engine of firelight?

But Shakespeare had already used the word for cannon, the 'mortal engines, whose rude throats Th' immortal Jove's dread clamours counterfeit'. He employed it also for trick. Men's lures and promises are 'engines of lust' and Iago, thus 'engining' Roderigo, said:

> If thou the next night following enjoy not Desdemona, take me from this world with treachery, and devise engines for my life.

A later use was as motive or source of persuasion. Some nineteenth-century philosophers would call punishment and reward 'engines of conduct'.

FADGE

FADGE in Scots is a bannock and has been annexed by our Ministry of Food as an attractive title for a potato-cake. In Robert Fergusson's picture of 'The Farmer's Ingle' the gudeman 'streeking' himself at his ease considers cat and collie and flings them 'mony a crum' of 'kebbuck whangd' (cut cheese) and 'dainty fadge'.

The English fadge is a verb, to fit, suit, or agree. People are made to fadge 'spite of antipathy' in Milton and everybody must remember that Shakespeare's Viola, when Malvolio offers her the ring, uses the word for 'agree with the facts or make sense':

> How will this fadge? My master loves her dearly
> And I, poor monster, fond as much on him.

Fond, as a verb, is a nice usage of the seventeenth century.

Armado in *Love's Labour's Lost* says, after discussing the proposed theatricals, 'We shall have, if this fadge not, an antic'. Seasoned playgoers must often have felt, somewhere about the middle of Act II of some dull, pretentious stuff, that this is not fadging at all and so have desired, if not total escape, at least an antic.

FIGGLE, with its mixture of fidget and wriggle, is a fine old English word and well suits an unweaned lamb worrying away at its mother. Fig and fige are also graphic forms of fidget. The participle figent was fairly common in the Jacobean dramatists. (A fig or figger is also one who fidgets his way into other people's pockets, a thief or cut-purse, and figgum was an old name for conjuror's tricks.) Hounds used to 'fig to and fro' upon the scent. I like 'fige' as Congreve used it. His Mrs. Marwood talks of legal proceedings thus:

> To be ushered in with an 'O yes' of scandal and have your case opened by an old fumbling leacher in a quoif like a man-midwife . . . and to discompose the gravity of the Bench and provoke naughty interrogatories in more naughty Law Latin, while the good judge, tickled with the proceeding, simpers under a grey beard and figes off and on his cushion as if he had swallowed cantharides or sate upon cow-itch.

Fidge is a commoner spelling now. But fidget is the commoner word. Fiddle-faddle expresses the exasperation of one who is kept waiting and is a ripe old word as well as a favourite of to-day.

FORLORN

RARELY is so much meaning carried in the sound of two syllables as in the case of forlorn.

> Forlorn, the very word is like a bell
> To toll me back from thee —

Keats summed it up. The deep clang of the two 'ors', with the liquid to introduce the second syllable, makes the true music of desolation. Shakespeare is sparing with forlorn, but, when he does employ it, the sense of solitude and destitution is absolute, as in 'Forlorn and naked hermitage' or 'rogues forlorn, in short and musty straw'.

Beddoes, indulging 'the mighty thought of an old world', wrote:

> My waking is a Titan's dream
> Where a strange sun, long set, doth beam;
> Through the fern wilderness forlorn
> Glisten the giant hart's great horn
> And serpents vast with helméd brow.

Fern is here used in its antique form as an adjective signifying 'far away and long ago'. 'Fern wilderness forlorn' is a wonderful phrase for the kind of England that is symbolized in Avalon and Egdon Heath and Stonehenge, the world of Lear and his Fool and others cast out and couched in musty straw.

There is a strong pathos in the prefix 'for' when used to signify excess. Forlorn is the past participle passive of forlese, to lose. Forlese is more than lese: so forlorn is more than lorn, as forspent is more than spent and forswunk more than swinked or swunk. (See note on Swink later.) None the less, alliteratively used with lone, the brief lorn can be powerful too, as that 'lone, lorn creature' Mrs. Gummidge knew. Forlorn has such poignance in its word-music as almost to make poetry whenever it appears. So, too, has forsaken.

FRAMPLE AND FRANION

W H Y did frample or frampold for peevish or sour disappear? It is a vivid, effective word. Tudor and Jacobean drama has a number of frample jades. Mrs. Quickly said to Falstaff of Mrs. Ford, 'Alas, the sweet woman lives an ill life with him (Ford). He's a very jealousy man and she leads a very frampold life with him, good heart'. Here frampold seems to mean soured rather than sour. As a rule it suggests an actively pettish person and might be applied (and perhaps somewhere is so applied) to its dictionary neighbour, franion, a favourite of George Peele, the author of *The Old Wives' Tale*.

Franions were usually licentious creatures, male or female, but Peele also used the word for a wandering, or idle person. His character Frolic, who is lost in a wood with Antic and Fantastic in the comedy mentioned above, claims to be 'frolic franion' and another character talks of 'the frolic'st franion among you', but elsewhere franions are not so innocently jocund and can be frample.

FUBSY

'FAT and fubsy Fellows of Colleges' hardly exist nowadays. Nor does fubsy, which used to mean squat and stout. The modern don is usually a lean young man. Instead of brimming with port and erudition, he avoids the former and conceals the latter, walking the quadrangle with a sad stoop, as it were a perambulant question-mark, dubiety on stilts. Even a war-diet, which is so wrongly discussed in terms of belt-tightening since it only bloats a man with starchy and enlarging substances, has not made Oxford or Cambridge richer in 'fubs', which is the noun for fubsy folk — and a good noun too. The verb 'fub' means, or meant, cheat, being a corruption of fob. In the North of England pubble is a dialect word for fubsy animals. 'At Michaelmas a pubble goose — at Kersmas, standin' pie.' Sir Thomas More used fobby for fubsy. 'Glotony maketh the body fat and fobby.' But fubsy is the obvious term here . It almost lards the page as one writes it, as sweating Falstaff larded the earth below him. But Falstaff, though a fubber-off of landladies, was not fubsy himself. He outranged the term altogether. Fubsy is for small, plump men, not for adiposity's masterpiece.

GALIMATIAS

I SHOULD have linked this with gallimaufry in my previous volume, for it seemed once to mean collection or assortment. But more often it means an assortment of noises, a babble, especially a nonsensical row. I came across it as a synonym for a torrent of silly chatter and sound in a work of Henry Siddons on Stage Gesture and Delivery. It was fairly common in the eighteenth century with that sort of significance and was used by Horace Walpole, that constant friend of the uncommon word. It sometimes implied what the

French mean by 'brouhaha'. We lack a good term for that now, but we should not, considering the noise we make (or used to make) at cocktail parties and their gabbling like. We might revive 'a galimatias' to connote that kind of dithering din and squealing pursuit of gossip and of wit.

GILLIVER

F E W English flowers have had a wider choice of names than the Gillyflower, which has run through the whole range of possible spellings from July-flower to giroflour or gilver. It means generally the flower connected with the clove, either in shape or smell. The yellow gilliver was our wall-flower, but pinks and sops-in-wine were also gillivers. At any rate the name became synonymous with beauty, an honour it has somewhat lost. For several centuries the gilliver was as honourable a title as rose or jewel. It blossomed in a thousand lyrics. No adored one was complete without it. I was reminded of this when reading John Heywood's *Praise of His Lady:*

> Truly she doth so far exceed
> Our women nowadays
> As doth the geliflower a weed
> And more a thousand ways.

Damask rose would have scanned just as well but gilliver was chosen. It held equal pride of place in poets' fancies.

The Scots, too, put the gilliver on the celestial heights. The question what comes of women who have died in childbirth ('strong traivelling') is asked in the 'Ballad of Clerk Saunders'. Here is the reply:

> Their beds are made in the heavens high,
> Down at the foot of our good Lord's knee,
> Well set about wi' gillyflowers;
> I wot, sweet company for to see.

Dunbar linked it with the rose in his noble, rolling praise of London:

Gemme of all joy, jasper of jocunditie,
    Most myghty carbuncle of vertue and valour;
Strong Troy in vigour and in strenuytie;
    Of royall cities rose and geraflour.

The geraflour's loss of status is lamentable, not least because the word in all its forms is a fair one and makes music wherever it goes.

GINGERLY

GINGERLY has nothing to do with ginger. The latter I recently found mysteriously ascribed to Queen Guinevere in a book called *Phrases and Names*, by Trench Johnson. The idea was that the lady had red hair and so Guinevere became a synonym for 'Carrots' in its popularized form of ginger. All this I take to be nonsense and I shall still refuse to attend the image of Miss Guinevere Rogers at my Palasseum, preferring simple Ginger and accepting the official explanation of that word as 'the rhyzome of the tropical plant Zingiber Officinale'.

Returning to gingerly, we can claim that the word, although more quaint than beautiful, has a lordly origin. Its parent appears to be the old French *gentior*, a comparative of *gent*, nice. (See note on Jaunty.) We think now of walking gingerly or handling things in a gingerly way, i.e. cautiously, but people could look gingerly too in Tudor or Stuart times. In a play of Webster's it is said of a lady: 'Oh, she looks so sugredly, so simperingly, so gingerly, so amorously . . . she's such an intycing she-witch.' This is a fascinating usage and suggests a deal of nice naughtiness. That fierce Puritan Stubbes, sworn foe of all things nice or naughty, denounced 'the dancing minions that minse it ful gingerly'. A maid 'looking gingerly' seems to have been what is vulgarly known as 'hot stuff', and of course a confusion between gingerly and ginger (*gentior* and Zingiber) soon became inevitable. It was easy to suppose that one picked a thing up gingerly because it was so hot. A curious slang use of ginger continues in the phrase 'Stone Ginger'. Stone Ginger is ginger-beer kept cool in a stone-bottle and the mingled conceptions of 'hot stuff' and 'cool customer' have turned the phrase into a synonym for athletic precision. I was once watching cricket at Lord's when, at a critical point of the game, a very high catch was sent to Elias Hendren, commonly known as Patsy, who had to run to be ready for it. Amid an anxious silence a voice cried from the outskirts of the Tavern: 'It's orl right, boys. Patsy's Stone Ginger.' And Patsy was.

GLIB

IT is nice to hear glib still used in its proper sense of smooth or slippery as applied to material surfaces. 'Be careful, the greens are glib here,' said an old golf-caddie to me once. (Scots caddies might describe the same fast, treacherous quality of worn grass as kittle.) A correspondent has likewise reminded me of glib roads. 'In Rutland recently,' he writes, 'I was talking to the local roadman, a man of fifty-five, born, bred in, and never out of that county!' (He was evidently a very static piece of England, this roadman, considering the size of Rutland.) 'Of a road on a hill that we both knew well, I happened to say that the County Council had wasted money tarchipping it at the wrong time of year. It had in consequence become dangerous for horses. His reply was "What, sir, has it gone glib already?"' Browning used glib so:

> The snow lies glib as glass and cold as steel.

Shakespeare, however, used glib only of people or arts. It occurs in Ulysses' magnificent dismissal of Cressida and her kind:

> There's language in her eye, her cheek, her lip,
> Nay, her foot speaks: her wanton spirits look out
> At every joint and motive of her body.
> Oh these encounterers, so glib of tongue,
> That give a coasting welcome ere it comes
> And wide unclasp the tables of their thoughts
> To every ticklish reader! Set them down
> For sluttish spoils of opportunity
> And daughters of the game.

The Poet in *Timon* contrasts the 'glib and slippery creatures' with those of 'grave and austere quality', while all must remember Cordelia's

> If for I want that glib and oily art
> To speak and purpose not ...

Glib is one of the words whose metaphorical usage has almost conquered and banished its simple meaning — except in a few country places.

GLIMMER

IT glimmers everywhere. Indeed, the word seems to be inevitably imbedded and refulgent in all the most justly familiar and most beautiful poems in the language.

For Macbeth's First Murderer:

> The west yet glimmers with some streaks of day.

(What lines the prodigal Shakespeare used to toss to his small-part men!)

Oberon at the close of *A Midsummer Night's Dream* asks:

> Though the house give glimmering light,
> By the dead and drowsy fire;

and in Gray's Churchyard:

> Now fades the glimmering landscape on the sight.

In Henry Vaughan's *Friends in Paradise* terrestrial glimmering is sadly contrasted with the radiance of the other-worldly light. Here too the quiet word enchants:

> I see them walking in an air of glory
> Whose light doth trample on my days,
> My days, which are at best but dull and hoary,
> Mere glimmering and decays.

Again it offers a faint but poignant beam in:

Squadrons and squares of men in brazen plates,
    Scaffolds, still sheets of water, divers woes,
Ranges of glimmering vaults with iron grates
    And hushed seraglios.

(The author? Tennyson would not be the first guess of most who were uncertain. But Tennyson is right. Source, 'A Dream of Fair Women'.

There is really nothing to be said about glimmer except that it ubiquitously, abundantly, and exquisitely gleams. Everybody will have his own passage to which glimmer adds a quality of delicate illumination. The romantics will certainly murmur the rich Shelleyan music of 'The Cloud':

That orbèd maiden, with white fire laden,
    Whom mortals call the moon
Glides glimmering o'er my fleece-like floor,
    By the midnight breezes strewn.

The Londoner will remember the slow and sweeping flight of Laurence Housman's heron:

High up he sails, and sees beneath
The glimmering ponds of Hampstead Heath;

while Dubliners will respond to Sean O'Casey's

A gold-speckled candle, white as snow, was Dublin once: yellowish now, leanin' sideways, an' guttherin' down to a last shaky glimmer in th' wind o' life.

But one could go on for ever with glimmer.

GUY

W H Y has Guy become slang for a man, especially for a good man, 'the regular fellow' or 'great Guy'? Although Guy has long been attached to Guido Fawkes and turned into an enemy of society meet for mockery and even for destruction, it still, strangely, can suggest a decent sort of chap. Can there be any connection with the earliest guy, who was a guide or leader or support? (Hence guy-rope.) Guy in that sense occurs in old Dunbar's fine, if flattering, poem on London with its cry of

> Gemme of all joy, jaspre of jocunditie
> Most myghty carbuncle of vertue and valour;

and its refrain of

> London, thou art the flour of Cities all.

The stanza which introduces the word in its oldest sense is that which honours the Lord Mayor:

> Thy famous Maire, by pryncely governaunce,
>   With sword of justice thee ruleth prudently.
> No Lord of Parys, Venyce, or Floraunce
>   In dignitye or honour goeth to hym nigh.
>   He is exampler, loode-star, and guye;
> Principall patrone and rose orygynalle,
>   Above all Maires as maister most worthy:
> London, thou art the flour of Cities all.

Plainly, a Great Guy, as the comedians say now.

HARBOURING

A NAUTICAL nation has come to regard a harbour mainly as a sea-shelter, although there is no particularly marine suggestion in the word. There is something strong and reassuring in the sound of it: the two r's are comforters. How it can help a quatrain and give the notion of protective bastion appears in Emily Brontë's famous lines about mystical Experience.

> Then dawns the Invisible; the Unseen its truth reveals;
> My outward sense is gone: my inward essence feels;
> Its wings are almost free — its home, its harbour found,
> Measuring the gulf, it stoops, and dares the final bound.

Harbouring for brooding or sulking is an old, but vivid, extension of the sheltering notion. It is now colloquial. I quote this perfect description of a rural English mating from a wildly comic story by R. C. Robertson-Glasgow called *No Other Land*. This Oxford and Somerset cricketer, journalist, and author is a fantastic, but he is also a realist and knows how the village manages its affairs and speaks its mind. Here is his record of a mating:

> Corlett called her 'the steady': and, on the morning after the wedding, said 'Elsie, you look after the cooking and the ducks; I'll look after the garden and the pigs. You ask for what money you want; I'll keep what money I want. And when you get something as you want to point out, just chuck it off and I'll catch it. No harbouring, Elsie, for you and me. How's that?' — 'Fine, Jack.' And it was.

'The steady' for the wife is perfect in its simplicity: also in its suggestion that giddiness may lurk elsewhere.

HAVEREL

'POOR hav'rel Will', wrote Burns in 'Hallowe'en', meaning a chatterer of nonsense or even a total 'daftie'. Carlyle wrote of 'a haveril lass', and the spelling haveral is also known. Haverel is a noun derived from the Scottish verb to haver, which means to talk rubbish. Haver (more commonly havers) is also a noun. Who invented 'Hoots, Toots, and Havers' I cannot discover, but certainly Barrie wrote of a bad piece of writing as 'a haver of a book'. Scott has the graphic, 'Dinna deave me with your havers' (Don't deafen me with your trash).

The English have almost completely altered the meaning of haver. Ask an Englishman what he means by havering and he would say hesitation, nervous, indecisive speech. When a Scot says that the speaker 'havered away' he means that he was a gaseous idiot. The Englishman, using the same phrase, does not imply idiocy: he suggests rather that the man on his feet was a yammerer or stammerer:

he may have spoken sense, but he was a long time about it. As a Scot, I am loyal to the native usage. A Scottish correspondent suggests that the English have made some muddle here with hover. Very often similarity of words produces this kind of confusion of meaning.

Haver is also a Teutonic word for oats which the Scots have preserved in the vegetable world while the English have retained it only in their bag and baggage. How many of the millions who have carried a haversack realize that it is an oat-sack or horse's nose-bag, carried by the cavalryman in many a war? The German *habersack* and French *havresac* proclaim the widespread use of haver as a farmer's term. It is odd that the Scots should have the same word for oats and nonsense, since no nation is more partial to the former or more intolerant of the latter.

HEY NONNY

W H Y were the Elizabethans so addicted to hey-nonnying? A nonino was a trifle and presumably the phrase beloved of the minstrel boys suggests a spirit of carefree ease or defiance. Certainly it seems to imply the latter in Middleton's lyric:

> Love for such a cherry lip
> > Would be glad to pawn his arrows;
> Venus here to take a sip
> > Would sell her doves and team of sparrows.
> > > But they shall not so;
> > > > Hey nonny nonny no!
> > > None but I this lip must owe,
> > > > Hey nonny nonny no!

In Shakespeare's 'Sigh no more', however, a simpler jollity seems to be the intention of the words:

> Sing no more ditties, sing no mo
> > Of dumps so dull and heavy;

> The fraud of men was ever so,
>   Since summer first was leavy:
>   Then sigh not so,
>   But let them go,
>   And be you blithe and bonny,
> Converting all your sounds of woe
>   Into Hey nonny nonny.

So also in the anonymous lyric, with its brave call for 'a laughing way in the teeth of the world':

> Hey nonny no
> Men are fools that wish to die!
> Is't not fine to dance and sing
> When the bells of death do ring?
> Is't not fine to swim in wine
> And turn upon the toe
> And sing hey nonny no,
> When the winds blow and the seas flow,
> Hey nonny no?

One can hardly imagine the Italianate scenes of Tudor Comedy without some carolling of hey-nonny verses to the gentle music of gallery musicians or of lutes unseen.

HIRPLE

HIRPLE, to limp, is a vivid word for slow and painful motion. It is common in Scots and occurs in Burns's ballad 'What can a Young Lassie do wi' an auld man?' Little indeed, if it be true that:

> He's always compleenin' frae mornin' to e'ening,
> He hoasts and he hirples the weary day lang;
> Hey's doylt and he's dozin', his bluid it is frozen,
> O dreary's the night wi' a crazy auld man!

(Doylt means scant-witted.) Hoast, for cough, is a vivid piece of

Scots. Perhaps the English 'hawk' is more accurate for the early-morning activities of the cigarette-smoker; hoasting I fancy to be a less aggressive business, an anxious, wheezy, strained affair. It reminds me of Max Miller, that unbiddable Cockney comedian of the bright and roving eye, as he taps his chest and says, 'Tight, lady. Just there. Tight.' I cannot spell the Cockney Tight. It is neither tate nor toit. But it has the whole of February's bronchial horror in it when Max Miller hoasts it out.

The two verbs for limp and cough are also associated by Burns in the 'Epistle to James Smith':

> The magic wand then let us wield;
> For, ance that five-an-forty's speel'd,
> See crazy, weary, joyless Eild,
>   Wi' wrinkled face,
> Comes hoastin', hirplin', ow're the field
>   Wi' creepin' pace.

Eild, the Southron need hardly be told, is old age. The 'magic wand' is pleasure which makes the hours dance.

Returning to Hirple, I am reminded that it can have a sombre beauty as well as sounding its note of awkwardness and pain. It occurs beautifully in Burns's lines 'On the Birth of a Posthumous Child':

> November hirples o'er the lea
>   Chill, on thy lovely form:
> And gane, alas, the sheltering tree
>   Should shield thee frae the storm.

'Hirples o'er the lea' is surely exquisite and renders a perfect image of the dull droop of a November day. We can see and feel the mist slowly clambering along the side of the brae, wreathing the purple of the stripped and leafless copse, and loitering in smoky patches on the fields once green but now famished into greyness or umbered with the visitation of the plough.

HOCUS POCUS and INCUBUS

THOMAS BURKE in *The Streets of London* quotes thus from an old story of Bartholomew Fair:

> Here a knave in a Fool's Coat, with a trumpet sounding, or a drum beating, invites you to see his puppets; there a Rogue like a Wild Woodman, or in an antic shape like an Incubus, desires your company to view his motion; on the other side Hocus Pocus, with three yards of tape or ribbon in his hand, showing his art of leger-de-main to the admiration and astonishment of a company of cockroaches.

Both Hocus Pocus and Incubus began as persons and became things. On the Tudor fairground Hocus Pocus was the conjuror, so named because that was the kind of bogus charm that he muttered. Now the word refers only to the trickery. In the same way an Incubus is now only a burden; but he was once a fiend, especially a rapacious fiend likely to descend on sleeping beauties. He thus came to be the symbol of a nightmare, as Master Hocus Pocus became the symbol of illusion and deceit.

So Milton knew him. Belial, in his opinion, was not only 'the dissolutest spirit that fell' and 'sensuallest', but also 'after Asmodai the fleshliest Incubus'. Poor Incubus! After being fouler than a Black Fiend, it has become the small brother of a White Elephant.

HOYT

MISS ROSE MACAULAY in her delightful anthology *The Minor Pleasures of Life* includes, under the caption 'Huntin',' an excerpt from an anonymous poem of 1675 called 'The Chase'. This describes Dian's young and virginal nymphs a-chasing the stag:

> A light-foot Host, green-kirtl'd all they came
> And leapt, and rollickt, as some mountain Streame
> Sings cold and ruffling thro' the Forrest Glades;
> So ran, so sang, so hoyted the Moone's Maids.
> Light as young Levretts skip their buskin'd feet,

Spurning th' enamell'd Sward as they did fleet.
The Wind that buss'd their cheekes was all the Kiss
Was suffer'd by the Girles of *Artemis*,
Whose traffique was in Woods, whom the winged Boy
Leaguer'd in vain, whom Man would ne're injoy,
Whose Bed greene Moss beneath the forrest Tree,
Whose jolly Pleasure all in Liberty,
To sport with fellow Maids in maiden cheere,
To swim the Brook, and hollo after Deer.
Thus, the winds wantoning their flying Curles,
So rac'd, so chas'd, those most Delightfull Girles.

The last couplet is indeed a gem.

Hoyt or hoit is to act the romp or hoyden. Winsome and spirited maids go hoyting across the English stage of the seventeenth century. Hoity-toity is an expansion of the same word and originally was applied to frolicsome women. D'Urfey in his *Pills to Purge Melancholy* wrote of a 'Hoity Toity Frowzy Browzy Covent-Garden Harridan' (Harridan meant originally a broken-down horse). The meaning of hoity-toity was altered to become an expression of petulance and surprised disgust, in which function it remains common. The verb to hoit has almost disappeared; it is a pity, for it went well with the racing and chasing of 'Delightfull Girles'.

IMPOSTHUME

D o you want Lamb at his most whimsy-whamsical? Then try this from *Amicus Redivivus*:

Had he been drowned in Cam there could have been some consonancy in it: but what willows had ye to wave over his moist sepulture? — or, having no name, beside that unmeaning assumption of eternal novity, did ye think to get one by the noble prize, and henceforth be termed Stream Dyerian?

And could such specious virtue find a grave
Beneath the imposthumed bubble of a wave?

This follows 'pails of gelid and kettles of the boiling element' for hot and cold water. Elia in this mood can be very tiresome. He anticipated the George Augustus Sala species of journalese. But I like his quotation for its 'imposthumed bubble'. The lines we owe to the Cavalier, John Cleveland: they occur in his contribution to the volume of elegies on the drowned Edward King, the book in which Milton's 'Lycidas' first appeared. Cleveland's words were slightly, but not substantially, different from Lamb's version. 'Imposthumed bubble' is his.

If you suffer from anything so painful and humiliating as a boil, why not, by way of compensation, dignify the odious lump with the fine old English title of imposthume? Imposthume started life, apparently, as aposthume, which is Greek for an abscess. Somehow it became emposthume in English and so imposthume, an imposing name for a mean affliction. Cleveland's 'imposthumed bubble' is really a most graphic term for the seething of a wave-top. Shakespeare's Thersites, when he wished to reel off the commoner plagues of miserable man, listed

> the rotten diseases of the south, the guts griping, catarrhs, loads o' gravel i' the back, lethargies, cold palsies, raw eyes, dirt-rotten livers, wheezing lungs, bladders full of imposthume, sciaticas, limekilns i' th' palms, incurable bone-ache, and the rivelled fee-simple of the tetter.

Hamlet, less clinically, describes war about little or nothing as 'the imposthune of much wealth and peace'. 'Imposthumed Braines' occurs in Dekker for poisoned minds.

Tetter, a general (and horrible) term for skin-disease, appears formidably in Hamlet's father's diagnosis of his own fatal affliction:

> A most instant tetter bark'd about
> Most lazar-like, with vile and loathsome crust,
> All my smooth body.

It is generally supposed that Shakespeare's interest in disease began with his friendship for Dr. John Hall, who married his elder daughter Susannah. Certainly, the later plays, written when Shakespeare was supposed to be seeing more of Stratford and of his neighbour Hall, show a lively interest in the maladies most incident to man. Hall, by the way, wrote a case-book with a superb title, *Select Observations on Human Bodies*. Shakespeare may have shared some of the Doctor's scrutinies — and so powerfully added, as Thersites showed, to a vocabulary already uncommonly rich. There are moments in Shakespeare's later plays when his surge of metaphor is so fierce and turbid as to suggest an apoplexy of the fancy and an imposthume of the phrase-minting brain.

INCONY

N O B O D Y seems to know the origin of this Tudor trifle. 'A darrlin' word, a darrlin' word', as Sean O'Casey's Joxer Daly would say . For incony is darling, although some link it with the French *inconnu* or our own uncanny for no apparently good reason. In any case, it means something delicate, nice, or 'amusing', as smart folk used to say. Marlowe has it and Shakespeare uses it twice, both times in the same play, *Love's Labour's Lost*. The dactyl runs so sweetly on the tongue that it is strange that, having once used it, he thereafter forgot it. (In my opinion Shakespeare was working over and adding to somebody else's text in this play and incony may have been his predecessor's darling.) However that may be, there the pretty word lies cosily. 'My sweet ounce of man's flesh, my incony Jew.' Again, there is talk of a 'most incony wit'. Marlowe employs it in the rough jesting of his crudest piece, *The Jew of Malta*. Says Ithamore to Bellamira:

> Love me little, love me long, let music rumble,
> While I in thy incony lap do tumble.

'Love me little, love me long' first appears, I think, in John Heywood's *Book of Proverbs* (1546). It is best known, perhaps, in Herrick's

> You say to me-wards your affection's strong
> Pray love me little, so you love me long.

Herrick, by the way, might be described as one of the most incony of English poets and parsons.

INDAGATE

WHEN in 1648 John Aubrey was a-hunting in Wilts and spied the majesty of Avebury's megalithic ruins, then far more impressive than now, thanks to eighteenth-century vandalism, he left the chase to inspect the monument. This scrutiny he termed 'a more delightful indagation'.

Indagate for inquire was a Latinity popular in the seventeenth century and held its own until the beginning of the nineteenth. The Caroline inquirers liked the classical flourish. 'Let us be indagacious and exact in the least punct', wrote another of them. Parsons of the time indagated the Scriptures and indagatrix was a fine she-title for the questing spirit. The term is apparently dead now, but would lie handsomely in any cathedral-piece of elaborate prose-architecture.

INFLUENCE

A SAD decay has overtaken this once magical word. It was originally associated with the effluent power of the stars as it entered into man. In Milton's Nativity Hymn,

> The Stars with deep amaze
> Stand fixt with stedfast gaze
> Bending one way their precious influence.

The Bible Translators had already made question, 'Canst thou bind the sweet influences of the Pleiades?' So, moving across from the sublime to the sinister, we find Edmund in *King Lear* denouncing the foppery of the world which excuses its vices by the stars and claims that men are 'drunkards, liars, and adulterers by an enforced obedience of planetary influence'. Parolles describes the fashionables as moving 'under the influence of the most received star'. Prospero also speaks of

> A most auspicious star, whose influence,
> If now I court not, but omit, my fortunes
> Will ever after droop.

Valentine in *Two Gentlemen of Verona* is surely also thinking of a star when he says of Silvia that by her 'fair influence' he must be

> Foster'd, illumined, cherished, kept alive.

He would hardly bring in 'illumined' otherwise.

Next comes the idea of a magic spell, or inspiration, and we hear from Milton of

> Ladies whose bright eyes
> Rain influence.

Crashaw too writes of a brisk cherub who sips 'sweet influence' from a lady's eyes and 'so adds sweetness to his sweetest lips'. The modern sense of the word as a social force or corrupting pressure is oddly anticipated in Milton:

> So spake the false Arch-Angel and infus'd
> Bad influence into the Unwarie brest
> Of his Associate.

Thus was the way prepared for the present meaning of importance or effect. Influence has become examination English. Are we not always inviting (or invited) to trace the influence of this or that? Certainly the magic has departed and bottom depth was touched when Influenza, itself first meaning an infusion of astral power, was exclusively devoted to 'a febrile, zymotic disorder, whose symptoms and sequelae are rapid prostration and severe catarrh'. We most of us know all about that, without recourse to such words as sequelae.

So influence comes streaming down our centuries of poetry, gradually losing its sense of starry or divine afflatus, dwindling into an ugly form of social pressure, and even sneezing itself into the humiliations of a streaming cold. Perhaps the most recent kind of stars are now in their own way vehicles of influence. It is by the image of the cinema's beauties that millions now appear to be

> Foster'd, illumined, cherished, kept alive.

So we can still quote Milton aptly when we talk of bright-eyed ladies raining influence. But of course the gentlemen must also be included in that galaxy of the influential, from the great Gable down to Mickey Rooney.

JAUNTY

THIS is one of the downward sliding words. Like Gingerly, it owed its origin to the French gent or gentil and meant well-bred, poised, easy of manner. Then the easiness became too easy and began to be associated with carelessness and impudence. By the beginning of the nineteenth century a slattern could be jaunty, which would have seemed absurd in the seventeenth and eighteenth when fashion was described as 'ganty' or 'jauntee'.

> A bag-wig of a jauntee air
> Tricked up with all a barber's care.

But a jaunty manner to-day means a pert insolence rather than a modest grace.

Jaunt, as a trip, which seems to have an independent origin and was sometimes spelt Jaunce, went the other way and climbed. It began as a troublesome journey and became a light or gay one, made in pursuit of pleasure. Twice does Juliet's Nurse speak of a jaunt as sore labour:

> Fie, how my bones ache! What a jaunt have I had

she cries in Capulet's garden; and again:

> Beshrew your heart for sending me about
> To catch my death with jaunting up and down.

(How many know that 'to catch your death' is Shakespearean English, though here it seems to refer to the head-ache and bone-ache caused by worry and exertion rather than to the catarrh with which it is usually associated now?)

The Irish jaunting-car was surely based on the old idea of a rough and jerky journey and not on the new one of a joy-ride.

JIMP

JIMP is mainly Scottish for slender or, by extension of meaning, scarce. Sir Walter Scott used jimp and jimply where we might employ scanty and scantily. Does any Scots grocer still remark that eggs are jimp instead of pompously announcing that eggs, non-reconstituted, are now in short supply? The earlier, physical jimp was applied to ladies' waists and limbs. Inquired the Lass of Lochroyan,

> O wha will shoe my bonny foot?
> And wha will glove my hand?
> And wha will bind my middle jimp
> Wi' a lang, lang linen band?

Burns knew a 'waist sae jimp' and the word came far enough south to reach the *Ingoldsby Legends*, where it accompanies 'a taper waist'. But it is jimply used in England.

KIM-KAM

THE admirable gossip John Aubrey, while recording his own affairs or 'accidents', as he justly said of a disturbed life, had a bad time in 1664. He went to France, reached Orleans, was prostrated by 'a terrible fit of the spleen and piles', returned home, fell off his horse, suffered, in a very uncomfortable corner, 'damage, which was like to have been fatall'. But he recovered sufficiently to go a-wooing, for he observes 'made my first addresse (in an ill houre) to Joane Sumner'. He next has to admit,

> This yeare all my businesses and affaires ran kim-kam. Nothing took effect, as if I had been under an ill tongue. Treacheries and enmeties in abundance against me.

Next we read 'Arrested in Chancery Lane, at Mrs. Sumner's suite'. Kim-kam indeed! But better was to follow: 'Triall with her at Sarum. Victory and 600 *li.* dammage, though devilish opposition against me'. What it was all about he does not explain. There was some more legal trouble, but from 1670 onwards he enjoyed 'a happy delitescency', a nice word for freedom from writs. Possibly Mrs. Sumner had been cast off. Aubrey must have had a gay time on the whole, but his chronicle of 'accidents' is formidable. He started very kim-kam, asserting that he had an ague while in his mother's womb, was 'born like to die' and 'got no health' till 11 or 12. After that he had 'sicknesse of vomiting for 12 houres every fortnight'. His undergraduate life went kim-kam too. 'The small-pox at Oxon, and shortly after left that ingeniouse place: and for three years led a sad life in the country.'

Not a great deal, beyond his autobiography of 'ill houres', is known of Aubrey: nor is a great deal known of kim-kam, an expression taken to mean contrary and mainly, but never very frequently, used in the seventeenth century. It appears to be much the same as Burns's 'agley'. The best-laid plans of ourselves and the mice go kim-kam south of the Border.

KITLING

A L L the diminutives seem to gain attractiveness by the termination in 'ling'. Could anything fall more heavily on the fishmonger's slab than Cod? Codling is almost lively. Darlings, younglings, striplings, moonlings (to be discussed later) skip lightly into the mind. And a kitling, to me, seems more captivating and vivacious than even the friendliest kitten. Kitlings are not so common nowadays, but they frisked in Elizabethan drama and were a symbol of wantonness to Swift. Herrick, always so sure a judge of the right and light word, was a kitlingite:

> Yet can thy humble roof maintain a choir
> Of singing crickets by the fire,
> And the brisk mouse may feed herself with crumbs
> Till that the green-eyed kitling comes.

Herrick dealt likewise in younglings. When he asked the cause of tears in the dewy primroses, he commands them

Speak, whimp'ring Younglings and make known
The Reason why
Ye droop and weep.
Is it for want of Sleep?
Or childish Lullaby?

Dogs appear to remain outside the 'ling' company. Has literature any puplings?

LIMMOCKED

THIS is a dialect word which a kindly correspondent sent me along with others no less expressive from rural Lincolnshire. It means made limp with heat. On a scorching day in that county, it seems, you might take a walk along a ramper (high, straight road running over wolds) in mulfering weather to get a good stare (view) sloshwise (diagonally) at the slamp (boggy) ground below. Then, as you came home in the duskling (twilight and pronounced 'dooslin'), you might have good cause to feel limmocked. Mulfering is a grand word for a thundery atmosphere. We have much to learn, it seems, from Lincolnshire.

MACARONI

ELIA's cashier at the South Sea House was 'one Ellis, a Cambro-Britain. . . . He wore his hair to the last, powdered and frizzed out in the fashion which I remember to have seen in caricatures of what were termed in my young days Maccaronies. He was the last of that race of beaux'.

The macaroni, or dandy, drew his name from Italy. He was a man of affected foreign habits and named after foreign fare. But to Boswell he was not foreign, just urban. 'You are a Londoner, you are a macaroni. You can't ride.' For a horse-proud age and race that was the final putting-down of a wretched Cockney pedestrian.

Macaroon seems to have had a similar origin among Italy's cereal foods. But, while a macaroni came to mean a fop, a macaroon became slang for a dolt or fool, which is odd for so delicate a sweet.

MALTWORM

THIS is surely a very satisfactory term for a drinker. It suggests everything that a cocktail-bar is not and has not: dark panelling, arm-chairs of rubbed and faded leather, old prints, frowst, and the inevitable Major — a bore, but somehow forgivable because so apt to the spot — chuntering away by the fire. In short, 'the snug'. (Some of our public-house vocabulary is wrong, e.g. saloon, but snug is proper.) The maltworm appears early in English song and revels, wriggling his way into the mid-sixteenth-century drinking catch 'Back and side go bare, go bare':

> And Tib, my wife, that as her life
> Loveth well good ale to seek,
> Full oft drinks she till ye may see
> The tears run down her cheek:
> Then doth she trowl to me the bowl
> Even as a maltworm should,
> And saith, 'Sweetheart, I took my part
> Of this jolly good ale and old'.
> Back and side go bare, go bare, etc.

Maltworm to me is the just word for the slim, weedy little man discoverable in most snugs who entirely belies all the common attributes of alcoholism by remaining lean, pallid, and rather melancholy, but not sourly so. Shakespeare certainly saw the maltworm otherwise, namely as a fellow formidably hirsute and tinted from the vat. Cries Gadshill (in a speech good enough for Sir John himself):

> I am joined with no foot land-rakers, no long-staff sixpenny strikers, none of these mad, mustachio purple-hued maltworms, but with nobility and tranquillity.

The original maltworm was a weevil and, despite Shakespearean authority, I shall continue to think of the human maltworm as a small, pale, and pertinacious drinker.

MAUDLE

'S it ye down and mardle awhile' is, I am told, carved on a seat near Wroxham in Norfolk, and mardle is a restful, pensive word which might be more widely employed. Close to it, and also East Anglian, comes maudle, which is to talk in a drunken or confused way or, actively, to besot. Maudle, as a verb, is a back-formation from maudlin, which signifies silly or sentimental through drinking, and is itself, strangely, derived from Magdalen. (Our pronunciation of Magdalen must be at least as old as Shakespeare, for the name is spelt and pronounced Maudlin in *All's Well*.) The old picture of Mary Magdalen showed her as a weeping penitent: the idea of a red-eyed and rheumy face was also associated with drinking. So first of all came the phrase 'maudlin drunk' (the fifth stage in Nashe's analysis of intoxication) and then maudlin alone to signify a soppy or sodden condition. Maudlin in the seventeenth century could still mean weeping without any alcoholic suggestion. Butler called the sad Heraclitus 'The maudlin philosopher'. Nowadays a maudlin creature is generally deemed to be sottish as well as tearful and helpless. The verb to maudle is a good one and deserves to be an East Anglian export. So does mardle.

MINIKIN

Minikin is a good word for anything small and nice. It had a special musical reference to the thin string used for the treble of the lute. Marlowe wrote:

> I cannot lisp, nor to some fiddle sing
> Nor run upon a high-stretched minikin,

and Pepys told of a Mr. Caesar who had a pretty experiment of 'angling with a minikin, a gut-string varnished over'.

A minikin-tickler was a general term for a fiddler, but minikin was also a pretty thing or creature of any kind. Minikins mince it in old songs of love and are linked with manikins in terms of affectionate regard for life's atoms and midgets.

MINIVER

H o w many who have followed the fortunes or gazed upon the image of Mrs. Miniver realize that she is Mrs. Ermine — or something similar? Miniver is 'little-vair', and vair could be either squirrel, weasel or stoat. Christina Rossetti ranked vair highly, when she rejoiced 'because my love is come to me'.

> Raise me a dais of silk and down
>   Hang it with vair and purple dyes;
> Carve it in doves and pomegranates
>   And peacocks with a hundred eyes.

Whatever it was, vair yielded fur for robes of authority, and so miniver came to be promoted and to stand for the costly and consequential ermine. But evidently Simon Eyre in Dekker's *The Shoemaker's Holiday* did not value it so very highly, for he dismissed his wife Margery with

> Vanish, Mother Miniver-cap! Vanish,* go, trip and go: meddle with your partlets and your pishery-pashery, your flewes and your whirligigs: go, rub, out of mine alley!

(Partlets are ruffs and collars. Flewes are flaps, like the hanging chaps of a hound, and whirligigs are, I surmise, hooped skirts, but the dictionaries are unhelpful here.)

Sean O'Casey couples miniver with ermine when he writes of 'Those safely sheltered under the lawn of the bishop, the miniver of the noble, the scarlet and ermine of the judge. . . .' One cannot help wondering why Jan Struther chose the name of Miniver for her middle-class madam. She is scarcely miniverial in the ermine sense.

MOMUS

J o h n A u b r e y wrote of Sir John Denham, with his usual genius for rapid portraiture, 'He was of the tallest, but a little incurvetting at his shoulders, not very robust. His hair was but thin and flaxen, with a moist curle. . . . His eie was of a kind of light goose-grey, not big, but it had a strange piercingness, not as to shining and glory, but (like a Momus) when he convers't with you, he looked into your very thoughts'. Momus was the Greek god of ridicule and so came to mean 'a captious critic'. (Aubrey adds: 'He was satyrical when he had a mind to it'.) Dekker in *The Gull's Horne-Booke* thus described the Elizabethan Theatre:

> Your Stinkard has the self-same libertie to be there in his Tobacco-Fumes, which your sweet Courtier hath: and your Carman and Tinker claime as strong a voice in their suffrage and sit to give judgment on the plaies' life and death as well as the prowdest Momus among the tribe of Critick.

Having moved among the Momi in my time, I find the word agreeable. Dekker's Momus was an amateur, the Inns-of-Court young man or University wit. Nowadays the tribe is professional, but it can be 'prowd' and witty still.

MOONLING

T o Mr. Desmond MacCarthy I owe the sweet Jonsonian moonling for a dreamy fool. One of Ben's women-characters rails at her husband as a moonling whom no wit of man can redeem from asininity. It seems a pity that so lovely a word as moon should have to be associated with idiocy. (In the matter of loveliness, I suppose the scanty use of the beautiful 'moonset' for the hour of the moon's vanishing is due to the scanty number who are about at that time to see it.) Moonling is a gentler word than moon-calf, which meant an abortion or monstrosity before it came to signify a simpleton. The moon has given its name to many a species: there are moon-ferns, moon-fishes, moon-flowers, moon-seed, and moon-wort. But only for men is the lunar prefix one of contempt. They can be moon-blind, moon-eyed, moon-faced, moonish, and moony. Shakespeare's Rosalind links moonish with apish, shallow, and fantastical and Shakespeare uses moon-calf with some frequency. But for once Jonson has the better of him. Moonling offers the most vivid notion of a nice weak-minded creature, a Mr. Skimpole.

Dickens has abundance of moonlings and a special genius for their kindly portraiture.

Mr. MacCarthy also gave me 'gowl', an old and excellent term for whine or scream. Does it differ from howl in meaning? It certainly looks magnificent and may contain something of a groan or gird. That Jonsonian wife may have gowled at her moonling husband.

MOPPET

M O P P E T is an affectionate form of mop or moppe, which was applied as a termination to the name of fish. A cod-mop was a codling; a whiting-mop was a young 'un of that unexciting tribe so curiously doomed by cooks forever to chase their own tails. It now seems strange that moppe or moppet should have become a term of human endearment, because we do not feel so tenderly about fish as did our ancestors. We call our dear ones honey or peach, kitten or flame, or any form of flower. But we somehow shrink from the imagery of the aquarium. Sprats and shrimps we reserve for unbiddable boys. Who would think of his beloved in terms of the minor clupeoids or call his Amaryllis his sardine, his elver, his stickle-back, his parr or his prawn? Yet such was the old way. 'I called her Moppe,' wrote Puttenham in *English Poesie*, 'understanding by this word a little pretty lady or tender young thing, for so we call fishes.' Moppets and Poppets have been the darlings of light comedy down the ages. Poppet is a corruption of puppet or doll and I am not sure that to call a young woman a doll seems any more complimentary than to view her as a tiddler. Moppet, however, comes amusingly and agreeably to the ear. It was applied jocosely to effeminate men and Horace Walpole several times dismissed such manikins as moppets.

MUCKENDER

W H A T a nice frank word for a handkerchief is muckender! (I take leave to doubt the polite ascriptions of its origin to a place-name.) Perhaps it has been too frank in its catarrhal suggestion to survive in centuries which have grown in gentility. It is the kind of word you expect to find in Ben Jonson — and do.

> Be of good comfort; take my muckender
> And dry thine eyes.

This is spoken by Turfe, a Kentishman, and the word may thus be deemed pastoral by its author. But it had its place in aristocratic English, or at least in lordly incivilities. The Earl of Dorset (1706) wrote of a playwright of his time:

> For thy dull fancy a muckender is fit
> To wipe the slabberings of thy snotty wit.

One gathers from this that the Earl might have applied a muckender to his own somewhat 'snotty' notions of dramatic criticism.

MULLIGRUBS

W H Y let mulligrubs become an antique only? A corruption, seemingly, of mouldy-grubs, the word first meant a depression, and then a fit of megrims or sometimes a stomach-ache. It is found in the singular and applied to a person. 'Thou art a puffe, a mulli-grube, a Metaphysicalle Coxcombe!' wrote Shirley before Dryden went back to the more orthodox 'She is in her mulligrubs'. It is more expressive than megrim, which is English for migraine. The megrim or megrims meant a headache, usually of the sickening, livery kind that descends on one side of the head. Then it means low spirits or even curious desire. Addison linked megrims with whims and freaks. But that sounds all wrong. A megrim should be a heavy article with nothing light and fantastical about it. It is a far sadder word than mulligrubs. 'To lie sick of the mulligrubs' sounds odd and might even suggest the Herodian affliction and death by worm-eating. Or mulligrubs might be some garden-blight. Yet the term also suggests to me an inner warmth, perhaps through its initial resemblance to mulligatawny, which is a Tamil word for pepper-water. Byron linked megrims with dullness.

Railing against the Stage Censorship, founded by Sir Robert Walpole as a protection against satirists far more than against salacity, the author of *Hints from Horace* wrote:

> Now to the Drama let us bend our eyes,
> Where fetter'd by Whig Walpole low she lies;
> Corruption foil'd her, for she feared her glance,
> Decorum left her, for an opera dance!
> Yet Chesterfield, whose polished pen inveighs
> 'Gainst laughter, fought for freedom in our plays:
> Uncheck'd by megrims of patrician brains
> And damning dullness of Lord Chamberlains.
> Repeal that Act! Again let Humour roam
> Wild o'er the stage — we've time for tears at home!

But the drama has had to endure the megrims and mulligrubs caused by official interference ever since.

MUMCHANCE AND MUMPSIMUS

M U M expresses the tightened lip. You cannot shout that syllable. To mum is also to mime or to act. This has led to some confusion. Mumchance originally meant a masquerade: it also meant a game of chance. And then, because the silent 'mum' was remembered as well as the mummer's 'mum', it came to signify silent or tongue-tied. So Lamb had it in that very whimsical essay' 'Upon the New Year's Coming of Age':

> Order being restored — the young lord (i.e. New Year) . . . in as few and yet as obliging words as possible assured them of entire welcome and, with a graceful turn, singling out poor *Twenty-Ninth of February*, that had sat all this while mumchance at the side-board, begged to couple his health with that of the good company before him.

Mumchance, thus used, may be deemed an error which has been justified by time and is now established as correct, in other terms 'a mumpsimus'. Mumpsimus is derived from the blunder of a priest who constantly said mumpsimus instead of sumpsimus in reciting the Mass. When corrected, he refused the instruction and continued to use the wrong term. Hence mumpsimus means a habit obstinately held, a mistake which has some sanction of time, or even the obstinate fellow who sticks to the wrong, old way.

MUSE-BROW

ELIZABETH BARRETT BROWNING has become a popular heroine of stage and screen, but I doubt whether this introduction to Wimpole Street has caused many to discover or revisit the poetry which she wrote there — or anywhere else. She must now be in the forlorn class of the Well-Neglected Classics. Yet *Sonnets from the Portuguese* are more than an exercise in passionate sonneteering. There (in No. XIX) you will find that she thus describes a gift of her adored one's poetic lock:

> As purply black as erst to Pindar's eyes
> The dim purpureal tresses gloomed athwart
> The nine white Muse-brows.

Of course Muse-brow here means a brow of the Muse, but, in view of our modern vogue for brow-estimation, surely a Muse-brow is a word to be retrieved as an adjective for minstrels of imposing forehead. Shakespeare naturally heads the team and, among the moderns, I think W. B. Yeats certainly merited a place.

Mrs. Browning had a sharp pen for the lesser breeds of Muse-brow, the miminy-piminy foot-in-the-grave young men later located by Gilbert in Castle Bunthorne.

In *Aurora Leigh* she observes:

> There are men
> Born tender, apt to pale at a trodden worm,
> Who paint for pastime, in their favourite dream,
> Spruce auto-vestments flowered with crocus-flames.

The last two lines are perfect for a species of Muse-brow Miminy.

Auto-vestments now somewhat suggest leather motoring coats, but I have not yet seen these spruced with crocus.

The consideration of Muse-brow led me to reflect on this brow business in general. When did the now inescapable 'highbrow' and 'lowbrow' arrive? Mr. Eric Partridge, chief authority on such affairs, tells me that highbrow came from America at the end of the last war and was established in a year or two. Lowbrow followed. Then we had mid-brow, which had become fairly common by 1930. I remember Sir Nigel Playfair, when defending the Lyric Theatre, Hammersmith from the charge of highbrowism, calling his programme mid-brow. The term was new to me then. The best definition of a highbrow I know is 'a person educated beyond his intelligence'. Some people would be glad to be called high-brows, but not many have such pride of brains. If Muse-brow came into use, would any accept the honour with delight?

NATURAL

WHAT word in the English language has more curious and various meanings than natural? That, of course, happens because man has never made up his mind as to what he understands by Nature. Is it the Creative or the Created Thing? Is it an essential moral principle, as in Natural Law and Natural Right, or is it an essential depravity of the sinner that is man. ('You cannot alter human nature' — most idiotic and false of parrot-phrases.) Roughly speaking, you can separate the optimists from the pessimists by their use of the word natural. The English seem to be on the gloomy side, at least in their popular usage. 'A natural' was employed to mean a blockhead or even an imbecile. 'This drivelling love,' says Mercutio, 'is like a great natural, that runs lolling up and down to hide his bauble in a hole.' Caliban is a natural to Trinculo. Pastoral English has re-tained the natural for simpleton or village idiot, the idea being, apparently, that wisdom and even sanity are abnormal.

So with wedlock. Again the English verdict is that virtue, at least if monogamy be virtue, is too much for human nature. So the bastard is called the natural, not the unnatural, child. G. K.

Chesterton said of marriage that it was a life-long battle which no man of honour could refuse and the notion of strain, which he, a combative Christian, welcomed as a challenge, has struck the averate man as excessive. To call the bastard a natural is to regard adultery as natural too. (Christianity has rarely been more than a top-dressing on the soil of English folk-lore and folk-language.) Puritanism regarded the natural man as sinful. 'You must not expect,' wrote Cromwell, 'that men of hesitating spirits, under the bondage of scruples, will be able to carry on this work, much less such as are carnal, natural.'

So we reach the extraordinary situation in which the word natural is used alike for good and for bad, for normal and for abnormal things. A perfect hand at cards, which cannot be improved by addition, is 'a natural' although it is rare, while 'a natural occurrence' is that which commonly and ordinarily happens.

One could write an entire book on the attitudes of reflective man to the myriad things called Nature and his consequent contradictory employments of the word natural. So, gravelled by abundance of matter, one abandons the colossal task. We can, on this occasion, leave it to a fine but somewhat neglected poet to provide an answer. The most pregnant summary of this problem, i.e. of the conflict between Natural Man (non-moral) and the Law of Nature which seems to imply a moral purpose, occurs in Fulke Greville's admirable lines in the last chorus of his drama *Mustapha*:

> Oh wearisome condition of Humanity!
> Born under one law, to another bound:
> Vainly begot and yet forbidden vanity,
> Created sick, commanded to be sound.
> What meaneth Nature by these diverse laws?
> Passion and reason self-division cause.
> Is it the mark or majesty of power
> To make offences that it may forgive?
> Nature herself doth her own self deflower,
> To hate those errors she herself doth give.

Has any English poet, from Shakespeare to Housman, ever

packed the burden of morality and the ache of life into a more cogent quatrain than did Greville in the opening lines of that tremendous passage?

NEIF

'GIVE me your neif, Mounseer Mustardseed', says Bottom, when he wants to have his face scratched. Nowadays one would think that he was breaking into Scottish in thus describing his hand or fist. Neif, or more commonly neive, survives abundantly in the Scots speech. Here is a passage from Lewis Grassic Gibbon describing, with his typical lilting speech that has so much of wind and weather in it, the drift of the rain on the hills of the Mearns.

> So she closed the door and went up by the track through the schlorich of the wet November moor, a windy day in the winter's neive, the hills a-cower from the bite of the wind, the whins in that wind had a moan as they moved, not a day for a dog to be out in, you'd say. But she found her father near tirred to the skin: he'd been heaving a great root up from its hold. 'Come in by and look on this fairely, lass. I knew that some childe had once farmed up here.'

Gibbon's Kincardine crofters were childes and their lasses were queans. (Quean into queen — one of the words that has risen in the world.) Is tirred for soaked at all general in use? Nobody knew better than the short-lived author of 'Sunset Song' the feel of north-easterly Scotland, with its parks (meadows) rippling in summer's green or frozen in the winter's neive.

NITHERED

THIS word has been brought to my notice as another of our picturesque words for cold. It is really a stronger term than either starved or dazed. To nither was an old word for overwhelm, crush, bring to naught. 'Winter nithers a' below' is an old Scottish saying. The richness of our vocabulary for the sensations of chill is not a compliment to our climate. Most rural dialects seem to have more graphic terms for the shivers than for the sweats. Nithered holds on in the Pennines. Where heights are Wuthering in the wild Decembers, well may the winds be nithering too.

NONPAREIL

MANY of Shakespeare's beauties, such as Olivia, Miranda, and Cleopatra, are described as 'non-pareils' in some fair-sounding line. So, less agreeably, the First Murderer in *Macbeth* just fails to be a nonpareil because he let Fleance escape. Later the word was widely scattered and came to signify various species of moth, finch, and parrakeet. Also, it was a kind of apple and so Lamb knew it. Writing of 'My First Play' Elia records his ecstasy of waiting at the pit-door. 'Oh, when shall I be such an expectant again? — with the cry of Nonpareils, an indispensable playhouse accompaniment in those days. As near as I can recollect, the fashionable pronunciation of the theatrical fruiteresses then was "Chase some oranges, chase some numparels, chase a bill of the play" — chase *pro* chuse.'

Early nineteenth-century Cockney seems to have struck a 'refaned' note now familiar to us in London's more genteel suburbs.

NUZZLE

NEARLY all anthologies rightly include Crashaw's 'The Weeper', which has:

> The dew no more will weep
> The primrose's pale cheek to deck;
> The dew no more will sleep
> Nuzzled in the lily's neck;
> Much rather would it tremble here
> And leave them both to be thy tear.

Nuzzle contains a confusion. The simplest form of nuzzling is nosing or nousling, i.e. rubbing one's nose against. 'A nousling mole' or moldiwarp is one which noses his way along. But nuzzled, as used by Crashaw, is more akin to nestled or nursled. There is an odd contradiction here. Lambs nuzzling are in fact the most fidgety and pushful of creatures, while creatures nuzzling (in the nestling sense) are tranquil and even motionless. Browning's 'A Villa nestling on Fiesole' is essentially still, still as dew 'nuzzled in the lily's neck', and essentially different from the young animal who nuzzles at his mother's nipples, 'dugging for victory' as a carnivorous human remarked in war-time when he saw the young and thriving muttons and the beeves all a-nuzzling and a-guzzling for the national benefit.

PERSON

PERSON has had a very odd history. It comes from the Latin *Persona*, which meant the mask of a mummer. So the first person was really a false, unreal person. But history has swung the meaning right round. A film-actor is to-day announced as 'appearing in person' to signify that he is there in the actual flesh and with no mere fictitious presence of mask or photograph. That is not the only reversal of fortune which has befallen the word. At one time a person meant a great person or what we call a personage. 'As I'm a person!' cries Congreve's Lady Wishfort. But nowadays to call a person a person is usually demeaning and derogatory. 'There's a person who comes in to do the rough work' is genteel house-keeper's English. The old kind of person lingers on Latinly in 'Personae Dramatis', but even by Shakespeare's time person was truly personal, as we would say, in 'Our royal person' and similar phrases. But a hint of the old notion of masquerade or assumed aspect lingers on in Quince's 'to present the person of moonshine' and possibly in Iago's line about Cassio: 'He hath a person and a smooth dispose'. Personnel became a war-time favourite of 'officialese' English. 'Anti-personnel bomb' was one of the finer flowers of this horrid growth. Our ancestors were savage in their attitude to poachers and scattered horrible devices for their capture. But at least they called these things simply and accurately 'man-traps'. Now they would be 'Anti-personnel pincer mechanisms'.

87

PETTIFOGGING

NOWADAYS nobody ever pettifogs except a lawyer. George Augustus Sala wrote of 'a pettifogging six-and-eightpenny', but usually it is 'pettifogging attorney'. This is one of many adjectives limited to a single noun. (What, for example, is ever inspissated except gloom?) The first part of the word is plain enough. But what of fogger? He is a huckster. Or, if it be true that fogger is derived from the great Bavarian merchant-house of Fugger, then he is a huckster on the grand scale, reduced by prefixing the word petty. In any case the huckstering became associated with swindling. It is assumed that the verb 'to fog', meaning to secure gain craftily, is a back-formation from fogger, but I cannot see why fogger should not be a forward-formation from fog, a nice, sharp word for cheat or cozen, as sharp indeed as its rhyme 'to cog'.

But let that pass. Why should the attorneys now have all the pettifoggery? There used to be pettifoggers in medicine and divinity and the retailing of news. The word moves well in heavy-weight company and the Tudor men knew how to load a pamphlet with this kind of weapon.

'The Packe and Fardle of these circumferaneous Jugglers and pedling Pettifoggers in Physique'. So did the old Pamphleteers make pills to purge the quack medicos.

PIGHTLE

A GEORGE BORROW word and still used in Yorkshire for a small field or croft. The origin is obscure, the variants many. A pightle of land is also a pickel of land or even a piddle of pasture. Pickel is the northern form and Pickles, a Yorkshire family name well known to radio-listeners, is explained as a derivation from the pickel of land. I take it that some of the many piddle-villages of England, which give the school-boy his laugh, are really named after pightle. An odd corruption of the pickel form of pightle is pigtail. This is in the later work of Southey and so, presumably, a Keswick usage. Miss Mitford talks of the crofts and pightles of a farm. Pight as a verb is old English for pitch or pitched. Tents could be pight on a pightle.

PILGARLIC

'Go up, thou baldhead', might have been written 'Ascend, Pilgarlic'. For the pil is peel or strip and garlic is the garlic head. Pilgarlic, from being a stripped pow or scalp, moves on from mere baldness to signify a poor old fellow or man in a bad way. It occurs thus, as I was informed by a colleague, in William Hickey's *Memoirs*. Hickey, after one of his wilder nights about town, alluded to himself as 'old Pilgarlic' coming home in woeful plight. Pilgarlic had some association with disease. There was a Jacobean treatise called *The Hunting of the Pox*, a quite pleasant Discourse between the Authour and Pild-Garlike', wherein was declared the nature, cause, and cure of this calamity. In the eighteenth and nineteenth centuries pilgarlic was fairly common for an old fool. It was usually preceded by the adjective 'poor' and employed by the author as a comment on his own follies. Sir Edmund Gosse made the adjective 'pilgarlicky' and applied it to a pitiable, decaying mind.

PIXILATED

IN the morning's *News Chronicle* I read this concerning the powerful impact of Madame Chiang upon Washington. That journal's able American correspondent, Mr. Robert Waithman, wrote as follows:

> Things which are being said and written here about Madame Chiang just now must be giving a widespread impression that a high proportion of Senators, Congressmen and correspondents, who have taken a lifelong pride in their political sales resistance, have become suddenly pixilated. But I saw it happen, and, at the risk of sounding pixilated too, I have to bear witness that Madame Chiang's voice, beauty, serenity and dialectical brilliance come very close to being irresistible.

Here again was this pixilation which had turned up in the film about Mr. Deeds. The English dictionaries, even the O.E.D., know nothing of it, but they all mention the Old English pixyled, for constrained or enchanted by an imp or fairy. Pixilated must, I resolved, be the American version of this term, since Americans so often prefer the classical form. (In America you take the elevator to your apartment instead of the lift to your flat.) There was an old English theory that, if you carried bread about with you, you would never be caught by the creatures

> Whom the untaught Shepherds call
> Pixies in their madrigal.

But that would never do in war-time.

PLEACH

PLEACH for fold or inter-twine seems now an antique, but it is a capital word and should live. Says Antony to his page Eros, when ruin is upon them:

> Would'st thou be window'd in great Rome and see
> Thy master thus with pleach'd arms, bending down
> His corrigible neck, his face subdued
> To penetrative shame, whilst the wheeled seat
> Of fortunate Caesar drawn before him, branded
> His baseness that ensued?

The 'pleached bower' in Leonato's garden is one overshadowed by interlaced branches and sprays, a nook,

> Where honeysuckles, ripened by the sun,
> Forbid the sun to enter.

Pleach survived until Tennyson and Swinburne, whose various dreams and visions of fair women included pleaching of the golden locks.

PLURISY

PLURISY is a pleasant piece of confusion. Pleurisy, the inflammation round the ribs, is Anglicized Greek, but it sounds as though it had some connection with 'plus'. Hence it became an effectively muddled term for excess carried to the limits of a disease.

Shakespeare's

> For goodness growing to a plurisy
> Dies of his own too much,

is paralleled by John Ford's

> Must your hot itch and plurisy of lust,
> The hey-day of your luxury, be fed
> Up to a surfeit?

Those lines, incidentally, might easily occur in the Closet Scene in *Hamlet*. The terminology is identical with Shakespeare's. The dramatists of that period had a tremendous stock of rich reach-me-down stuff for the deeds both of Venus and of Mars.

On the other hand, the sub-Shakespeareans, while they handle this wealth of lusty lingo, usually betray themselves in the end as being less than William. Ford, in the already quoted speech of Soranzo's from *'Tis Pity She's a Whore*, continues:

> Now I must be the dad
> To all that gallimaufry that is stuffed·
> In thy corrupted, bastard-bearing womb!
> Why must I?

To which Annabella replies, with some justice,

> Beastly man!

Ford, the Inns of Court Man, could be a good deal rougher in describing affairs of love and wedlock than was 'Shagsper, the Stratford clown', as some are pleased to call him. In short, Ford sooner fell into a plurisy of sexual explicitness.

I T is not generally known that popularity, now so popular a term for being popular, i.e. generally liked, began in a far higher estate. It was a political term for the principle of democratic or popular government. Clarendon, in his *Portrait of John Hampden*, first suggests that he would have been the perfect K.C. in a modern law-court and sovereign of any jury:

> He was of that rare affability and temper in debate, and of that seeming humility and submission of judgment, as if he brought no opinions with him, but a desire of information and instruction, yet he had so subtle a way of interrogating, and under the notion of doubts, insinuating his objections, that he left his opinions with those from whom he pretended to learn and receive them.

He then adds that Hampden, even among those least susceptible to his skill,

> always left the character of an ingenious and conscientious person. He was indeed a very wise man, and of great parts, and possessed with the most absolute spirit of popularity, that is the most absolute faculties to govern the people, of any man I ever knew.

Here Clarendon defines popularity in his own way. The noun it intensely active. Nowadays it is passive, a state of being admired or liked. In the seventeensh century it meant, not only the condition of democracy, but the active ability of a democrat to lead and to command the populus.

Incidentally Clarendon may here be guilty of confusing ingenious with ingenuous. That muddle is old and common and persists in the use of ingenuity for skill or cunning as though it were the noun of the adjective ingenious. It should, by rights, mean, as it once did, probity or candour.

PRECIOUS

In his letter to Colonel Walton on the death of his son, Oliver Cromwell wrote with his incomparable brevity:

> Sir, God hath taken away your eldest son by a cannon-shot. It brake his leg. We were necessitated to have it cut off, whereof he died ... Truly, he was exceedingly beloved in the Army of all that knew him. But few knew him, for he was a precious young man, fit for God.

The adjective precious might nowadays seem to be unflattering and suggest the prig or the poseur, especially when applied to a soldier who, apparently, was not a 'mixer'. But Cromwell, who uses the word twice in the letter and calls young Walton 'a precious child, full of glory', had no such meaning in mind. Precious had, indeed, begun to be used ironically before that. In Shakespeare scoundrels and varlets can be called precious. Othello calls Iago 'Precious villain' when he stabs Emilia. In general precious was applied to jewels, virtues and the blood of Christ, as it still is. But the idea of something affected and pretentious grew steadily and the word 'preciosity', which once meant value, now refers only to a mincing and finicking type of culture, such as that of Mercutio's 'antic, lisping, affecting fantasticoes, new tuners of accents, strange flies, pardonnez-mois'. Precious and preciosity have come into hard times and unkindly usage. Stones can still be honourably labelled thus; not so the dying soldier.

PROPER

When Skelton rhymed 'the proper violet' with 'gelofar well-set', i.e. the sturdy gilly-flower or gillyvor, he meant, I suppose, demure, for the variations of meaning attached to this word had already begun. Proper, of course, first implied ownership and then characteristic quality. Then, since what you own should be, and may be, suitable and fitting, property acquired a sense of rightness. It was on its way to become propriety. The property (characteristic) of property is to be proper. Hence we come on to the

Shakespearean and now rather pastoral English in which a proper man is a right good one and not a goody-goody one. Later on, after the ethical implication, came the distrust of ethics. The proper people were no longer worthy, but unctuous, fussy, and pretentious. So propriety, once meaning suitability, came thus to mean primness and moral exactitude. When Othello denounced the clanging of the bell in Cyprus, with 'it frights the isle from its propriety', he meant its quietude, a state both natural and decent.

The history of this word, like that of Nature, is one of fascinating interest, because it contains so much philosophy and is such a revelation of man's opinion of himself. To begin with, things proper to our state are good because we have a fair esteem of ourselves. Then morality becomes over-weening and tyrannical and we tend to dismiss propriety as a dull and oppressive condition and proper people are bores and prigs. But all the time in the English of the countryside proper lives on in a complimentary sense and is applied to anything fine, large, genuine and what Lancashire would call 'jannock'. It can even be a synonym for anything prominent or conspicuous. 'A proper young rascal' only means an outsize in rascality. Skelton, writing about 1500, deemed the violet proper and probably meant to imply that its demure beauty was suitable to its lowly but often exquisite station.

PURDONIUM and TORALIUM

I WAS reminded of Purdonium, which is Auctioneer's English for a coal-scuttle, by a correspondent who told me of Toralium, which is similar lingo for an eider-down. Latin *torus* (bed) gives the latter its veneer of scholarship, but the origin of Purdonium is a mystery, unless it is somehow based on Greek 'pur' (fire), in which case it should be Pyrdonium. The O.E.D. admits Purdonium but not Toralium. Does Purdonium survive in catalogues? Perhaps not, for my memory of its grave splendour comes from boyhood. The jargon of salesmen has many fascinations; in 1943 it is only a sorrow's crown of sorrow to think of wine-merchants' lists and their sprightly use of the flattering, if incongruous, epithet. 'This courtly and

consequential claret.' 'A reverend, indeed an episcopal, Burgundy.'
The Purdonium was obviously destined to grace the hearth of what
is now announced as a Cozy Palace in Ye Little Manorial Style by
the developers of suburban estates. House-agents' English is an
everlasting treasure. Toralium as well as Purdonium should be on
the inventory list of (may I suggest?) 'Tudor-Style Bijou Bargain
in Essex Highlands. Facing South with fine views over E. London.
Veritable Sun-trap. L'pool St., 35 mins. Handy three stations, two
golf-courses, eight cinemas, greyhounds (two tracks), foxhounds
(two packs), and super road-house. Suit City gent. with sporting
tastes'. Or again: 'Six Centuries of Romantic History, but still standing in own grounds, Nobleman's Period Seat. Stately Baronial
Home-County Gem, completely renovated, just on market. Wealth
of old oak and modern plumbing. All usual offices on ducal scale.
Timbered park a picture. Company's and ornamental water.
Forty mins. City, House of Lords, Shaftesbury Avenue.'

This High-Life jargon will doubtless return in spate, when the
housing market is itself again. May it restore purdonium to the
fireside and toralium to the bed-chamber!

QUEACHY

QUEACHY land always sounds to me as though it should be
heavy clay, stolchy stuff. One can almost hear one's boots queach-
ing as one drags them out of the tenacious mire. Perhaps it should be
wet chalk-land rather than clay, for a piece of well-sodden chalk
beats all British soils in the horrible combination of the slippery and
the sticky. But queachy is not primarily a muddy term. First of all,
it is woody, shrubby, bosky. The Elizabethan dramatists, but not
Shakespeare, have quite a deal of queach (noun for thicket) and of
queachy (or bosky) ground in their scenery. But, as is perhaps
natural in our climate, where there's a shrubbery there's a puddle
too, and queachy begins, under pressure of our wet westerly winds,
to be swampy after all.

'The damps that rise from out the queachy plots' is a line that mistily suggests to me a November morning by Magdalen Bridge in Oxford. Queachy was last of all applied to people and then meant sick or feeble. Possibly there was some confusion with queasy in this case.

QUEAN

QUEAN and queen are an odd couple. The word is the same, yet altered spelling makes a considerable difference in meaning, at least in England where quean has gone steadily downhill, while queen was passing onward and upward from throne to throne. A Scottish quean was just a sonsie lass — Burns wrote of his sonsie quean — solid, healthy, spirited, but with no suggestion of depravity, and Sir Walter Scott frequently calls a peasant girl a quean without any derogatory intention. Both quean and childe have lived on so in Scottish rustic conversation. The English quean, however, descended to the tavern and the brothel, while the alteration of a single letter gave the term an entirely different significance. 'Common queans' abound sluttishly in the old plays. There is always some suggestion of mischief, if not of vice, about our queans. The 'flaunting, extravagant quean' of Sheridan is a flighty baggage, if nothing worse. Is there any other case of a word which has thus split in two and marked the separation by two spellings, the one to import supremacy of birth and position, the other to imply baseness of degree and conduct? Byron's 'queen of queans' is applied to 'a martial scold': it might even describe, according to much English usage, the worst girl of a bad bunch.

QUIDDLE

TO quiddle is to be idle, to trifle, to be nice or finicky about things. In the sense of toying it was possible, in the Restoration drama, to quiddle with a young lady's hand and affections. Nowadays picture-houses might be described as palaces of quiddle. The other meaning of quiddle appears both in verb and noun. Emerson, commenting on the fussiness of the English gentleman, called him 'petulant and precise about his accommodation' and 'a quiddle about his toast and chop'. Several wars have since taught the Englishman to be less dainty. There is no quiddling over chops in this year of 1943. But 'When the lights go up again, all over the world', as the popular song of that year rather mournfully proclaimed, perhaps we shall recover, along with other liberties, the right to quiddle. Yes, the day will come when a housewife will be a quiddle with impunity at the fishmonger's or the butcher's counter, dismissing a sole as second-rate and rejecting a steak as trash. It is difficult to believe, as I write, that quiddling of this kind ever existed. But, now that I come to think of it, there were moments when one put aside the very notion of a fillet steak as being likely to prove unsatisfactory to one's mood. No doubt we have been taught a salutary lesson: still, may quiddling once more become a frailty within our reach!

QUODLIBETARIAN

' N o t long ago,' said Sir Max Beerbohm in his Rede lecture upon Lytton Strachey, 'I heard that agile and mellifluous quodlibetarian, Dr. Joad, saying in answer to a questioner who wanted to write good letters that anybody could write good letters; one had but to think out clearly what one wanted to say, and then set it down in the simplest terms.' The advice was criticized by Sir Max, who believes that a true gift for writing is something more than lucidity. He is generally considered to prove the truth of this belief in his own writing. Meanwhile, what is a quodlibetarian? A quodlibet (Latin for what-you-will) is a question in philosophy or ethics set as an occasion or exercise for argument. The Brains Trust is largely engaged with quodlibets. Sir Thomas More wrote of the quodlibets before 'a pot parliament', which is indeed a complimentary title for a public-house argle-bargle. Quodlibet has sprouted some imposing stems. Quodlibetical is an epithet which I shall reserve for several of my friends, one of whom, on being casually told that it's a fine day, would certainly retort in the Joadian manner, 'That all depends on what you mean by the word fine and what you mean by the word day. Do you mean a total absence of rain for twelve or twenty-four hours?' And so tenaciously onward. There is a verb 'to quodlibetificate'. My friend deserves it.

RAMBUNCTIOUS

THIS, for an uppish fellow who cannot carry corn, seems to be purely American now. It is a good, fat, formal term and might well be a re-import (so might *pernucative*, sent to me by a student of Canadian and obviously a more solemn form of our *pernickety*, whose meaning it shares).

Words beginning with 'ram' are specially dedicated to obstreperous folk and the kind of child whom nursemaids used to call a young limb, jockey or Turk. A rambunctious lad was surely a rampant 'rampallion' in childhood. 'She's back on the Ram-page,' said Joe Gargery to Pip when Mrs. Gargery, 'Tickler' in hand, was launching one of her domestic offensives. The latter end of a rambunctious fellow must be to join that loose and liquorish company whom Burns described as,

> The hairum-scairum ram-stam boys,
> The rattling squad.

The ram-stam boys would, of course, be met in a bar 'ram-jam' to the doors.

REFOCILLATE

REFOCILLATE is rare, but commoner than focillate, meaning to refresh or reanimate. Presumably it is related to focus, the hearth, and means renew the fire. Coleridge liked to have his spirits refocillated and there is a lovely use of it in Aubrey's *Life of William Prynne*, whose zeal for scholarship did not disdain refocillation through a frequent recourse to what is now commonly known as wallop:

> About every 3 hours his man was to bring him a roll and a pott of ale to refocillate his wasted spirits. So he studied and

dranke, and munched some bread; and this maintained him till night; and then he made a good supper. Now he did well not to dine, which breakes off one's fancy, which will not presently be regained: and 'tis with invention as a flux — when once it is flowing, it runnes amaine; if it is checked, flowes but *guttim*: and the like for perspiration — check it, and 'tis spoyled. Goclenius, professor at —— in Germany, did better; he kept bottles of Rhenish wine in his studie, and when his spirits wasted, dranke a good rummer of it.

We most of us know that sinking feeling which beset the learned Goclenius. Nowadays sherry or a whisky and soda are commoner refocillants; but a good rummer of Rhenish sounds well enough to me.

RESPECTABLE

I T was written of Sir Kenelm Digby, that curious Caroline figure, that 'he was such a goodly handsome person, gigantique and of great voice, and had so gracefull elocution and noble addresse that had he been dropt out of the clowdes in any part of the world, he would have made himself respected'. This use of respected may seem a little odd to us now. The adjective has come down in the world owing to our contemptuous use of the word respectable. But it was retained by old-fashioned people. A battered but genial old Corinthian who used to wiite remarkable paragraphs in the London letter of *The Manchester Guardian* once described the much-attended funeral of a well-known bookie. He ended majestically: 'Mr. Solomon was the most respected book-maker in South London.' An eighteenth-century writer would have substituted respectable for respected without change of sense. But respectable has very largely lost its old quality: it now means either moral in tone or moderate in size. 'A respectable army' suggests that it is just sufficient. 'A respectable citizen' means a worthy, black-coated, perhaps rather priggish little man, a blameless ratepayer. But a respectable army of old was a formidable one and a respectable man was a person to whom one genuinely looked up.

RICKLE, or sometimes ruckle, is a heap and often has the secondary connotation of an untidy collection of worthless stuff. The word is mainly northern and Scottish in usage and is often extremely effective. I remember an old Scots body referring thus to the gear in a house taken furnished by my father. 'Furniture indeed! There's nicht but a rickle of auld sticks.' The adjective ruckly occurs in a similar way in R. B. Cunninghame Graham's grim story called *Beattock for Moffat*, in which a dying Scotsman is somehow conveyed from Euston across the Border in order to gasp his last in Scottish air. Here is some of his brother's cheerful conversation, designed to get him yet breathing into the nobler air past Gretna:

> Ye ken, we've got a braw new hearse outby, sort of Epescopalian-lookin' wi' gless a' roond, so's ye can see the kist. Very conceity too, they mak' the hearses noo-a-days. I min' when they were jist auld sort o' ruckly boxes, awfu' licht, ye ken, upon the springs, and just went dodderin' alang, the body swingin' to and fro as if it would flee richt oot. The roads, ye ken, were no nigh and so richtly metalled in thae days.

The change in mortician's modes from the ruckly to the conceity has a certain macabre charm.

The rick of hay or corn is a shorter form of rickle. Also tidier. Rickles and ruckles are slap-dash assortments. Tumbledown houses are rickles of brick and plaster, just as flimsy furnishings are rickles of wood and nails, poor rickly, ruckly things.

RUNAGATE

THE runagate is a seventeenth-century type of renegade or man who reneges. (Many correspondents, by the way, have assured me that renege is still common coin in some card-rooms.) Milton used the word simply to mean opponents or opposites. 'Go on, both hand in hand, O nations never to be disunited!' he wrote (with a certain prophetic aptitude to the Anglo-American relations of to-day and to-morrow), 'then shall the hardest difficulties smooth out themselves before ye; envy shall sing to hell, craft and malice be confounded, whether it be homebred mischief or outlandish cunning: yea, other nations will then covet to serve ye, for lordship and victory are but the pages of justice and virtue. Commit securely to true wisdom the vanquishing and uncasing of craft and subtlety, which are but her two runagates: join your invincible might to do worthy and godlike deeds; and then he that seeks to break your union, a cleaving curse be his inheritance to all generations.'

So much for Isolationist runagates! The runagate, from being a rebel or deserter, became (mistakenly) a wanderer and outcast and so a generally disreputable person. Cain in the older Bibles was condemned to be 'a vagabond and runnagate in the earth'. The seventeenth century was fond of the word, whether for translation of Scripture or political declamation. But now the runagates continue in their scarcity. A pity, for the term runs well off the tongue.

SALLOW

SALLOW is not so beautiful a word as willow, to whose species it belongs. But it seems to share the mournful loveliness with which willow is always clothed in English poetry and it continually appears to grace our water-music.

> Then in a wailful choir the small gnats mourn
> Among the river sallows

is perfect Keats.
While

> Look, look! A May-mess, like on orchard boughs:
> Look! March-blooms, like on meal'd-with-yellow sallows

is typical Manley Hopkins.
I take it that when he sang

> Down by the salley gardens my love and I did meet;
> She passed the salley gardens with little snow-white feet,

Yeats was thinking of willow-shadowed lawns.

Sallow as an adjective is linked by the lexicographers with the French *sale* and given a mean and grubby significance, but I believe that Hopkins offered us the right idea in his 'meal'd-with-yellow sallows'. That is surely the kind of tint which Collins had in mind when he wrote of Evening that 'sallow Autumn fills thy lap with leaves'. He was not demeaning autumn, but thinking of 'the sere, the yellow leaf', whose variations on creamy and light golden hues so embellish the small bushes at the fall of the year.

SANCTIMOODY

THIS engaging word I owe to a friend's report of rural tavern-talk. Sometimes there bubbles up from the subconscious, stimulated by a pint of beer, such verbal felicities as this. Were not Sankey and Moody great evangelists and surpassingly righteous? Is not the sanctimonious fellow also inclined to dark looks and moody ways? Very well, then sanctimoody is the adjective for him. 'Thou concludest,' said Lucio, 'like the sanctimonious pirate that went to sea with the Ten Commandments but scraped one out of the table.' Captain Hook and Smee between them had their sanctimoody aspects. But we need not limit so grand a condemnation to the sea-dogs. Sanctimoody is good enough for such land-animals as the great Dickensian humbugs.

These rustic confusions with happy results are fairly common and sometimes lead to satire quite beyond the notions of the speaker. Of a rich gentleman who had just taken and altered an old farm, a labourer said to me, 'He's had it all re-moderned'. The word re-modern is delightful in its ironic reflection on the vanity of vogues and the transience of the up-to-date. An accidental sarcasm, but most pregnant.

SCOBBERLOTCHER

THE O.E.D. knows only of this strange monster that it may be connected with Scopperloit, an old word for leisure or idleness.

Scobberlotcher I found along with some other weird terms of abuse. It occurs in Aubrey's description of that 'don of might', Dr. Ralph Kettell, President of Trinity, Oxford, in the sixteen-forties. Here is the passage:

> Dr. Kettell, when he scolded at the idle young boies of his colledge, he used these names, viz. Turds, Tarrarags (these were the worst sort, rude rakells), Rascal-Jacks, Blindcinques, Scobberlotchers (these did no hurt, were sober, but went idleing about the grove with their hands in the pocketts and telling the number of the trees there or so).

Scobberlotchery does not seem, on the whole, to be a desperate form of dissipation. Nowadays it might pass for a prelude to silviculture. Rake-hell I always like, especially in its adjectival form, rake-helly. The learned inform us that rake-hell does not mean a hell-raker, but comes from an Old English adjective rakel or rackle, meaning disorderly. But does it matter? Anyhow, the rake-hells and scobberlotchers won't care.

Kettell, who had 'a terrible gigantique aspect with his sharp grey eies', was not always ferocious. True, he was 'irreconcileable to long haire' and would carry 'a paire of cizers in the muffe which he commonly wore' and with these pounce on the superfluous tresses of his more hirsute undergraduates while they sat in hall. But he 'sang in a shrill, high treble' and he had a humane cure for tippling and a shrewd knowledge of how to 'keep the boys at home':

> He observed that the houses (i.e. Colleges) that had the smallest beer had most drunkards, for it forced them to go to the town to comfort their stomachs: wherefor Dr. Kettell always had in his College excellent beer, not better to be had in Oxon: so that we could not goe to any other place but for the worse and we had the fewest drunkards of any howse in Oxford.

It is a fascinating picture that Aubrey gives of his College. Did he ever acquire the curious vice of tree-counting in the grove with hands in pocket? Was he a Scobberlotcher in the President's eye or was he — perhaps worse — a Tarrarag? Or even a Blindcinque?

SCOW

A SCHOOLMASTER, writing from Merseyside, has given me scow for play truant. It would be too easy (and also a pity) to let this book be overladen with slang or argot of any kind, but it is noteworthy that schoolboy (or girl) slang has retained many good old English terms which have fallen out of general use. Is scow one of them? Examples are cog for cheat, which in my previous book I recommended our political speakers and writers to recover from the lexicons of Shakespeare and Burke. Several correspondents (one from Ireland) have informed me that cogging is still common for cribbing in their schools, while miching for playing truant, i.e. scowing in the North-West, is reported from South Wales. Miching was Elizabethan English for trespassing or making mischief. I never heard of cogging at school, but 'chiselling' (for cheating) was common with us. That seems to be still frequent in Ireland. Sean O'Casey's characters frequently speak of their enemies as 'chiselurs' - as he spells them.

SHAME-FAST AND SHENT

OUR words ending in fast, meaning fixed, dwindle away. Steadfast is steadfast still, but the admirable bed-fast has yielded to bed-ridden, good enough but not so expressive as the older term with its hint of real imprisonment. Bed-fast lingers, I know, in the north of England, but I never hear it in the south. Shame-fast has been altered by error to shame-faced. The mistake took place early. Chaucer's 'shame-fast chastitee', that is purity firmly rooted in modesty, had become shame-fac'd by Shakespeare's time and was the general spelling of the seventeenth century. Shame-faced is, of course, a striking epithet, but not quite as powerful as in its earlier form. A word for shamed which has vanished is shent, past participle of 'shend', which meant to scold, put to shame, or even destroy. It seems an archaism and out of place in Keats:

The Centaur's arrow ready seems to pierce
Some enemy: far forth his bow is bent
Into the blue of heaven. He'll be shent,
    Pale unrelentor,
When he shall hear the wedding lutes a-playing.

Shent is Shakespearean. Hamlet applies it to his mother and Mrs. Quickly has it too. But even here it has an elderly air and Spenser, whose fashion was to be a little out of fashion, is your true author for shending. With him loyaltie is not only 'foully shent', but naturally too.

SKELLUM

THIS is an old Dutch immigrant which has survived best in the north. Scolding words are naturally vigorous and picturesque and skellum seems to be the right term for a wrong'un. So it was lustily used by Jonson and Pepys. It occurs in a familiar passage at the beginning of Burns's 'Tam o' Shanter':

She tauld thee weel thou wast a skellum,
A bletherin', blusterin', drunken blellum.

I came across it recently in one of Dorothy Una Ratcliffe's lively Yorkshire sketches. She is a writer who has many good Pennine tales and terms. This, for example, of an odd job man (more odd than job): 'A raffling skeellum ragabash'. Raffle, for rubbish, is old English and so is ragabash for an idle fellow. I have seen this charming description of the illiterates in 1609: 'The veriest lack-latines and un-Alphabeticall raggabashes that ever bred lowse.' If skellum and ragabash still hold out in the hill-country, it is a good sign that the flattening influence of urban, educational, 'Southern English' has not crushed all our lively old words. I should like to think that a shepherd on either side of Tweed or at large in Swaledale or Craven would understand what you meant by a 'raffling skeellum ragabash'. How many would do so in Leeds?

SLEAVE

To the vast majority of *Macbeth's* readers and audiences 'the ravelled sleave of care' means, I suppose, a frayed or loose sleeve. But sleave has nothing to do with sleeve. It is a thin silk obtained by parting thicker silk, a floss-silk. So the 'ravelled sleave' is ragged, unstitched silk. The word is also a verb, and was so used by John Donne in his invitation to the river, but not to angle; such savage practice was for others:

> Come live with me and be my love
> And we will some new pleasures prove
> Of golden sands and crystal books
> With silken lines and silver hooks.

He would spare 'the enamell'd fish':

> Let coarse bold hands, from slimy nest
> The bedded fish in banks outwrest:
> Let curious traitors sleave silk flies
> To witch poor wand'ring fishes' eyes.

Sleave here is tease out (and so contrive) a lure of silken floss.

SLOTTERY

My note on stolchy and clarty brought considerable comment from the North, where clarty is a favourite for muddy. There is much to be said for remembering slottery in November.

> Now that the Fields are dank and ways are mire,

as Milton wrote to his 'Lawrence of vertuous father vertuous son'.

Slotter is old English for dirt (hence slut) and the fifteenth century called dirty folk 'slotterbugges', which is a lively anticipation of the recent 'jitterbugs' and gives it medieval precedent. 'Sl' is the favourite beginning of our mucky words. Slobber, slub, slubber, slubberdegullion (a variant for slotterbugge which occurs in Butler's *Hudibras*), slime, sludge, slur, slush — they go squelching nicely along on the clarty, stolchy, slottery way.

SLUG-HORN

To come across the word slug-horn is not impossible, without recourse to the Gothic pretences and bogus antiquarian diction of a Chatterton. Browning's 'Childe Roland', a poem with a deal of odd and energetic vocabulary, ends

> And yet
> Dauntless the slug-horn to my lips I set;
> And blew. 'Childe Roland to the Dark Tower Came'.

A slug-horn suggests a dark and shiny tube of an odious nature; in fact it is only a mistake. Slug-horn is a corruption of the Gaelic Sluagh-ghairm (cry of the host), which is more familiar to us as a slogan. You cannot blow a slogan or even a slug-horn, unless you think that Browning's authority is sufficient to turn the word into a trumpet. One might, of course, introduce slug-horn as a variant for the now abominably over-worked slogan. So the Big Advertising Chief, entering his office in the morning, might greet his wights and scullions with, 'To it, varlets! What slug-horn for to-day?'

SMITTLE

THIS adjective appears to be Northern only. A Cumbrian correspondent sent it me. 'We used it for "likely". If you were shown a pool or run in the Derwent likely to hold trout, or came to a marsh (when shooting) where duck might be, you'd say, "Hist, yon's a smittle spot".' Since then I have come across smittle in some dialect reading and it has apparently found its way to the verge of Dictionary-English. It primarily meant infectious and was used of diseases. 'This house is smittle of rheumatics' or 'The village is smittlish with fever'. Then it came to have a more favourable implication and signified that which 'takes' or yields. Indeed, it became almost a synonym for fertile. A bull whose cows never failed to calve was smittle. So, too, as my correspondent pointed out, was land or water which provided the hunter with his prey.

It is an effective little word, but never seems to have travelled far from the fells and dales, of which it has an excellent and native smack.

SNEAP, SNOB, and SNUB

FEW words have stood on their head more completely than snob, which began as a shoemaker, was 'town' as opposed to 'gown' in Cambridge, and so generally proletarian. 'A person belonging to the lower ranks of society: having no pretensions to rank or gentility.' Then it became exactly the opposite, 'A person admiring, apeing, and pretending to gentility.' Nobody knows the origin of snob. Everybody, especially the foreigner, likes to use it. 'Très snob' has endeared itself to the French, even as an expression of praise and delight. Could not a Gents' Suiting, *pour la chasse*, be labelled 'Très snob'?

Words beginning in 'Sn' frequently betray contempt. So, if snobs are fawning creatures, they are exceptions to the rule. But when the snob is spurning or rebuking his supposed inferiors, he conforms to the habit of his first letters. Here is a catalogue of proud, contemptuous 'Sn's' — sneer, snib, snicker, sniff, sneap, snotty or snooty, snub, snuffy. Sneap is the most dignified of these, a word of pedigree as well as of pride. Falstaff used sneap for rebuff: 'I will not undergo this sneap without reply.' The adjective sneaping was employed for a pinching or withering quality in the weather:

> Biron is like an envious, sneaping frost
> That bites the first-born infants of the spring.

(Sneaping winds in Scotland are also snell, another 'Sn'.) It is regrettable that snub should have so far grown in favour as to make us forgetful of sneap. Alison Uttley in her book, already quoted, of a north-country childhood's memories writes:

> Anyone who had been snubbed or repressed into silence before other people was said to have been 'sneaped'. A haughty woman would sneap another, an overbearing man would sneap his wife, the wintry-wind sneaped us to silence.

Snirrup or snurp is (or was) a Northern term for turning up the nose.

> As seun as she fund I depended on labour
> She snirpt up her nose and nae mair leuked at me

occurs in a Cumbrian ballad.

SORNER

I WAS puzzled by 'sorner' when I came across it in a theatre notice by James Agate. He talked of Falstaff as an old sorner and fribble. Fribble, I knew, but sorner was a stranger, though its meaning of 'sponge' fairly plain. The word is commoner in Scotland than England. To sorn originally meant 'to trouble or harass by exacting free quarters and maintenance' and then came to suggest cadging in general. Sir Walter Scott used it now and again and spoke of himself, when beset by visitors, as a sornee. Legally it was applied to 'masterful beggars' whose vagabondage included demands for free lodging. Scott included sorners with thiggers: these latter were beggars. The two words were common companions north of the Tweed and applied especially to cattle-thieving vagrants who took a free sleep in the farm before they lifted its stock.

SOVEREIGN

A MYRIAD shades of meaning has this well-sounding word possessed, ranging from majesty to money and being applied by poets to every kind of supremacy and indeed to any species of excellence. Cures, charms and simples were sovereign in their efficacy: flowers could be sovereign simply in elegance. When Skelton praised

> The ruddy rosary
> The sovran rosemary
> The pretty strawberry

he was not, one feels, putting rosemary at the head of the list. Sovran was his compliment, not his marking in the examiner's sense. Shakespeare used the word lavishly, attaching it to anything from a kiss to a medical prescription. A glorious morning could

> Flatter the mountain-tops with sovereign eye

and a night could equally be

> The sovereign mistress of true melancholy.

Olivia's rejection of Orsino's suit made her 'yon same sovereign cruelty'.

Nowadays we keep sovereign mainly for political power. The Treasury note has ousted the golden piece, though I think that the announcements of prizes in horse-races and other sporting events still carry that solid-sounding brevity, 'Sov.' 'Of a thousand sovs.' It rings true as the best coin and sounds like real money.

SPUNGY

SPUNGY, or as we now spell it, spongy, always strikes the eye and ear. Its softness of sound perfectly suggests the absorbency of its nature. Long before Mr. Soapy Sponge was invented, human sponges had been sucking up liquor or money or advantage. Portia, declining to be married to a spunge, referred to drink, but Hamlet called Rosencrantz a spunge for soaking up the king's rewards and for being in turn squeezed dry. Hector in *Troilus and Cressida* said:

> There is no lady of more softer bowels
> More spungy to suck in the sense of fear . . .

But Lady Macbeth meant drunken by spungy, when she described the well-dined and well-wined chamberlains of the king

> When in swinish sleep
> Their drenchèd natures lie as in a death,
> What cannot you and I perform upon
> The unguarded Duncan? What not put upon
> His spungy officers?

Elsewhere Shakespeare uses spungy of weather and climate. April and the South are both spungy to him. With his love for verbs beginning with 'dis' he makes Enobarbus say in his despair:

> The poisonous damp of night disponge upon me.

When Donne was bidding his mistress remain in England and warning her against the foreigner, he observed:

> Nor spungy, hydroptic Dutch shall thee displease
> If thou stay here.

Hydroptic does not apparently refer to the moist eyes of the Old Soak, but to his generally dropsical condition. In the same elegy, by the way, Donne describes our nearer neighbours as

> Men of France, changeable chameleons,
> Spitals of diseases, shops of fashions,
> Love's fuellers and the lightest company
> Of players which upon the world's stage be.

The Dean of St. Paul's had not a smooth pen nor did he rhyme with grace. But he could be as sharp in his censure as profound in his morbidity of contemplation. And 'changeable chameleons' seems to be justified by so much of recent French history.

Coming to our own time, we have one of Sean O'Casey's characters crying, 'This spongy leaden sky is Dublin: these tomby houses is Dublin too — Dublin's scurvy body. And we've Dublin's silver soul.' After which the young lady, perhaps a little spongy in another sense, spits.

SWINK

IT is odd that Shakespeare missed the rustic Swink, meaning labour, both as noun and verb, and sometimes used as a verb meaning to 'drink or carouse'. Spenser had used it and Milton's 'swink't hedger' remains familiar. Francis Thompson described 'The Poppy',

> lethargied with fierce bliss
> Hot as a swinked gipsy is.

I am assured that it is still in use on the Cotswolds, and a Tewkesbury friend also recounts a surviving use of the superb past-participle, forswunk. Could any word better express the collapsing state of one who has been all day at some hot and galling drudgery of house or land?

I trenched and hoed and weeded

sang A. E. Housman, not, I surmise, having done anything of the sort. If indeed he had so turned from Latin texts to garden-tools, he would certainly have been forswunk. Trenching and hoeing and weeding are genuine swink.

SYLLABUB AND TATNAM

S Y L L A B U B , or sillabub (sometimes syllybub), was a dish of milk curdled with wine and given various flavours. Is the word, or the article, ever served up nowadays? One hears of syllabubs in Early Victorian England: Tom Brown knew about them and so did Mr. Soapy Sponge. One meets them commonly in the accounts of Restoration pleasuring. An outing in the gardens usually led to a syllabub for two before it proceeded to become a more serious escapade. This, from Wycherley's *The Gentleman Dancing Master*, gives a handsome list of the recreations awaiting the London miss in 1672, that is if she had more freedom than the young ladies in the play:

> PRUE: 'Tis true, Miss, two poor young creatures as we are!
> HIPPOLITA: Not suffer'd to see a play in a twelve month!
> PRUE: Nor to go to *Punchinello* nor Paradise!
> HIP: Nor to take a Ramble to the Park nor Mulberry-garden!
> PRUE: Nor to *Tatnam-Court* nor Islington!
> HIP: Nor to eat a sillybub in new Spring-garden with a Cousin!
> PRUE: Nor to drink a Pint of Wine with a Friend at the Prince in the Sun!

HIP: Nor to hear a Fiddle in good Company!

PRUE: Nor to hear the Organs and Tongs at the Gun in *Moorfields*!

The allusion to Tatnam-Court is interesting, since that a. de of bliss left its name behind. (Mulberry-garden was replaced by Buckingham Palace.) The long, cumbrous, and now meaningless name of Tottenham Court Road is an odd survival. When the early London tubes had conductors to open and shut the train-gates they had to warn the passengers by announcing the next station. In this case it soon became 'Torra Corra next' and Torra Corra lives upon the tongues of bus-conductors. Tothill, Totenhall, Tatnam or Tottenham Court was a famous manor on whose grounds Fitzroy Square was ultimately built. But, while it remained a nobleman's seat until the middle of the eighteenth century, it had long been surrounded by pleasure-gardens and famous for its syllabubic confections. There is a reference in Ben Jonson to 'courting it to Totnam to eat cream' and in 1648 people were fined a shilling a-piece for drinking at Tattenhall Court on the Sabbath. Gay wrote of spring, when

> Love flies the dusty town for shady woods,
> Then Tottenham Fields with roving beauty swarm.

The Adam and Eve was a great beer-garden of that area and the name still lingers, but without benefit of gardens, at the corner of Euston Road. None the less the view of Hampstead heights seen from 'Torra Corra' is still one of the sylvan surprises and delights of London, a syllabub for the senses.

TOADY

HERE seems to be the perfect term for a fawning, sycophantic creature. It is short, slimy, odious and brilliantly hits the mark either as verb or noun. Its origin is curious. It is an abbreviation of toad-eater. The toad-eater was the hanger-on of a charlatan or medical mountebank who went about demonstrating his cures.

The wretched assistant had to eat toads (or a mock-toad, much as turtles are mocked), since toads were generally believed to be poisonous, and then he was publicly and profitably healed (I refuse to say rehabilitated) by his master's art. The toad-eater was thus what we now call 'a stooge', and the abbreviated term toady did not oust the full term until the nineteenth century. In the eighteenth a politician's hanger-on was called his toad-eater. Doubtless, when the change was made to toady, the fact that toady had long been an adjective meaning toad-like and so slimy or despicable helped the alteration. But toady in essence is not the man who resembles a toad but the poor wretch who, to earn his living, used to swallow it.

TREACLE

A CORRESPONDENT who is a devotee of old shop-signs sent me the following from Cornwall:

> Bibles, Buckets and Boots,
> Godley Bukes and Grinding Stones,
> Trousers Testaments and Tea-Kittles,
> Everything to buy and sell here
> Except Treacle. Best prices paid
> For Whale-Bone Staze.

J. W. NINNIS.   1835

The strong objection to treacle taken by the devout Mr. Ninnis set me thinking about that queer word. It began its English life as triacle, a cousin of therapy (Italian teriaca), and meant an antidote for a bite. Salves and treacles went as much together as pills and potions. It is odd now to think that Milton could write of 'the Sovran treacle of sound doctrine', following the common medieval usage of treacle as a means of salve and salvation. The name of Jesus was called 'holsomest tryacle' by Lydgate. (Triacle or treacle used for balm gave its name to the Treacle Bible.) Then treacle flowed out of the pulpit onto the counter and left the apothecary's for the grocer's shop. It became the 'uncrystallized syrup produced in the process of refining sugar'. Also 'an inspissated saccharine juice obtained from trees and plants'. It is fascinating to find the word inspissated applied to something other than gloom. There are certain adjectives which are only used in general with a single noun and inspissated is one of them, as I observed in my note on pettifogging. The really bad writer never ever mentions gloom, especially in relation to works of art, without putting inspissated in front of it; probably he has no idea what it means.

So treacle, which had once been the symbol of strong, curative, cleansing power, became the common metaphor for suggestion of cloying and sickly matters. It was the eighteenth century that set treacle oozing on the downward path and reaching its present 'sticky end', as the slang phrase goes; a sticky end, but not a bad one, for a good dollop of treacle or of the gentler 'golden syrup' is an article generally approved, and the 'treacly puddin',' of which Jay Laurier used to sing with such relish in the music-halls, is an excellent comfort on a wintry day. Shakespeare never used treacle for salve, and as a sweetmeat it was still unknown in his time. The Tudor for lollypop was 'candy' and here, as so often, the Americans have kept the old usage. Talk of candy never seems quite normal English in England, but Shakespeare used candy as an adjective ('What a candy deal of courtesy') and also in the verb discandy for melt away or desert. Candy was commonly a verb for sweeten or crystallize in Tudor English.

TRINKLEMENT

THERE is something nicely dismissive about the termination 'ment'. When Bacon was considering the superficial elegances of the Tudor and Jacobean masque with its lavish outlay on costumes, disguises, perfumes, lights and so on, he dismissed these grandeurs as toys and 'petty wonderments'. He might have used the term 'trinklement' which lingers in the North. A correspondent has sent me 'tranklement' as her version of the word. Trinklement is a happy collision of trinket and oddment. Trinklements include everything in a pedlar's pack, the whole range of Autolycan stock-in-trade, and can be applied derisively to larger matters.

READING that General Eisenhower had 'slept in his truckle-bed', I remembered how often truckle-beds had appeared in old stories of my boyhood's pleasure. Yet I was vague about the article. What precisely was it? What exactly earned it the name of truckle? Had it anything to do with the Scots trachle or trauchle, which means to tire out, with trauchle also employed as a noun for hard toil. So 'he went off to his trauchle' wrote Lewis Grassic Gibbon of the slaving crofter, greedy for more earth, in his fine short story of land-hunger called *Clay*. Was the trauchle-bed that of a poor, tired man? No, truckle-bed does not mean the labourer's simple cot. It was the small trolley-bed on truckles or castors which used to be pushed under the large standing bed, with which it was frequently contrasted. The lowlier party had the truckle. 'To bed all alone and my Will in the truckle-bed' (Pepys). The old-style tutor could expect nothing better. Bishop Joseph Hall (1574-1656), in his amusing picture of the usher in private service, explained that:

> A gentle squire would gladly entertain
> Into his house some trencher chapelain;
> Some willing man that might instruct his sons,
> And that would stand to good conditions.
> First, that he lie upon the truckle-bed
> Whiles his young master lieth o'er his head.
> Second that he do on no default
> Ever presume to sit above the salt.
> Third that he never change his trencher twice.
> Fourth that he use all common courtesies:
> Sit bare at meals and one half rise and wait.
> Last, that he never his young master beat,
> But he must ask his mother to define,
> How many jerks she would his breech should line.
> All these observed, he could contented be
> To give five marks and winter livery.

(Jerk, of course, is here a cut with the cane.)

From the inferior position of the truckle-bed, under the standing-bed, came the idea of truckling as acting in an inferior way, fawning, surrendering. Truckle was also a verb for sleeping in a lowly way, but the usage has vanished. Hall suggests that the truckle-bed remained under the standing-bed, but its name hints strongly that it was pulled out. If the beds remained one on top of the other, the gentleman below must have had a stuffy night, but our ancestors usually preferred the snug to the snell in the matter of aeration.

TWANKY (ALSO SERENDIPITY)

I HAD often wondered why into the story of Aladdin our Pantomime tradition should have imported a lady called the Widow Twanky, usually to be seen in an a-kimbo condition or washing out 'the short and simple flannels of the poor'. Possibly for the same reason that Pantomime imported Will Atkins v.c. into the story of Robinson Crusoe, namely that parts have to be found for comedians, whatever the story may contain. Widow, yes. But why Twanky? Was she a spanker, for 'twanking' is old, and in some places enduring, school-boy slang for caning. No, the true origin occurred to me when I realized that Twankai in China was a Victorian term for China tea and so for tea in general. 'We'll have a roaring pot of Twankay' occurs in Thackeray. So Widow Twanky is the Pantomime English for a tea-swilling old woman.

The naming of a woman from a tea-garden reminds me of another gift from tea-country, that is Serendipity. Serendip was the old name for Ceylon and Serendipity is Horace Walpole's creation, based on a fairy-tale about three men of Serendip who were always making lucky discoveries. The essence of Serendipity is to go in search of one thing and find another. Bloomsbury used to have a Serendipity Bookshop, but now the term is scarce. The last time I heard it was in one of the mock-Victorian lectures so superbly delivered by Robert Eddison at the Players' Club. To go to these entertainments is usually to enjoy some serendipity in vaudeville.

P E O P L E who are fond of words have a perpetual banquet spread for them in any garden. Kipling gave a musical expression to an obvious truth when he wrote that our flowers 'sing themselves': it was the kind of statement which he could easily prove in rhyme by marshalling the examples, dittany, elecampane, and the rest. What of the fishmonger's slab? The commoner sea-fish, cod, haddock, hake, etc. fall heavily on the ear. The fresh-water fish are also unlucky in their naming. Trout, for example, a creature dapper and dappled, lithe and swift beyond description, demands a far more expressive title. So squat and absurd is trout that we apply it in slang to foolish old folk. To call somebody 'a silly old trout' is not rude only to the object of the remark. It is an insult to the liveliest of creatures and the lively water in which he ruminates and darts.

The coarse fisherman's monosyllabic prey, pike, chub, dace, perch, roach, bream, etc. are scarcely the stuff that poetry is made of, but the old rhymers could make a ballad of an angler's basket none the less. John Dennys, that happy water-poet of England's Middle-West, has this, for example, when discussing the Worm as Bait (date 1613):

> And with this bait hath often taken been
> The Salmon fair, of River fish the best;
> The Shad that in the Spring-time cometh in,
> The Suant swift, that is not set by least.
> The Bocher sweet, the pleasant Flounder then,
> The Peele, the Tweate, the Batling, and the rest;
> With many more that in the deep doe lye
> Of Avon, Uske, of Severne and of Wye.

This has brought me to Tweate (or Twaite) with which I headed the note. The Shad is a 'clupeoid' fish of which the British species are the Allice and the Tweate. (Clupeoid means small river fish akin to the herring.) Shad, I am told, come up the Severn as far as Tewkesbury. But let us not become too learned. As far as exact identity goes, we may leave 'the Bocher sweet' and also the Batling

to the erudite piscators. We shall be happy to roll the words upon
our tongues. Peele, Tweate and Batling, what an admirable firm
of accountants or solicitors! They would be perfect for handling
the business of The Worm Fishers' Club, a society which I have
secretly longed to form, especially when enjoying (free) the saddle
of lamb and claret of the Fly Fishers. Was it wrong of a pampered
guest to resent the Club's seigneurial disdain of any methods but
their own? My idea of fishing is to catch something in order not to
look a fool — and the sooner over with all this tangle of line, hook
and trouble the better. Worm fishing, when you have cajoled or
hired a small boy to get the worms, is the simplest way out. When
Worm Fishers have their place in Piccadilly, the immortal memory
of John Dennys shall be drunk. Incidentally, if any maker of plays
or films lifts the firm of Peele, Tweate & Batling from this page, I
stipulate only that, while he may cast Peele as he will, Tweate shall
be played by Mr. Robertson Hare and Batling by Mr. Alfred
Drayton.

VERMILION

A s fair a sonnet as any in all Shakespeare's book is that which
opens,

> From you have I been absent in the spring
> When proud-pied April, drest in all his trim,
> Hath put a spirit of youth in everything,
> That heavy Saturn laught and leapt with him.
> Yet, nor the lays of birds nor the sweet smell
> Of different flowers in odour and in hue
> Could make me any summer's story tell,
> Or from their proud lap pluck them where they grew.
> Nor did I wonder at the lily's white,
> Nor praise the deep vermilion in the rose:

To me the last line is the loveliest. Rose is a word which always
reverberates beautifully and how well vermilion rides with it!
Vermilion is 'cinnabar or red crystalline mercuric sulphide' and
the paint derived therefrom. Poets have preferred vermeil. Gray's

morn has 'vermeil cheek and whisper soft', but vermilion for me is the finer-sounding epithet. Blushes and blood are frequently vermilion, but especially it is the rose which claims the term. Here is Lovelace on that flower:

> Vermilion ball that's given
> From lip to lip in heaven:
> Love's couch's coverlid;
> Haste, haste to make his bed.

Darley dismisses as less than

> A tender heart, a loyal mind

the allurements of

> A blooming pair of vermeil cheeks
> Like Hebis in her ruddiest hours
> A breath that softer music speaks
> Than summer winds a-wooing flowers.

The ruddy adjectives are certainly the most attractive in our tongue. Compare vermeil, vermilion, cherry, coral, crimson, cremasie, russet, rubious, scarlet and so on with indigo, ultramarine, Prussian and the other blues. The greens are sadly limited. Yes, for good looks and good noises the Reds have it in this election.

VESUVIAN

DOES any member of the Old and Bold still call a match a Vesuvian, a term which paid fiery and handsome honours indeed to the eruptive splutter of a fusee? Matches were Vesuvians to Ouida and her Guardsmen:

> The hangings of the room were silken and rose-coloured, and a delicious confusion prevailed through it pell-mell — box-spurs, hunting-stirrups, cartridge-cases, curb-chains, muzzle-loaders, hunting-flasks, and white gauntlets being mixed up with Paris novels, pink notes, point-lace ties, bracelets, and bouquets to be dispatched to various destinations, and velvet and silk bags for bank-notes, cigars, or vesuvians,

embroidered by feminine fingers and as useless as those pretty fingers themselves.

This astonishing den belonged to

> . . . the Hon. Bertie himself, second son of Viscount Royallieu, known generally in the Brigades as 'Beauty'. The appellative, gained at Eton, was in no way undeserved.

Of this Beauty it was later stated:

> His features were exceedingly fair, fair as the fairest girl's; his hair was of the softest, silkiest, brightest chestnut; his mouth very beautifully shaped; on the whole, with a certain gentle, mournful love-me look that his eyes had with them, it was no wonder that great ladies and gay lionnes alike gave him the palm as the handsomest man in all the Household Regiments. . .

Lionne is a nice 'appellative' that we appear to have dropped.

What seems so odd now is the effeminacy in which the Hon. Bertie, himself most masculine of taste if not of appearance, appeared to revel. Nowadays he would have been terrified of being given the 'appellative' of Spenser's 'prettie paunce' (more vulgarly 'screaming pansy') had he thus appeared and surrounded himself with such curious elegance. Beauty on Horse Guards' Parade combined the 'martyrdom of cuirass and gorget' with carrying no masculine 'muckender', but a 'dainty filigree handkerchief, all point, embroidery, and perfume'. But, however velvety or silken the texture of their Vesuvian and bank-note receptacles, Ouida's he-men were of a 'he-ness' awesome, intense, and unchallengeable.

WADGET

A L L words ending in -dget have a certain domestic quality and are likeable. (Budget was originally a wallet and even something so friendly as a bottle. Fancy asking a publican now for a nice budget of whisky! Its translation to national accountancy, treasury and taxation occurred in the eighteenth-century.) Wadget is a bundle and is not family English only, but has strayed into the confines of Dictionary Status. It is a good fat untidy sort of word for a perhaps not very successful attempt to gather up scattered and untidy things. 'Here's a wadget of stuff.' It suits clothes, papers, and homely litter of all kinds. One might even have a wadget of gadgets. Gadget comes from the sea and I remember first hearing it at school from a boy of naval family whose delight it was to parade the latest Portsmouth lingo. The nautical gadget made a triumphant landing and has become any land-lubber's usage. Yes, those -dgets do endear themselves. Midget is a kindly diminutive and is no insult to a child. It is tempting to tell the too mercurial midget to make a wadget of his gadgets and not to fidget with the wadget.

WALLOP

W A L L O P has a strange assortment of meanings. It appears to come from French 'galop' and first means light and speedy motion. Thus it was used by Allan Ramsay in his *Up in the Air*:

> Now the sun's gane out o' sight,
> Beat the ingle and snuff the light;
> In glens the fairies skip and dance
> An' witches wallop o'er to France.

Then wallop began to mean a heavier motion. (Both our fighter and bomber aircraft have, like the witches, walloped over to France in one sense or the other.) Next the heavy movement became really clumsy, as in walloping along, and then it moved on, as a noun, to mean a blow. It would be understood as a helping at table, 'a good wallop of pudding'. (Perhaps a confusion with dollop, a word of Nordic origin for clump or lump.) Finally it has become slang for mild beer and many a bar resounds with demands for a pint of wallop. Why?

WALY

W A L Y both in Scottish and English signified lamentation.

> Oh waly, waly up the bank
> And waly, waly down the brae,
> And waly, waly yon burn-side
> Where I and my love wont to gae.

John Galt wrote of 'a willy-wallying at every door' of the parish whose annals he so pleasantly told. And so woefully on to Gilbert's Grosvenor, with his 'Oh, but I'm doleful, willow, willow, waly'.

The likeness to wail and the association with the weeping willow are sufficient explanation of this expressive word.

But waly, or wally, in Scotland was also fine and dandy. In Burns's 'Rantin', rovin' Robin',

> The gossip keekit in his loof
> Quo' she 'Who lives will see the proof,
> This waly boy will be nae coof,
> I think we'll call him Robin.

Then there was the 'waly nieve' (fine fist) of Burns's gudeman slicing into the haggis and, elsewhere,

> Auld Souter Rabby
> That dresses sae brawly
> And Auld Barber Watty
> Sae smirky and wally.

Wally has been made odious by the kind of lad, really called Walter, who now makes, or allows this to be, his nick-name. (How much more agreeable was Wat!) But waly does somehow suggest a cheerful smartness as well as the woebegone mood. A waly lad seems an apt enough phrase; so also does 'waly, waly up the bank', which is odd.

WAME

WAME, a form of womb, is Scottish and Northern for stomach, and how well it suggests queasiness therein! The very sound of it has a hint of undulant unrest. Scottish popular poetry rumbles with wames.

> Food fills the wame and keeps us livin';
> Though life's a gift no' worth receivin',
> When heavy dragged wi' pine and grievin';
> But, oiled by thee
> The wheels of life go down-hill, scrievin',
> Wi' rattlin' glee.

'Thee' refers, of course, to John Barleycorn. Burns writes of the City Gent as 'Purse-proud, big wi' cent per cent, and muckle wame'. So we would expect Burns to have the word wame expanding warmly in his 'Lines to a Haggis', but there he spoke of swelling kytes which

> Are bent like drums;
> Then auld guidman, maist like to ryve,
> Bethankit hums.

'Kyte' is still used in vulgar English for a belly. 'Every night, blow out your kyte with boiled beef and carrots', roared Harry Champion in the music-halls of my boyhood.

Robert Fergusson used wame simply for the front of the body in his praise of 'Braid Claith', respectability's uniform. He counselled the aspirants to prosperity and fame to

> Hap them weel, both back and wame,
> In gude Braid Claith.

The same poem, incidentally, has the nice word 'gawsy' for consequential. The barber spark, when done with 'scrapin' wark', goes out on the Sabbath trig and gawsy, 'in gude Braid Claith'. George Douglas in *The House with the Green Shutters* describes that home of disaster as 'planted firm and gawcey'. That story, by the way, is not only a notable piece of tragedy, but a treasury of Southern Scottish speech.

Returning to wame, I have been delighted to find it as a verb, indicating acute gastric distress. A-wameling in the passage quoted may be in confusion with the more common wambling, which means both to stagger about and to feel nausea. Both staggering and vomiting seem to be implied by an eighteenth-century Scottish traveller in her diary's description of a voyage to the Continent. She was a Mrs. Margaret Calderwood, who went from Scotland into England and on to Brussels in 1756:

> Marinasa the opera dancer was in the company, and a companion of his, a Swiss, who was either a singer or a dancer. ... All the company were sick, less or more, for first we plyed down the river with a cross wind, tacking every half hour till the tide was spent, and about three o'clock afternoon, when

we were off Orford, on the coast of Suffolk, we were obliged to cast anchor; which was no sooner done than every one fell a-wameling, as the ship did, and there was such sighing and groaning in the two cabins, as I never heard the like.

At the upper end of the cabin, a bed lyes across the stern, in that lay the Swiss dished up like a boiled salmond (for it has no cover over it), sick to death; on the right hand of it lay the almost expiring dancer; on the left lay the old lady; at her feet lay I as quietly as I could; on the side with the dancer lay Mr. Webb; John Rattray was laid before my bed, with his head on a clog-bag and his feet in the state-room.

A dreadful scene. 'A-wameling' for both the tossed vessel and its spent voyagers is express and admirable; the 'boiled salmond' is a curious simile, but striking.

WANHOPE

THE 'wan' words — the prefix signifying want or wane — have faded away. But wanhope, for despair, seems exquisite now; no doubt the added notion of wanness in colour as well as of waning gives special poignance to the word. R. C. Trench, Archbishop of Dublin, in his book on *English, Past and Present*, collected a number of these 'wans' — wanthrift, wanluck, wanlust, wanwit, wangrace, wantrust. They rarely survived Middle English: the cause of their disappearance is hard to comprehend. Mention of wanwit recalls 'witwanton' used as a verb in the sixteenth century. The Scots were more retentive. They had a beauty of this kind in 'wanwauchtie', unable to take the hearty draught. (Waucht must be known the world over through Burns's guid-willie waucht, the dram of kindliness.) 'He's unco wanwauchtie that scunners at whey', is an old Scots proverb. Scunners, for the benefit of the English, means dislikes or shrinks away from.

WANION

WANION or waniand means 'in the waning of the moon' and the moon is deemed to wane unluckily. Hence 'with a wanion' meant with a curse or with a vengeance. So it occurs once in Shakespeare: 'Come away or I'll fetch thee with a wanion.' It became possible to wish a wanion on to a person as a form of pest. It sounds too agreeable a word for this despiteful usage, but nearly everything connected with the moon acquired an unfortunate sense at one time. Nowadays we are more tolerant; sentimental balladry and music-hall lyrics have made the moon a symbol of happy romance as well as of frustrated yearning. So a wanion might come back to favour if anybody would use the word.

WANTON

I HAD always thought that wanton had much to do with wandering, but apparently it is Old English for untrained: hence it means ungoverned or rebellious. Mankind has ever taken two directly conflicting views of the unschooled and ignorant state, i.e. that it is either blissful innocence or abominable sin. Thus the beautiful word wanton came to be used in two contradictory senses. Usually it implies cruel, lascivious aberration: Shakespeare constantly employed it so. A notable example is in the wonderful picture of the Dark Lady in *Love's Labour's Lost*:

> A whitely wanton with a velvet brow.
> With two pitch-balls stuck in her face for eyes.
> Ay, and by heaven, one that will do the deed
> Though Argus were her eunuch and her guard.

So the plays are full of wanton lads with wanton blood and of maids no colder or more staid. But the innocent wanton, betokening the state of nature, is also there. Listen to Friar Lawrence (sometimes a bore, but here at his best):

> Here comes the lady: O, so light a foot
> Will ne'er wear out the everlasting flint;
> A lover may bestride the gossamer
> That idles in the wanton summer air
> And yet not fall; so light is vanity.

What could be more sinless than the breath of June? Herrick could think of wanton purity, claiming to sing of cleanly wantonness. Another of his century, Quarles, used wanton to signify a gracious meandering. In his 'Divine Rapture' he obviously thought of wanton as wandering:

> E'en like two little bank-dividing brooks
> That wash the pebbles with their wanton streams,
> And having ranged and search'd a thousand nooks,
> Meet both at length in silver-breasted Thames,
> Where in a greater current they conjoin.
> So I my Best Belovèd's am: so He is mine.

Reflection on this. Did Quarles pronounce conjoin conjine — or is it just a false rhyme? His subsequent rhymes with mine are twine and coin. One gathers coin was kine to him.

Further, what a change of tint the Thames appears to have undergone! How often does the Thames seem silver-breasted now? I have always been puzzled by the colours attributed by the poets to English rivers, especially the southern ones, whose normal hue is a dull, muddy brown. Milton, for example, calls Sabrina (the Severn) 'glassie, translucent and coral-paven'. Our oozy English streams certainly have a romantic effect upon their bank-side minstrels. Often the 'wanton streams' are seen through colour-tinted glasses and so move in silvery splendour far different from the dun floods of our acquaintance.

WINE-DARK

YEATS wrote:

> At wine-dark midnight in the sacred wood,

and the adjective works powerfully, though I cannot remember a midnight of exactly that hue. Wine-dark is the customary translation for the Homeric epithet applied to the Aegean Sea, which I have visited entranced, but did not find to be an empurpled flood. Radiantly, gloriously blue, yes; but scarcely claret or port, Samian or Chian — to be more local in the vintage. Yet the sound and suggestion of wine-dark do evoke in the mind the richness of the Archipelago where European civilization rose, like Aphrodite, from the waves. The surge of wine-dark waters in a line of poetry now inevitably brings to fancy the isles of Sappho and Alcaeus. Yet that aspect of nature which to me is truly wine-dark, or at least wine-misty, is much more native. I mean our English woods in winter.

In the Chilterns, the naked beech-woods of the short and misty days seem to me even lovelier than when they wear the tenderest greenth of May or blaze to heaven in October's frost before, consumed, they cast their leaves to earth. Day after day in the dark months the woods, especially the copses of birches and other smaller trees in the hollows, yield a tint of the utmost delicacy for which I think we have no proper word. It lies upon them like bloom on fruit; sometimes it seems to be given off and to take the air, like a visible essence, a fume, an emanation. This colour is not quite purple: yet it is richer than any brown. Umber is an epithet that somehow comes near to it. On December walks, when

> Trod beside me, close and dear,
> The beautiful and death-struck year,

I have fancied that tawny, as applied to port-wine, is just this shade. Certainly the exquisite effluence of the wintry spinneys reminds me of a rather light port drawn from the wood. So I would not call these noble groves of the chalky ridges and bottoms wine-dark; but wine-vaporous would not be inaccurate. Winter after winter, I have walked amazed at the fine hues of the long timbered slopes, but never lovelier than when the leaf has fallen. Their brownypurple is as soft as the coo of their doves in spring and indeed has something feathery about it too. Country folk strive to capture in simple terms this vapourish mystery of rural colour. I am told that in Wensleydale fog is used to mean the young shoots of grass that mist over the hayfield after the first crop has been cut. To call young grass fog is like calling a hill a cloud. It is natural poetry.

INDEX

JUST ANOTHER WORD

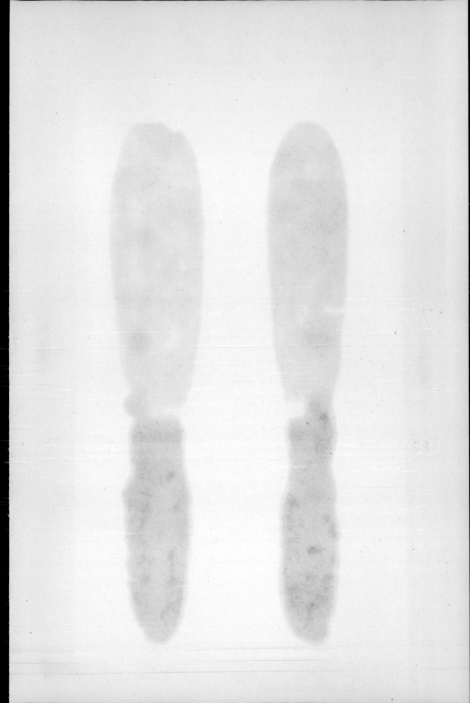